AF262833

THE WISDOM AND WEALTH SOLUTION

UNLOCKING *the* SECRETS *of* HAPPINESS, PURPOSE, *and* FINANCIAL SECURITY *with* LIVING360

FEROZ ANSARI

This publication is designed to provide accurate and authoritative information regarding the subject matter covered. Nothing herein shall constitute legal, accounting, or investment advice, or a solicitation to offer such. Further disclosures and information can be found in Appendix 7 under the heading "Important Regulatory & Compliance Disclosure." We encourage you to review such information before making any investment decisions.

Kiplinger Books
New York, New York
www.kiplinger.com

Distributed by Greenleaf Book Group

For ordering information or special discounts for bulk purchases, please contact Greenleaf Book Group at PO Box 91869, Austin, TX 78709, 512.891.6100.

Design and composition by Greenleaf Book Group
Cover design by Greenleaf Book Group
Cover image used under license from ©Adobestock.com

Publisher's Cataloging-in-Publication data is available.

Print ISBN: 978-1-969190-00-1

eBook ISBN: 978-1-969190-01-8

To offset the number of trees consumed in the printing of our books, Greenleaf donates a portion of the proceeds from each printing to the Arbor Day Foundation. Greenleaf Book Group has replaced over 50,000 trees since 2007.

Printed in the United States of America on acid-free paper

26 27 28 29 30 31 32 33 10 9 8 7 6 5 4 3 2 1

To Fauzia, my wife and my quiet miracle:
Your love has shaped every good part of me.

To my family and dearest friends:
Thank you for walking beside me through every season.

To my brother, Moe: Your devotion to the family
and the brave leap across continents
became the turning point in our family's story.

And to my beloved sons, Farooq and Ali:
Thank you for filling my life with joy, purpose,
and the deepest happiness a father can know.

Contents

PREFACE

Beyond the Concrete Box: Where Meaning Meets Money

The lecture hall hummed with energy—a low, electric thrum of ambition. Sixty MBA students streamed in, their faces a mix of youthful intensity and early-career exhaustion. Some carried laptops like shields; others clutched coffee like a lifeline. It was the first day of my wealth management class at the University of California–Irvine, and the air seemed to vibrate with one unspoken question:

How do I get rich? And how can I do it quickly?

I let the conversations fade, stepped forward, and smiled. "Imagine it's your sixtieth birthday," I began. "Someone offers you a choice—no strings attached: twenty million dollars in cash or a Nobel Prize. Which would you take?"

For a moment, the room was still. Then a confident voice from the back broke the silence: "Cash—no question!" Laughter rippled through the rows, followed by a chorus of agreement. Nearly every hand shot up for the money. The choice felt instinctive, almost primal.

And then one hand rose slowly. It belonged to Maya, a quiet, observant student in the third row. Her eyes met mine. "I'd take the Nobel Prize," she said softly.

The room turned toward her. I leaned in slightly. "Why?"

She hesitated, then spoke with calm conviction. "Because the Nobel Prize means I did something that mattered—something lasting, something bigger than me. The money? I could find a way to earn that, maybe. But I don't think I could ever buy meaning."

Silence. You could feel the air shift.

I've asked that same question dozens of times since—in high school classrooms, Wall Street boardrooms, and Silicon Valley workshops. The results rarely change. More than 95 percent of people choose money. It's almost automatic. After all, we've been taught the same formula from birth:

Money = Happiness. Money = Freedom. Money = Security.

Over the past three decades, I've viewed wealth and life from every angle—as an adjunct professor at the University of California–Irvine, teaching future leaders how to create and manage Total Wealth; as chairperson of the Todd & Lisa Halbrook Center for Investment and Wealth Management, promoting financial literacy and ethical stewardship; and as a senior principal at a registered investment advisory firm, helping thousands of families align their money with meaning. Across classrooms, boardrooms, and living rooms, I've seen the same truths emerge: Beneath every financial plan lies a web of emotion, fear, aspiration, and meaning. True wealth, I've learned, isn't measured in numbers but in wisdom—the ability to align your money with your purpose.

I've sat in the breathtaking penthouse of an ultrarich client as he confessed his marriage was a shell, his children were strangers, and his health was slipping—even as he worked another deal to add twenty-five million to a fortune he couldn't spend. I've watched a couple go from rags to riches, only to let a brutal divorce turn victory into ashes. I've seen ambitious graduates land six-figure jobs and burn out within a year, while others working two jobs to pay tuition discovered peace, joy, and connection that money could never buy.

Why does this happen? Why do so many of us chase only Financial Wealth, to find emptiness when we get there? The answer, I believe, lies in the structures that shape our desires themselves; it's the box we are born into.

The Concrete Box Theory

We are all born inside a *concrete box*. It's not a choice; it's the starting point. The box is built from the geography of your birth, the socioeconomic status of your parents, the religion you're raised in, the language you speak, the culture you absorb, the political beliefs you inherit, and the genetics written quietly into your DNA (see figure 0.1).

Inside, it feels soft: lined with comfort, familiarity, and belonging. But the walls are hard. They limit what you question, who you can become, and what you believe is possible.

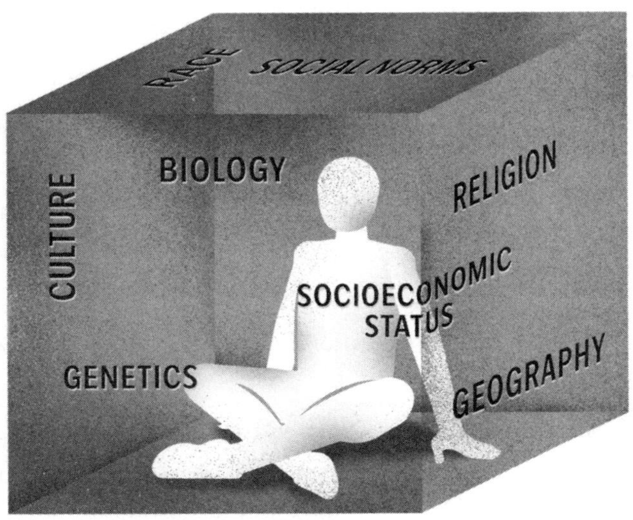

Figure 0.1: The concrete box theory.

This box is reinforced by the stories we tell ourselves and each other:

"This is the only truth."

"This is what success looks like."

"This is what I should want."

Over time, these inherited truths harden into walls you learn to defend—even when they no longer serve you. What feels like home may actually be a cage. What feels like truth may simply be tradition. To live a meaningful life, you must first see your box—and then summon the courage to step outside it.

That first step is never easy. It challenges your comfort, your circle, even your sense of identity. But it offers something infinitely greater: a life that feels authentically your own.

I know this because I spent much of my life inside my own concrete box. I didn't build it; I inherited it—my parents' religion, my community's politics, my friends' ambitions. I chased what I was told to chase: a career, a family, a house with a pool, the symbols of success. I achieved nearly all of it. But somewhere along the way, I stopped feeling alive and connected.

And then, in my late forties, I did something unthinkable. I stopped running.

One evening, I picked up a book that would quietly alter the course of my life—*The How of Happiness* by Dr. Sonja Lyubomirsky.[1] When I finished it, I sat in silence for a long time. I realized that I had mastered the art of growing Financial Wealth but not the art of nurturing Wisdom Wealth. That was the night I began dismantling my box, brick by brick.

That book left me with a question I couldn't ignore: *What am I really chasing, and why?*

As I began searching for that answer, I started to see the hidden cost of my own pursuit: relationships neglected, victories hollow, moments unlived. For years, I had been chasing *Financial Wealth* while starving my *Wisdom Wealth*—the inner compass that brings awareness, gratitude, and purpose.

That realization changed everything.

The answers to what makes a "good life" will be different for you than they were for me. But the *process* of finding them is universal. We've been conditioned to measure life in numbers—income, net worth, titles—while neglecting the invisible currencies that give those numbers meaning: love, relationships, gratitude, and purpose.

The result? Money without fulfillment. Success without connection. Achievement without joy.

I wrote this book because I believe you can find the balance between Wisdom and Wealth, a foundation of lasting happiness and enduring success. This is your invitation to step outside the concrete box, to rediscover what truly matters, and to begin your own LIVING360 journey—a path toward enhancing your life experience with purpose and lasting financial security.

If you've ever wondered whether there's more to life than what fits inside your box, you've already begun. Let's take the next step together.

INTRODUCTION

The Zero Moment

Every meaningful journey begins with a pause—that moment when the noise fades, and the truth you've been avoiding finally gets loud enough to hear. For some, it happens in a doctor's office. For others, it's a sleepless night, a bank statement, or a quiet realization that success doesn't feel like it should.

Think of the climber who stops at the base of a mountain, looks up at the distant peak, and asks, *Am I ready for what lies ahead?* That moment—the zero moment—is where awareness begins. Before you can scale your own mountain of a fulfilling, balanced life, you must stop, and ask: *Where am I, really?* Are you living in a state of struggle, or have you reached prosperity without peace? Are you enriched with wisdom but without a financial foundation? How will you know where to start if you don't know where you're beginning?

As we've discussed, everyone has been conditioned to live inside their concrete box, to measure markers of Financial Wealth: bank balances, stock portfolios, property values. But the wealthiest people I know are those who also focus on developing their Wisdom Wealth—a profound understanding of themselves and the world, a clear inner compass, and the courage to make choices aligned with their deepest values. Money matters, absolutely. It is a vital tool. Money is a necessary but insufficient condition for happiness. It is only one half of the real prize. Here is the right equation:

Your Total Wealth = Financial Wealth + Wisdom Wealth

This simple equation rewrites what it means to live well. It turns wealth from a race into a relationship—between your mind, your money, and your meaning.

Before you get the wrong impression, let me be clear: joy, purpose, and meaning are noble aims, but they are not sustainable without a strong financial foundation. It's hard to be grateful when you're worried about rent. It's almost impossible to feel free when you're uncertain how you'll support your family. Financial insecurity is the single greatest thief of peace of mind. Having financial security allows you to live your life with freedom, intention, and joy.

LIVING360

This book is a roadmap to Total Wealth—not just the dollars you accumulate, but the clarity, purpose, peace, and freedom you cultivate. True wealth is living with intention and confidence. That is the promise of LIVING360—a framework built on four pillars: know yourself, know the world, know your purpose, and build financial security (see figure 0.2).

The first three parts of this book build your Wisdom Wealth—the inner strength, awareness, and understanding that guide every meaningful decision, personal or financial. Part IV, along with the Comprehensive Investment Guide, gives you the tools and strategies to build Financial Wealth—the kind of security that protects your freedom and supports the life you want to live.

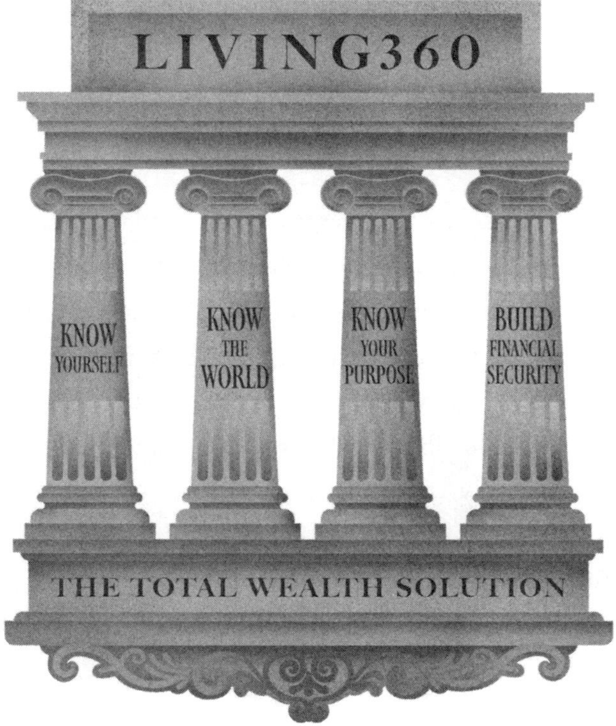

Figure 0.2: The four pillars of Total Wealth.

My own journey began differently. As a first-generation immigrant, locked inside my concrete box, I chased the American dream with a single focus: financial success. I believed money would solve everything. But looking back, I now recognize what was missing—authentic awareness and true acceptance. I built a career, but I had not yet built myself.

Decades of working with clients and students have taught me this: the most profound transformations begin on the inside. That is why this book starts not with money, but with a way of thinking—the 3As: Awareness, Action, and Acceptance. This framework reshaped my life and has guided thousands of people I've had the privilege to coach, teach, and walk alongside.

THE 3AS: AWARENESS, ACTION, AND ACCEPTANCE

In the chapters that follow, you will build your path to Wisdom Wealth and Financial Wealth with a simple but profound framework of the 3As: Awareness, Action, and Acceptance.

- Awareness: Everything begins with awareness—of who we are and the world we live in. Human metacognition to comprehend ourselves and the world is a unique gift. Not being able to nurture awareness of our thinking and living inside the box would be a great failure. Without it, our understanding falters and our actions misfire. "Knowledge is power," they say—and they're right. But only when that knowledge is clear, comprehensive, and factual. Acting on illusions or half-truths leads to suboptimal choices. Over time, bad choices compound to really bad outcomes; acting on wisdom changes everything. This book will push you to question, to see from new angles, and to awaken a deeper awareness of self and world.
- Action: This is where you take control. You leverage your awareness and knowledge into thoughtful action to grow your Wisdom and Financial Wealth. You will move beyond theory to create a framework to step outside the concrete box and execute a tangible plan to enhance your life experience. Each step of the process will be inspired by your vision of life that aligns with your authentic values and aspirations.
- Acceptance: The final, most crucial step. Even when we do our best to understand, to act wisely, and to choose the right path, outcomes are never guaranteed. When things go well, acceptance means receiving success with humility. When they don't, acceptance means meeting disappointment and heartbreak with grace and empathy. True acceptance comes from recognizing,

with kindness and compassion, that we did what we could—and that part of life ultimately lies beyond our control. While acceptance brings peace and comfort, its full impact also lies in learning from the outcome, which adds to your awareness, shaping your next action.

Over time, every cycle of Awareness, Action, and Acceptance enriches the compounding growth of your Total Wealth (see figure 0.3).

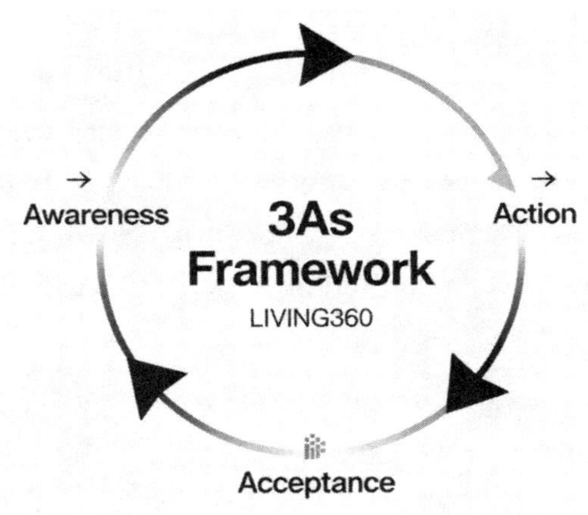

Figure 0.3: Cultivating Total Wealth with the 3As.

Find Your Starting Point

To answer the question, "Where am I, really?" in a way that honestly reflects your current reality with clarity—you'll need two more tools: the LIVING360 Grid, which shows you where you stand, and the LIVING360 Compass, which helps you see whether your life is balanced with Wisdom Wealth and Financial Wealth. Together, they provide the coordinates and the direction for your journey. You can find the Grid and Compass online at www.wisdomandwealthsolution.com.

ASSESSMENT: THE LIVING360 GRID

Imagine opening your phone's GPS. Before you can navigate to any destination, the screen must first locate the blue dot: *You are here.* That's exactly what the LIVING360 Grid can do for your life.

The LIVING360 Grid measures two essential dimensions of a fulfilling life:

- Financial Wealth: your level of financial security and resources
- Wisdom Wealth: your depth of knowledge, purpose, relationships, and self-awareness

These two dimensions can be combined in four unique arrangements, which are represented by the four quadrants of the LIVING360 Grid (see figure 0.4). Your personal combination will place you in one of four quadrants. In the grid that follows, read each quadrant's description carefully. Then, do the following:

1. Place a check mark next to the bullet-pointed statements in each quadrant that describe you.
2. Tally your check marks for each quadrant.
3. The quadrant with the most check marks is your dominant quadrant. It represents the current orientation of your life.

Now that you understand the philosophy and the method, let's locate your starting point. Think of this as your personal Total Wealth X-ray—a snapshot of where you truly stand before the transformation begins.

THE LIVING360 GRID

Quadrant II	Quadrant I
☐ I have significant assets and investments. ☐ I earn strong income from my career or business. ☐ I focus heavily on luxury, status, recognition, and success. ☐ I see my professional success as my identity. ☐ I approach relationships with limited emotions and maintain distance. ☐ I spend minimal time in self-reflection. ☐ I sometimes feel an inner void despite my success. ☐ I have low interest in global issues or learning new ideas. ☐ I maintain a work-dominated schedule. ☐ I seek fulfillment through consumption or achievement. **Count and Enter Total Checked Boxes in Quadrant II = _____**	☐ I have a strong retirement and investment plan. ☐ I consistently save and maintain surplus income. ☐ I have a clear life purpose and align my actions with it. ☐ I practice gratitude and emotional balance. ☐ I have deep, supportive relationships with family and friends. ☐ I stay curious and informed about the world. ☐ I actively give back to society. ☐ I balance work, leisure, and rest. ☐ I prioritize lifelong learning and growth. ☐ I make thoughtful decisions and try my best to maintain objectivity. **Count and Enter Total Checked Boxes in Quadrant I = _____**
Quadrant III	**Quadrant IV**
☐ I live paycheck to paycheck. ☐ I carry persistent debt without a repayment plan. ☐ I lack emergency savings. ☐ I have no long-term financial plan. ☐ I lack a reliable support network. ☐ I feel unclear about my life purpose. ☐ I experience high stress and frustration. ☐ I react impulsively to life challenges. ☐ I have low awareness of new opportunities. ☐ I often feel stuck or left behind. **Count and Enter Total Checked Boxes in Quadrant III = _____**	☐ I experience income instability or low earnings. ☐ I have limited savings or investments. ☐ I feel concern about retirement. ☐ I value purpose over possessions. ☐ I nurture deep, meaningful relationships. ☐ I am active in my community. ☐ I practice gratitude and mindfulness. ☐ I value learning, reflection, and self-awareness. ☐ I live a simple lifestyle, but money is a concern. ☐ I live in a rental apartment and worry about making rent. **Count and Enter Total Checked Boxes in Quadrant IV = _____**

Figure 0.4: The LIVING360 Grid reveals where you are at the start of your transformational journey.

On the next page, place yourself in the LIVING360 Grid area with the highest score or the greatest number of check marks from Figure 0.4 above. You may find that there are two or three areas with a similar number of checks, which indicates the balance or tension in your life today. While the dominant quadrant is important to understand your assessment of your thinking and life circumstances, the scores in other quadrants also reveal important insights. Figure 0.5 reveals what each area means and where you are on the LIVING360 Grid.

THE LIVING360 GRID

Quadrant II Prosperity Without Peace	Quadrant I Total Wealth: LIVING360
I have significant assets and investments. I earn strong income from my career or business. I focus heavily on luxury, status, recognition, and success. I see my professional success as my identity. I approach relationships with limited emotions and maintain distance. I spend minimal time in self-reflection. I sometimes feel an inner void despite my success. I have low interest in global issues or learning new ideas. I maintain a work-dominated schedule. I seek fulfillment through consumption or achievement. From the Previous Page, Count and Enter Total Checked Boxes in Quadrant II = _____	I have a strong retirement and investment plan. I consistently save and maintain surplus income. I have a clear life purpose and align my actions with it. I practice gratitude and emotional balance. I have deep, supportive relationships with family and friends. I stay curious and informed about the world. I actively give back to society. I balance work, leisure, and rest. I prioritize lifelong learning and growth. I make thoughtful decisions and try my best to maintain objectivity. From the Previous Page, Count and Enter Total Checked Boxes in Quadrant I = _____
Quadrant III **Surviving, Not Thriving**	**Quadrant IV** **Stifled Enlightenment**
I live paycheck to paycheck. I carry persistent debt without a repayment plan. I lack emergency savings. I have no long-term financial plan. I lack a reliable support network. I feel unclear about my life purpose. I experience high stress and frustration. I react impulsively to life challenges. I have low awareness of new opportunities. I often feel stuck or left behind. From the Previous Page, Count and Enter Total Checked Boxes in Quadrant III = _____	I experience income instability or low earnings. I have limited savings or investments. I feel concern about retirement. I value purpose over possessions. I nurture deep, meaningful relationships. I am active in my community. I practice gratitude and mindfulness. I value learning, reflection, and self-awareness. I live a simple lifestyle, but money is a concern. I live in a rental apartment and worry about making rent. From the Previous Page, Count and Enter Total Checked Boxes in Quadrant IV = _____

Vertical axis: High Wealth – Medium – Low Wealth
Horizontal axis: Low Wisdom – Medium – High Wisdom

Figure 0.5: The LIVING360 Grid with labels.

The Four Quadrants of the Grid

- **Stifled Enlightenment: (Quadrant IV)** You've built a rich inner life. You read, reflect, perhaps even meditate. You know who you are—but you lack financial security to fully live your vision. Consider the passionate artist whose work touches hearts but whose empty bank account limits the life they want to create.
- **Surviving, Not Thriving: (Quadrant III)** Life feels like a constant uphill struggle. Bills press in, worries pile up, and deeper meaning feels out of reach. Survival takes center stage, leaving little space for reflection. Think of the young couple working two jobs just to keep the lights on—exhausted, anxious, but still dreaming of a freer tomorrow.
- **Prosperity Without Peace: (Quadrant II)** On the outside, you look successful. The bank account is full, the resume polished, the lifestyle enviable. But inside, something is missing. Relationships feel shallow, purpose feels thin, and the question lingers: Is this all there is? Consider the executive or a successful business owner who "has it all" but lies awake at night, haunted by loneliness and unspoken regret.
- **Total Wealth: LIVING360 (Quadrant I)** This is the destination, the goal of LIVING360. Here, financial security is not a burden but a foundation. Relationships are rich, purpose is clear, and life feels whole. Think of the person who has enough, loves deeply, and wakes up each day with both security and meaning.

This book is a comprehensive guide to pinpointing where you are on your LIVING360 journey and gives you the tools and mindset you need to reach your goal of a balanced, meaningful, 360-degree life. Each chapter offers insights, theories, and reflection questions to help you on your way. If you are committed to building the most solid foundation possible for your newly redesigned life, you will be best served by following along closely with each section of the book, even if you currently fall into the Prosperity Without Peace or Stifled Enlightenment quadrants.

THE LIVING360 COMPASS

Knowing your quadrant is only the first step. Life is not just about where you stand, but how balanced you feel within yourself. That's where the LIVING360 Compass comes in.

If the Grid is your map pin—the *You Are Here* moment—the Compass is your navigation tool. It breaks life into four essential directions:

1. Know Yourself: your beliefs, biases, and inner awareness
2. Know the World: your understanding of history, progress, risks, and global megatrends
3. Know Your Purpose: your relationships, gratitude, health, and sense of fulfillment
4. Build Financial Security: your money habits, stability, and long-term planning and vision

Take the following survey or find it online at www.wisdomandwealthsolution.com, mark your scores, and place yourself on the Compass. This is where your journey begins.

ASSESSMENT: MY LIVING360 COMPASS

This is a self-reflection survey calibrated to determine how balanced and fulfilling your life is right now and where you have room for improvement. Answer to what extent you agree with the following statements.

Part 1: Know Yourself

1. I have reflected on religion and faith (or lack of it) and can respect both my own beliefs and those of others.
   Answer: Yes / Somewhat / No
2. I understand where my political views come from and why others might think differently.
   Answer: Yes / Somewhat / No
3. I have thought about free will and how much control I really have over my choices.
   Answer: Yes / Somewhat / No
4. I understand how genetics and biology influence health, personality, and opportunity.
   Answer: Yes / Somewhat / No
5. I know that my thinking is shaped by my biases and blind spots.
   Answer: Yes / Somewhat / No

Part 2: Know the World

1. I see how history, politics, science, and culture have shaped the world I live in today.
   Answer: Yes / Somewhat / No
2. I believe life for most people has improved in the last fifty years (e.g., less war, poverty, and hunger).
   Answer: Yes / Somewhat / No

continued

3. I recognize the existential threats humanity faces as a species (e.g., climate change, pandemics, and nuclear conflict).
   Answer: Yes / Somewhat / No
4. I pay attention to new technologies such as AI and think about how they may affect my work and life.
   Answer: Yes / Somewhat / No
5. I stay aware of major political and economic changes that could impact my home, work, and community.
   Answer: Yes / Somewhat / No

Part 3: Know Your Purpose

1. I have at least one person in my life I can trust fully and share anything with.
   Answer: Yes / Somewhat / No
2. I have at least three close people in my life who I connect with often and who would be there if I needed them.
   Answer: Yes / Somewhat / No
3. I make time for people I care about, listen deeply, and offer real support.
   Answer: Yes / Somewhat / No
4. I regularly reflect on what's good in my life and practice gratitude.
   Answer: Yes / Somewhat / No
5. I take care of myself—healthy weight, good sleep, regular exercise, and some spiritual or community activity.
   Answer: Yes / Somewhat / No

Part 4: Build Financial Security

1. I know my income, expenses, net worth, and credit score, and I feel I'm on track financially.
   Answer: Yes / Somewhat / No

2. I save regularly, maximize retirement accounts, and invest with discipline based on my goals.

   Answer: Yes / Somewhat / No

3. I own my home (or have a clear plan to).

   Answer: Yes / Somewhat / No

4. I believe I'll have enough savings to fund the lifestyle I want in retirement.

   Answer: Yes / Somewhat / No

5. I have thought carefully about risks (illness, disability, long-term care, lawsuits) and use insurance or planning to protect myself.

   Answer: Yes / Somewhat / No

Scoring

- Each Yes = 2 points, Somewhat = 1 point, No = 0 points.
- Maximum 10 points per part, 40 points total.
- Plot your scores on the LIVING360 Compass (see figure 0.6) to see how balanced your life is. Transparent bars are left open for you to write your score directly on the chart—a visual snapshot of where you shine and where growth is calling.

MY LIVING360 COMPASS—SELF-REFLECTION SCORING

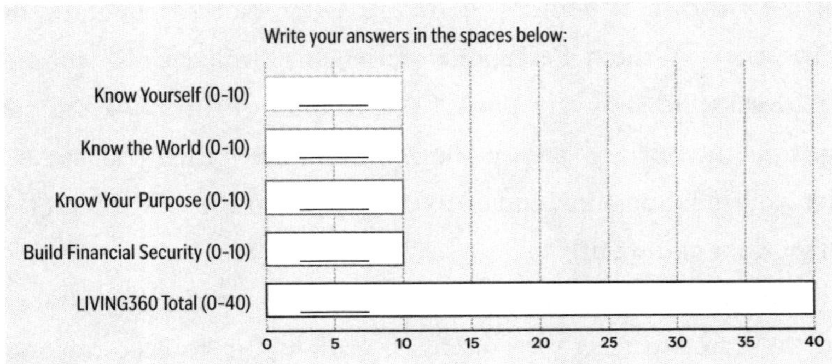

Figure 0.6: The LIVING360 Compass helps you determine areas in which growth is calling.

The compass you just completed isn't about judgment; it's about awareness. Every "Yes," "Somewhat," and "No" is a clue to where you can focus your energy and attention. The LIVING360 Grid gives you a big-picture view of the kind of life you're living right now. The LIVING360 Compass gives you a practical way of seeing if you're balanced across the four pillars of a fulfilled life. Together, they provide a complete picture: where you stand, where you're strong, and where your next step should be.

From Awareness to Action

This is your zero moment—the point where Awareness sharpens into clarity for Action.

- The grid has shown you your home quadrant: your current reality.
- The compass has revealed your trajectory—the areas in which you are strongest and the areas that yearn for attention. Together, they provide the most honest snapshot of your life today.

But here's the LIVING360 promise: *Your starting point does not define your destiny.* Whether you are Surviving, Not Thriving, dwelling in Prosperity Without Peace, or experiencing Stifled Enlightenment, the path forward is always open. Each chapter of this book is a stepping stone intended to deepen your wisdom, strengthen your finances, enrich your relationships, and move you closer to the LIVING360 life with wisdom and wealth.

Remember: This isn't about perfection. It's about *direction.* Your goal is not to score a perfect forty points overnight, but to keep moving—steadily, consciously—toward a life that feels balanced and whole.

When you finish this book, you'll return to this compass and grid to measure again. You'll see what's shifted, what's grown, and where you've moved. Progress won't just be something you feel. It will be something you can see, right in front of you. For now, this is your baseline. This is your moment of truth. From here, your LIVING360 journey begins.

Your LIVING360 Quadrant Location:

____

Your LIVING360 Compass Score:

____

Your moment has arrived—the breath before the climb. Ahead lies the life you were meant to live: grounded in wisdom, fortified by wealth, guided by purpose. Take a deep breath. Let's begin.

PART I

Know Yourself

Before you can build a joyful life—and the financial security to support it—you must first understand the most important person in your world: you. Money decisions, career choices, relationships, success, happiness—every one of them flows from a single source: the beliefs, emotions, and invisible stories inside your own mind.

To know yourself, you must begin by asking questions most people avoid:

- Why do I believe what I believe?
- Where do my desires come from?

- What triggers my joy, my fear, my ambition, my love, my anger?
- And how much of "me" is an inheritance of other people's ideas?

Before you can expand your Wisdom Wealth, you must see the hidden architecture of your inner world—the concrete box you were born into. Its walls are built from your family's beliefs, your culture's expectations, your childhood experiences, and the fears you never chose but learned to carry (see figure I.1). These walls do more than shape your mindset—they influence your relationships, limit your opportunities, and quietly govern the choices that determine both your life's joy and your financial future.

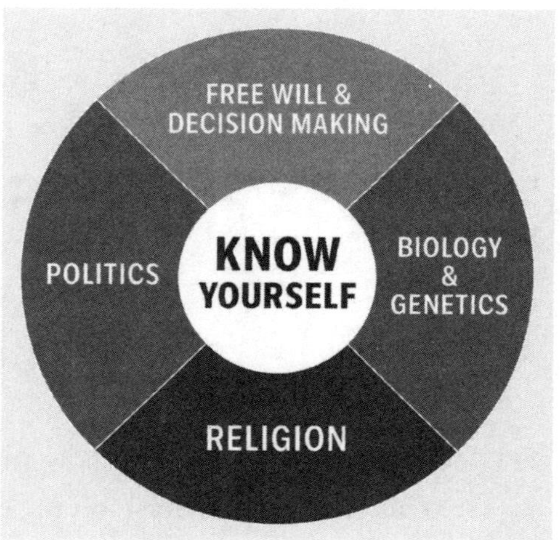

Figure I.1: Who you are reflects multiple interacting forces, most beyond conscious awareness.

If you want a meaningful life, self-knowledge isn't optional; it is the foundation of financial clarity and emotional freedom. You cannot invest wisely, choose confidently, or plan your future with conviction unless you understand the forces shaping your decisions. What you confront in this section becomes the compass for everything that follows—in your worldview, in your pursuit of purpose, and in every financial decision you will make.

In the pages ahead, you are not destroying your identity—you are illuminating it. The work may be unsettling. At times, it might even feel like breaking something sacred. But every piece of concrete you remove lets in more light—light that reveals who you truly are beneath layers of conditioning and conformity. Some walls—like genetics and biology—may never fully disappear. Others—like inherited beliefs or unexamined fears—will crack the moment you shine light on them.

Everyone thinks they know what they want. But true self-awareness means understanding not only your first-order desires—the things you currently pursue—but also your second-order desires: what you want to want (second-order volition).[1] It means projecting your mind beyond the version of you that exists today toward a wiser, more intentional version of yourself in the future, a version that may value different things than you do now. This alignment between who you are and who you aim to become is what some philosophers describe as true freedom of will.

And so, we begin our journey where the walls are thickest, and the emotions run deepest—with the force that has shaped human behavior more than almost anything else: religion.

CHAPTER 1

Religion

I've seen religion heal and harm. It can comfort the grieving and divide the living. It builds civilizations and breaks them too. It can bind people to one another—or blind them to their shared humanity.

This chapter is an invitation to look beyond labels and see faith as something more: a philosophy of life, a living practice, and a force that continues to shape the human condition.

In the pages ahead, you will explore a fresh perspective on spirituality, faith, and religion. Whether you identify as an atheist, an agnostic, or a theist—whether your belief leans toward monotheism, pantheism, or somewhere in between—this chapter invites you to widen your perspective. You may resonate with mystics, secularists, humanists, or freethinkers, but there is immense value in understanding how people come to believe what they believe, and how those beliefs profoundly shape their lives.

It was a warm San Diego afternoon when I sat down for lunch with my client, Deepa. She always reminded me of my favorite aunt—the one I used to visit every summer as a child—gentle, warm, and full of quiet wisdom. Deepa had just turned eighty. As we finished ordering, she folded her frail hands on the table, her eyes distant yet steady. Only weeks earlier, she had lost her husband of sixty years, and her grief had seemed immeasurable.

Yet on this day, something in her demeanor had softened. A small, peaceful smile played on her lips as she spoke about him. She told me that what brought her comfort was a simple belief: her husband's "good karma" would guide him toward a blessed rebirth (*Samsara*)—perhaps even toward *Moksha*, liberation from the cycle of life and death and union with the divine (*Atman*).

As I listened, it struck me how faith—across every tradition—speaks a universal language. The vocabulary may differ, but the longing for meaning, continuity, and hope is the same in all of us.

In another quiet moment, a different client sat before me, his voice barely above a whisper, eyes red from sorrow. His beloved wife had died suddenly, leaving him in an abyss of loneliness. Yet, with remarkable strength, he whispered, "I survive only because Jesus carries me through each day," finding solace in the unwavering support of his faith. Different prayers, same plea: the human search for acceptance when grief and sorrow appear unbearable.

And then there was the mother, graceful and serene, even in the face of unimaginable tragedy—the loss of her vibrant, healthy son at the age of just twenty-two. Standing among family and friends, she radiated a quiet strength that held everyone together. With gentle authority, she reminded the grieving hearts around her of their spiritual anchor, softly reciting, "Indeed, to Allah we belong, and to Him we shall return." In every tradition, grief seeks refuge in the sacred.

I've learned through profound moments such as these that for many people faith can be an integral component of their Wisdom Wealth, guiding them through life's storms and illuminating their path even in the darkest times.

Your religious beliefs shape identity, inform choices, and define worldview. This force of belief, together with politics and cultural norms, has been a cornerstone of human civilization for millennia. But when was the last time you critically examined the historical, psychological, and social foundations of your own belief system?

When Religion Is a Concrete Box

Religions are expressed through stories—some awe-inspiring, some miraculous, and some pointing beyond literal interpretation. Yet, billions of people live and die for them. Some dedicate their entire lives to spiritual practice, while others find in religion a deep source of comfort, purpose, and community.

Religious conviction that your own faith is the only truth—or that deep spiritual connection is possible only through specific rituals—can become one wall of the concrete box. Often poured lovingly by family, place, language, and community, it feels like warmth and belonging from the inside. Most people carry a label: Catholic, Sunni Muslim, Hindu, Buddhist, agnostic, and so on. But how often have you paused to truly ask: Why do I believe what I believe? The aim is not to unsettle anyone's house of faith, but to open its windows and widen the doorway. In doing so, preserving the pillars and the beams that support you (e.g., compassion, community, and meaning) while gently easing back whatever narrows your growth or grace. That is Wisdom Wealth in practice: The 3As—Awareness of what shaped you, Action aligned with your deepest values, and Acceptance of mystery and difference.

To understand how faith took root so deeply in the human story, we must first look at what religion claims about itself.

THE THEOLOGICAL CASE FOR RELIGION

Many see religion as a genuine response to something real and beyond yourself. Across faiths, there is the idea that you are born with an inner compass pointing toward the divine—a quiet restlessness only stilled by connection to something greater. The Qur'an calls this *fitrah*, a natural inclination toward God. The Bible, in Romans 1:19 (The Passion Translation), states: "In reality, the truth of God is known instinctively, for God has embedded this knowledge inside every human heart."[1] In the Hindu tradition, the Upanishads (600 BCE to 300 BCE)—the concluding and philosophical part of the Vedas—describe *Atman*, the divine self within, waiting to be awakened.

Whether called *sensus divinitatis* or divine spark, these ideas suggest that religion arises not from fear or social pressure, but from something encoded into your being, a whisper that there is more to life than meets the eye. Al-Ghazali, the influential eleventh-century Islamic theologian and mystic, captured this sentiment: "The truth is known not by means of reasoning alone, but through a light which God casts into the heart."[2] Some hear eternal truth in sacred revelations—scriptures, prophets, and moments of divine encounter that have shaped communities for centuries. From Moses at Sinai to the Prophet Muhammad in the cave of Hira, from the teachings of Jesus to the hymns of the *Rig-Veda*, many believe that religion is rooted in revelations that call you toward higher truths and a way of living aligned with them. The medieval Christian philosopher and theologian, Thomas Aquinas, expressed this view clearly when he wrote, "It was necessary for man's salvation that certain truths which exceed human reason be made known to him by divine revelation."[3]

Others turn to morality itself as evidence for religion and the existence of a higher power. How is it that across cultures, values such as justice, honesty, and compassion arise again and again? Does this universal moral grammar point to a higher moral lawgiver? For some, an internal sense of right and wrong is less about cultural convenience and more a signpost pointing toward God.

> "The Moral Law tells us the tune we have
> to play: Our instincts are merely the keys."
>
> —C. S. LEWIS

EVOLUTIONARY, SOCIAL, AND PSYCHOLOGICAL EXPLANATIONS OF RELIGION

Not everyone interprets faith as revelation. Some see it as evolution: a byproduct of how the mind seeks safety and meaning. Religion, they suggest, is not planted by the divine, but by evolution. Long ago, when our ancestors saw rustling in the grass, it was safer to assume it was a predator than the wind. This instinct to detect agency—hyper-alertness to intention—helped us survive and evolved into seeing spirits in the trees and gods in the thunder. Our ability to imagine other minds, including minds greater than ours, gave rise to gods who could see us, judge us, and care for us, offering comfort in a chaotic world.

Others approach religion through the lens of evolution and culture. They note that religious communities often thrive and outlast others, bound by mutual aid and shared purpose. Religious beliefs spread like viral ideas that replicate because they are memorable and emotionally resonant. From this angle, religion is a cultural tool that helps groups thrive.

Freud saw religion as a shield against existential fear, a story we tell ourselves to soften the terror of mortality. Pascal Boyer and Justin Barrett argued that belief in gods arises from mental processes tuned for survival rather than truth.[4] Religion, in this view, is an echo of how our minds work rather than a message from beyond.

"Religion is the opium of the people."

—KARL MARX

Sociologists see religion as the glue of society. Shared beliefs and rituals build trust and cooperation. Costly practices such as fasting or tithing signal commitment, strengthening group identity. The belief in an all-seeing deity encourages ethical behavior, even when no one is watching. For thinkers such as Émile Durkheim, religion is society reflecting itself, creating a shared moral order that holds communities together. Durkheim is credited with saying, "Gods are social facts. Religion is society worshipping itself."[5]

In 2025, nearly 85 percent of the world's population identified with a religion.[6] Yet no scientific method has proven God's existence. And yet—faith endures. Perhaps that's because truth in religion does not reside in test tubes or telescopes, but in mystery, meaning, and lived experience.

A MATHEMATICAL METAPHOR FOR RELIGION

Throughout my life of faith, I have found myself engaged in long and hard discussions about my own beliefs and religious practices, and of other traditions. And as I wrote this chapter, I kept asking, "How do I capture, in one clear expression, the complex journey of how religions take shape over time?"

I took some time to consider the question, to identify the forces that act on religions and cultures over time. I traced the path religions follow, from ancient inspiration to modern practice.

For example, most religions practiced today began with a historical personality—a figure who stepped into their age carrying answers to humanity's deepest moral and social questions. That voice, at its core, was powered by a divine epiphany: a revelation or an encounter with the sacred that elevated their words beyond ordinary human insight.

Yet, as centuries pass, those original truths do not remain untouched. They are filtered, reshaped, and sometimes reinterpreted by the tides of political expediency—the needs and strategies of rulers, institutions, and communities seeking to survive and thrive. Layer upon this the cultural amalgamation—the blending of traditions, languages, and customs as faith spreads across borders and generations, further transforming the original ideas.

And then there is time itself—the multiplier. The longer the distance from the original epiphany, the more these human elements imprint themselves upon the faith in terms of original principles and practices.

When I considered these truths, what came to me was not another parable, but a simple equation—a metaphor that speaks to both the heart and the mind:

Practiced Religion Today = Original Message + [Time (Political Expediency + Cultural Amalgamation)]

Religion, as we practice it today, is driven from the "sacred revelation" and human story. It is the echo of the divine that was heard by the historical personality, carried through the centuries by fragile and flawed but inspired human hands. Religion, in this light, is not diminished. On the contrary—its endurance is a testament to both the timelessness of its spiritual core and the adaptability of human communities who have carried it forward.

Religious Inheritance

We often speak of choosing a religion, but the truth is, most people inherit their faith—passed down through family, tradition, and early life experience (see figure 1.1).

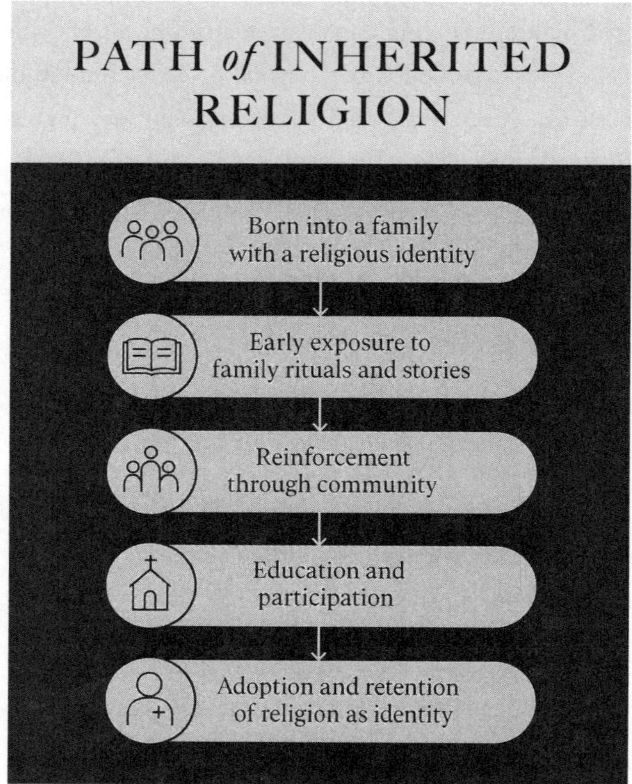

Figure 1.1: This chart illustrates the path of inherited religion.

Let's test this idea. Evolutionary biologist Richard Dawkins predicted that faith, like genetics, would show strong inheritance.[7] The data proved him right: religion is the stickiest form of cultural transmission.

- Christianity: 73 percent in the US; 98–99 percent in places like Hungary and the Philippines[8]
- Islam: Over 99 percent retention globally[9]
- Hinduism: 82 percent in the US; >99 percent in India[10]
- Judaism: 76 percent retention[11]

EXERCISE: RELIGIOUS TRANSMISSION

1. Identify your religious inheritance. What religion were you raised in? ________________
2. Were you told stories about it growing up? Yes / No
3. Were those stories repeated by your family/community? Yes / No
4. Were you asked to participate in religious rituals? Yes / No
5. Do you still follow that religion today? Yes / No
6. How did answering these questions make you feel? Curious? Defensive? More open-minded?

This chapter's intention is not to shake your faith or to encourage you in following a particular religious tradition. It is meant to help you see it with fresh eyes—more clearly, more compassionately, and more consciously. It is part of our 3As framework: Awareness, Action, and Acceptance, helping us move toward the Total Wealth-LIVING360 destination on the grid.

By understanding religion more deeply, you grow your Wisdom Wealth, equipping yourself to live with intention rather than habit. After a lifetime devoted to practicing my own faith and exploring others with a spirit of reverent curiosity, I have learned that beneath the surface differences in language, rituals, and sacred texts—the moral core of all religions—converges. Strip away the garments of tradition, and you'll find shared values—compassion, justice, humility, forgiveness, and love. I have come to a quiet conclusion: The essence of every faith is the search for connection with a higher power. That truth leaves us with the profound choice to accept that either every tradition reflects a part of the whole—or none of them do. The question that remains is not which path is right, but whether we walk our chosen one consciously, with awareness of the roots of our faith, action that is grounded in humility, and acceptance that all faith traditions carry a common thread.

Reflection Questions

These reflection questions aren't about what is right or wrong—just awareness. Write honestly, without judgment.

1. After reading this chapter, how do you feel about your own beliefs?
2. How do you feel about religious traditions that other people follow?
3. Which of the following theories of religion's origin and persistence most appeals to you and why?
    - Religion is rooted in true revelations that call us toward higher truths and a way of living aligned with them.
    - Our sense of right and wrong is not merely about cultural convenience but is a signpost pointing toward religion and God.
    - Religion is a shield against existential fear, a story we tell ourselves to soften the terror of mortality.
    - Religion is a cultural tool that helps groups survive, reproduce, and navigate an uncertain world.

CHAPTER 2

Politics

One afternoon during President Biden's tenure, my phone buzzed with two very different messages. The first was from a conservative client, angrily venting that the economy was "ruined," citing excessive government spending, high inflation, and crippling regulations. He was convinced the nation was on the brink of ruin. Just thirty minutes later, a liberal client called to enthuse about the same economy, praising record employment, vibrant innovation, and unprecedented prosperity. Here's the paradox: both clients had similar financial situations and identical investment portfolios with identical results. They were living in the same reality . . . or so it seemed. In truth, they inhabited entirely different realities, each one filtered through a political lens. Why? In politics, perception supersedes reality. What you *expect* to see often colors what you *do* see.

When President Trump was elected in 2024, I witnessed an immediate role reversal in these two clients. The conservative's pessimism turned into bright optimism and the liberal's positive view of the economy and the country's direction suddenly became dark and gloomy. Nothing had fundamentally changed, but the switch in outlook was instantaneous and startling. It reminded me of a famous line by Mark Twain, who once observed, "You tell me whar a man gits his corn-pone, en I'll tell you what his 'pinions is."[1]

In plain English, Twain meant that if you show him where a person gets his *cornbread* (aka, his sustenance or social belonging), he can tell you what that person's opinions are. You might like to think you form your beliefs through independent reasoning, but more often, your beliefs come from the concrete box you inherited. You adopt the opinions that feed your sense of identity and ensure social acceptance. In politics especially, tribalism comes first and the facts a distant second. This tendency can have disastrous unintended consequences. If your investment decisions are significantly determined by partisan opinions, they have a high probability of being hazardous for the health of your finances.

The Corn-Pone Effect

Mark Twain's essay "Corn-Pone Opinions," explores how opinions and ideologies are formed. He argues that our views are shaped not by careful reasoning, but by a deep desire for approval and belonging. He may have first written this in 1901, but the observation still rings true, that "The poor man who has lost his job and is hungry and frightened . . . is not a Republican because he has studied out the doctrine and believes it; no, he is a Republican because he can't help it—he is a Republican because the men he hopes to work for are Republicans, and he wants to please them and get their good will."[2]

In Twain's view, many so-called convictions are just corn-pone opinions—ideas inherited or absorbed from your surroundings—because holding them wins approval. He writes about a man who was a Democrat, "not because he believes in that doctrine, but because he was born that way . . . It is a matter of association and sympathy and habit, not reasoning and conviction."[3] In short, what is often called personal belief is frequently little more than borrowed allegiance. Twain saw it before Twitter. We want to be liked more than we want to be right.

If Twain's world seems conformist, consider how much more powerful this effect is today. You live in an information age with 24/7 access to news and media. Many people tune into the news source or social feed that reassures them that *they are right*. You might watch Fox News religiously or prefer CNN. You might read *The New York Times* versus *The Wall Street Journal* or listen to Ben Shapiro instead of The Young Turks. Each side feels confident their source is the logical, factual, *truthful* one. And when you happen to hear the *other* side's version? Your stomach turns at what sounds like lies and propaganda. Most people are quick to catch bias in others yet remain blissfully unaware of the biases clouding their own thinking.

The greatest irony is that most people believe they arrived at their political opinions freely and rationally. They tell themselves a nice story: "I've weighed the facts, and I've thought this through." My experience tells a different story. We rarely choose our political beliefs by analytically comparing policy proposals. Instead, we inherit them, absorb them, and then defend them to the death, often without realizing it. Developing the ability to step back from this instinct—to dispassionately and objectively evaluate politics and economics—is a hallmark of wisdom. It's a skill that many people sadly lack, but one that is integral to acquiring Wisdom Wealth.

Digital Echo Chambers

Think about how your environment shapes your views (see figure 2.1). Twain pointed out that humans are natural conformists who take their cues from those around them. In the twenty-first century, "those around us" doesn't just refer to family and neighbors. It also includes the media

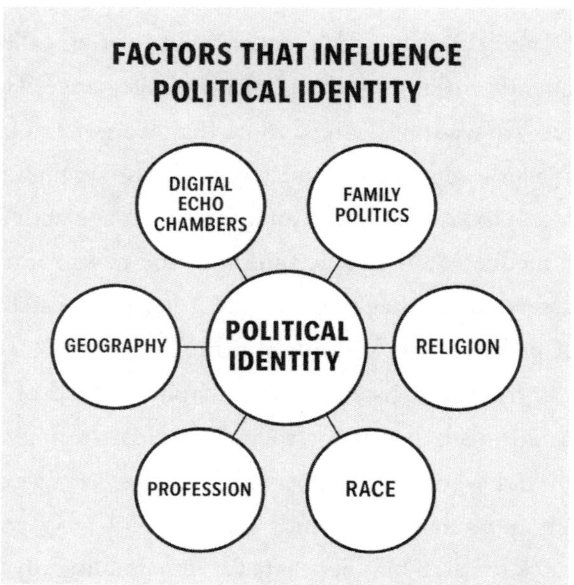

Figure 2.1: This diagram shows six factors that influence political identity.

you consume and the online communities you join or frequent. The last decade has supercharged echo chambers through social media algorithms. Picture a young woman who clicks on one political video online. By the end of that day, her feed will serve her five more videos echoing that same message—and ten more tomorrow morning. Within a month, she may be utterly convinced the world is black-and-white, without nuance or middle ground. Not because she researched deeply or heard multiple perspectives, but because an algorithm decided what she should hear. She has been quietly nudged into a digital tribe.

Whether on X, Facebook, YouTube, or TikTok, these platforms learn what makes you tick—or rather, what makes you *click*. If outrage over healthcare or immigration keeps you engaged, you'll see more of it. If you linger on videos celebrating one politician and trashing another, the algorithm obliges with an onslaught of the same. The result is millions of people sealed into digital echo chambers, each reinforcing corn-pone opinions. This way, you are in danger of becoming not only convinced that you are correct, but also increasingly hostile to those who disagree with you. Opposing viewpoints aren't just wrong to you; they start to feel alien, immoral, or even dangerous.

The Partisan Divide in America

Let's pause and look at some cold, hard numbers. In the United States today, about 47 percent of registered voters formally affiliate with one of the two major parties.[4] As of 2024, roughly 45.1 million Americans are registered Democrats (about 24 percent of all registered voters) and 36 million are registered Republicans (about 19 percent).[5] The remaining are independent or third-party. Yet these partisans wield outsize influence: in recent elections, more than 65 percent of all ballots were cast by party-affiliated voters, far above their share of the population. Simply put, party loyalists vote, and they vote in droves.[6]

This is a loyal group. According to Pew Research Center's validated voter survey, more than nine-in-ten self-identified Republicans (95 percent) voted for their party's presidential candidate in 2024—and the same 95 percent of Democrats voted for theirs.[7] Even when pollsters include "independents" who privately lean toward a party, the figures barely budge: 92 percent of Republican-leaning independents chose Trump, and 94 percent of Democratic-leaning independents chose Harris in 2024.[8] These numbers are astounding. It means that despite all the policy twists and candidate quirks, Americans largely vote *by team*. Red votes red; blue votes blue. Period.

When political identity becomes this dominant, it often reflects something deeper than ideology alone. Through the lens of the concrete box and the LIVING360 Grid, this pattern tends to emerge when political affiliation provides security, status, or belonging. This unquestioned loyalty can take root when someone is striving not thriving or enjoying prosperity without peace—without authentic self-knowledge or awareness of the broader world. In those states, political affiliation becomes less a set of ideas and more a source of certainty and identity.

As a result, relatively few voters change their minds. Those most likely to do so tend to be independents—a smaller but influential group whose turnout can shape election outcomes. Entertaining the possibility of voting for "the other side" requires more than information; it requires Wisdom Wealth—the capacity to step outside inherited identities and choose deliberately rather than reflexively.

Community Determines Politics

Where you live can be one of the strongest predictors of your politics. Your ZIP code may actually be a better clue to your ideology than your self-described "independent thinking." In some states, one party so dominates registration that being in the minority is truly being *a stranger in your own land*. The following is a snapshot of the top five states where one party utterly dominated voter registration in 2024:

Top Five Republican-Leaning States by Share of Registered Voters Who Are Republican[9]

1. Wyoming: 81 percent of registered voters are Republicans (yes, you read that right—in Wyoming, Republicans outnumber Democrats *four to one*)
2. Idaho: 58 percent Republican registrants
3. Oklahoma: 52 percent Republican registrants
4. Utah: 50 percent Republican registrants
5. South Dakota: 50 percent Republican registrants

Top Five Democratic-Leaning States by Share of Registered Voters Who Are Democrat[10]

1. Washington, DC: 76 percent of registered voters are Democrats (DC isn't a state, but its partisan makeup tops any state)
2. Maryland: 53 percent Democrat registrants
3. New York: 50 percent Democrat registrants
4. Delaware: 47 percent Democrat registrants
5. California: 47 percent Democrat registrants

It's striking to see that in Wyoming, more than four out of five voters walking into the polling booth are Republicans, whereas in DC, three out of four are Democrats. These super-majority locales create self-perpetuating political cultures: a Democrat in rural Idaho might feel she's in enemy territory, while a Republican in Brooklyn, New York, might feel like a lone wolf. In such environments, the dominant ideology becomes socially reinforced at every turn—your neighbors, your local officials, your news, all sing from the same hymn sheet. It's "corn-pone opinions" on a statewide scale that form the walls of our concrete box.

Politics as a Concrete Box

In addition to where you live, other factors that form our concrete box of political ideology include family influence, religion, race and ethnicity, and profession and class. Let's unpack a few of those.

FAMILY INFLUENCE

The strongest predictor of your political views is often your parents' political views. Political socialization begins early—kids absorb the talk at the dinner table, the news that's on TV in the background, the comments their parents make about politicians. If your parents are staunch partisans, chances are you will be too. In fact, Americans raised by consistently partisan parents tend overwhelmingly to adopt the same party. One extensive survey found that 62 percent of Americans raised by parents who consistently voted Democratic still identify as Democrats, and 57 percent of those raised by consistently Republican parents identify as Republicans in adulthood.[11] These are huge numbers when you consider all the other influences in life; clearly the apple doesn't fall far from the political tree.

Not every child follows their parents (family dynamics are complicated, and some rebel in politics as in everything else). But strong parental cues create a default concrete box that many never bother to change. The partisan inheritance is roughly symmetric—Democratic parents and Republican parents are about equally effective at passing on their allegiance. However, there's an interesting wrinkle: daughters raised in Republican households are markedly less likely to stick with the GOP than sons are. Only 44 percent of young women with Republican parents stayed Republican, compared to 67 percent of young men.[12] Can we say that girls are more open to stepping outside the box, when it comes to politics? Social factors such as abortion, gender, and LGBTQ issues may be pulling young women leftward despite their parents.

RACE AND ETHNICITY

Race intersects with geography and family, but it's worth noting broad trends. Black voters today overwhelmingly identify as Democrats. Republicans typically get under 10 percent of the Black vote in national elections (Trump got 15 percent in 2024, a slight uptick).[13] Hispanic voters have leaned Democratic, though that is changing. By 2024 Trump nearly split the Hispanic vote, losing it by only three points.[14] Asian

American subgroups vary, but overall lean Democratic. Meanwhile, a majority of White voters, especially those without college degrees, now lean Republican. These racial patterns are cultural as well as ideological. They shape the partisan atmosphere in households and communities. A young Black woman in Atlanta and a White farmer in Nebraska are likely to experience very different political socialization from their respective peer groups.

Each racial group carries its own historical relationship with political ideologies, and race becomes one of the walls in our concrete box. It shapes the stories we inherit and the lens through which we interpret the world.

PROFESSION AND CLASS

What you do for a living can also influence your political leanings more than you might realize. People often self-select into professions that attract "their kind" of people, and workplace culture can create its own political bubble. Consider these contrasts: Surveys and voter data show that police officers are nearly twice as likely to be Republican as the general public (one study of ninety-nine big-city police forces found about two times the proportion of Republicans compared to the civilian population, and campaign contribution records indicate roughly 68 percent of police officers lean Republican).[15]

On the flip side, K–12 teachers lean Democratic. A 2024 Pew Research study revealed that about 58 percent of public school teachers identify as Democrats or Democratic-leaning, versus 35 percent Republican-leaning.[16] This could be because police and military roles tend to attract conservative, order-oriented individuals (and the subculture reinforces that), whereas educators and academics operate in environments that emphasize social welfare, tilting them left. Our jobs don't *force* us to be Democrat or Republican, but they envelop us in an environment where certain views are the norm. Over time, the norm starts to feel like "the truth."

To illustrate, here are a few professions and how partisan they are in today's America (based on surveys of political donations and self-identification):

Republican-Leaning by Profession

1. Real Estate Agents/Brokers: About 55 percent Republican-leaning and 24 percent Democrats (business interests often align with GOP tax and regulatory preferences)[17]
2. Financial Advisors: Around 45 percent Republican and 21 percent Democrat (money managers tend to favor the GOP's free-market, low-tax stance)[18]
3. Farmers and Ranchers: Surveys show about 61 percent identify as Republican versus only 10 percent Democrat (rural agricultural communities have trended heavily Republican)[19]
4. Military Veterans: About 60 percent of US veterans align with the Republican Party (the military tradition has long leaned conservative)[20]

Democratic-Leaning by Profession

1. Journalists/Editors: About 36 percent Democratic leaning and 3.4 percent Republican (news media and publishing are more liberal in identification)[21]
2. Social Workers: Around 80 percent lean Democrat and 13 percent lean Republican (those in social services strongly favor the party of social programs)[22]

3. Scientists and Researchers: Roughly 55 percent lean Democrat and 6 percent lean Republican (academia and science communities skew left, valuing public funding and international cooperation)[23]
4. Psychologists/Therapists: Around 62 percent lean Democratic and 7 percent lean Republican (fields focused on social issues lean blue)[24]
5. Artists and Musicians: Approximately 80 percent lean Democrat and 20 percent lean Republican (creative industries thrive in liberal urban centers and embrace progressive values)[25]

Why do professions matter? Because they create daily peer groups and incentive structures that push political identities. A young police cadet quickly learns the prevailing attitudes among his fellow officers. A new teacher absorbs the discussions in the break room. Over time, the professional tribe can become as influential as the family tribe. You might "support small government" or "believe in universal healthcare," not always because you sat down and *worked it out* from first principles, but because the people around you—your parents, your friends, your coworkers—signaled that these beliefs are *acceptable* or *desirable* to them. As Twain noted, *approval* is the mighty force at work.

Identity over Issues

Interestingly, if you ask voters *why* they align with their chosen party, they often talk about broad values: "Republicans stand for freedom" or "Democrats fight for equality," and so on. But if you press for specifics, many struggle to name actual policies. This suggests that political identity often comes first, policy reasoning second. We join Team Red or Team Blue for a sense of belonging and identity and then we retrofit justifications for *why* our team's policies are "the best." It's human nature: we rationalize to make our group loyalty sound logical. The reality is that for most people, *belonging* precedes *believing*.

Political scientists describe party attachment almost like a sports fandom or a religious affiliation—something deeply emotional and not easily swayed by facts. That's why scandals or policy failures that seem like they *should* sway voters often don't. If "your guy" does something questionable, you may not believe it, or you may dismiss it as a one-off, or even find an equivalent sin on the other side to justify your continued loyalty. This is cognitive dissonance.

WHO IS LEADING WHOM?

Are leaders putting people back in new and shiny concrete boxes that serve their purpose? Charismatic leaders can absolutely shift public opinion—sometimes dramatically, even shattering the concrete box of entire voting blocks. Think of Ronald Reagan's sunny optimism in the 1980s, which helped usher in an era of conservative confidence. Or Barack Obama's message of hope and change, which energized a new generation. Or Donald Trump's fiery populism, which realigned the Republican Party around an anti-establishment, nationalist agenda. A powerful narrative from a single individual can make millions of people see the world differently almost overnight.

While leaders shape narratives and ideologies, they are constantly monitoring voter sentiment. Modern politicians have polling down to a science. They hold focus groups to test which phrases get applause. They scan social media to see what their base is excited or angry about. In many cases, politicians end up following the public mood rather than leading it. If they detect that voters are restless about, say, immigration or healthcare costs, they'll pivot their message to match the anxieties of their base.

So who's driving the bus? It's a bit of both. Leaders and the public are in a dance, each responding to the other. A shrewd politician amplifies what their supporters already feel, giving it voice and shape. Those supporters in turn become even more convinced and fervent because now their feelings have been validated from the podium. It's a feedback loop of conviction. Politicians don't always *lead*; often, they *echo*. And voters don't always *think*; often, they *react*.

Understanding this loop is important for anyone seeking wisdom. It reminds you that what you may consider your own opinion might actually be a reflection of a reflection—an echo of a narrative that was designed to resonate with you. Objective thinking requires you to oppose and debate your own thoughts.

EXERCISE: FIND THE ROOTS OF YOUR BELIEFS

Let's pause here for a personal exercise. Grab a pen or just think through these questions to examine your own political socialization:

1. Your dad's political leanings: ____________________
2. Your mom's political leanings: ____________________
3. When you were young, did your family talk politics at home? Yes / No
4. Did your family mostly support one political party? Yes / No
5. If yes, which? ____________________
6. Are your close friends' or your partner's politics similar to yours? Yes / No
7. Do you find that you lean toward the political ideology that is common among your family members or friends? Yes / No

continued

Now, challenge yourself: Think of three policies or ideas that are generally supported by the party you identify with *that you actually disagree with*. Write them down:

1. Policy/Idea 1: ______________________
2. Policy/Idea 2: ______________________
3. Policy/Idea 3: ______________________

The preceding exercise may not have changed your fundamental beliefs, but it can deepen your understanding of *where* those beliefs come from. It might also open the door to respecting others who have walked a different path. It's a step toward Wisdom Wealth—moving forward in your LIVING360 journey with greater self-awareness.

The goal isn't to foster doubt for doubt's sake, but to cultivate a healthy sense of perspective. When you know, for example, that you're inclined to favor policy X because everyone around you does, you become more open to evaluating policy X on its merits, not just its popularity in your circle. That is intellectual independence, Wisdom Wealth—a priceless asset.

When Politics Feels Like Religion

Humans have a tendency to treat politics with a fervor once reserved for religion. Both shape how we see the world, who we trust, and what we fear. There's a key difference: most religions call on us to believe in something *transcendent*, whereas politics calls on us to choose sides in very *earthly* conflicts. Yet the loyalty and emotion inspired can be strikingly similar. Many people approach their political party with the same devotion someone else might give to their church. Defying the party can feel like heresy. Switching parties? An act of apostasy.

There is, however, more room to change in politics than in religion. Political ideologies are *somewhat* more malleable. Parties shift platforms over time (consider how the Democrats and Republicans essentially traded places on many issues over the past century). Voters do change affiliations (though not frequently; when they do, it often realigns the whole system, as happened in the South from Democrat to Republican in the late twentieth century). Movements rise and fall—yesterday's fringe idea can become tomorrow's mainstream position, and vice versa. In other words, politics evolves as society does.

Knowing this can be liberating. If you acknowledge that your own views have roots in your upbringing, your social circles, and your news sources, you become less reactive and more reflective. Instead of instinctively demonizing the "other side," you can step back and ask: *How did they come to see the world that way?* Often, it's not because they are stupid or evil, but because their life experience delivered them a different story than yours did. Recognizing this complexity doesn't mean abandoning your convictions. It means holding them more *consciously*. You can still fight for what you believe is right, but you do so with an understanding that good people can sincerely disagree, because each of us is partly a product of our environment. This mindset is where Wisdom Wealth truly begins. It's not about being wishy-washy or sitting on the fence; it's about having conviction paired with curiosity.

Think of it like this: politics, like religion, is part of our story but it's not the *whole* story. No ideology has a monopoly on truth or virtue. Often attributed to Aristotle, the following quote, "It is the mark of an educated mind to be able to entertain a thought without accepting it," is an illustration of intellectual humility. In practice, that means listening to opposing views without immediately labeling the speaker as an enemy or a fool.

The American Exception

Having lived and traveled through more than twenty-five countries, I've seen the full spectrum of political environments, from open democracies to one-party states, from military dictatorships to theocracies. This global perspective gives me a profound appreciation for what we have in the United States. Despite all its polarization and partisan warfare, the US remains in many ways a beacon. We have a system, however imperfect, that is founded on the rule of law, created in a spirit of innovation, and still bears the capacity for reinvention. In some countries, if you join the "wrong" political tribe, your life opportunities, even your safety, could be at risk. In America, you can be a passionate Republican or Democrat or neither, and still live next door to someone of the opposite persuasion in peace. That is a *remarkable* achievement in human history. Our system encourages vigorous debate and dissent; it's noisy, it's messy, but it's also dynamic and resilient.

The freedom the US system provides to pursue not just material success, but a fuller life is also unusual by global standards. In many places, those who feel trapped by circumstance or constrained in thought have little room to maneuver. In America, even those who are striving yet not thriving, or who feel inwardly awakened but outwardly constrained, encounter fewer structural barriers than almost anywhere else on earth. The space to grow—economically, intellectually, and spiritually remains rare by global standards.

This American dynamism relies on an informed, curious, and engaged citizenry. We can't take it for granted. Each of us, whatever our politics, shares a responsibility to keep the civic fabric intact. That means recognizing that our political opponents are not our enemies—they are our neighbors, our coworkers, and our fellow Americans. *E pluribus unum*—"out of many, one." We can disagree vehemently on policy and still unite around the idea that the system must endure.

So, whatever your politics, remember that this grand democratic republic is bigger than left or right. It's a framework that allows left and right to duke it out with ballots instead of bullets. Cherish that. Protect it. And perhaps most importantly, be willing to step outside your partisan box to engage with ideas on their own terms.

Political beliefs often feel like facts. But wisdom begins when we question not just *what* we believe—but *why*. In a world that rewards outrage and certainty, choosing reflection takes courage. Now you see the roots of your own beliefs: the family conversations, the hometown echo, the profession you chose, the algorithms that learned your every click. You can feel the walls of the concrete box that were built for you, not by you. What will you do with that information?

Reflection Questions

After reflecting on your political beliefs and their origins, consider the following questions:

1. Why do you prefer a particular political party? In the past decade, have you thought about switching sides?
2. Has anything changed about how you see your own political identity?
3. Do you feel more empathy for those on the other side?
4. What conversations are you now open to having about your most deeply held political beliefs?

CHAPTER 3

Biology and Genetics

At seventeen, Adam seemed to have it all. He lived in a safe neighborhood, had two loving parents who never missed a school play or soccer game, and carried a GPA that made his Ivy League dreams feel like inevitabilities. On paper, his life was enviable. But inside, everything felt . . . muted. Joy, the kind that others seemed to experience in effortless bursts—spurred by a song on the radio, a sunset, a good grade—rarely made it past his emotional firewall. His world was a grayscale movie playing in a room full of people watching in color.

Teachers called Adam "serious" and "thoughtful." Friends said he was "too intense." His parents were bewildered by the persistent cloud that seemed to follow their son. One well-meaning adult told him to "just smile more." Another said he needed to "choose happiness." But Adam wasn't choosing sadness. He was just trying to survive the weight of it.

It wasn't until college, after a particularly difficult depressive spell, that a psychiatrist suggested genetic testing to Adam. The results came back with something unexpected: He carried a specific variation of the serotonin transporter gene (5-HTTLPR), known to be linked with lower emotional resilience and increased susceptibility to depression under stress. His brain wasn't broken; it was built differently.

What Adam discovered wasn't weakness or failure—it was wiring. And in that revelation lies one of the most humbling truths of the human condition: we are all shaped by biology before we ever choose our beliefs.

Whether it was genes, or dopamine, or serotonin, this information meant a certain kind of freedom and, for Adam, it was a turning point. He stopped blaming himself for not feeling what others felt. He began tailoring his life around his neurobiology. He prioritized sleep. He changed his diet. He exercised more regularly—not just to look good, but to generate dopamine. He built a life with structure, support, and awareness. He traded ambition for sustainability. He no longer chased someone else's version of happiness. He started building his own.

Understanding his biology didn't cure Adam, but it gave him awareness. And with awareness came acceptance and compassion—for himself and for others who quietly fight their own genetic battles. Most importantly, it gave him agency. It gave him the power not to rewrite his code, but to respond wisely to it.

In America—and increasingly across the world—we are told that anything is possible. That we can be anything we want to be. That with enough grit, hustle, and self-belief, we can rise above all odds. The American dream, after all, is built on this ethos. But biology doesn't read motivational posters. As you explore ways to elevate your life experience, it's essential to confront a sobering truth: Biology and genetics shape us all more than we may care to admit.

The myth of total control is powerful—but incomplete. Wisdom Wealth begins with the humility of the 3As: Awareness of what biology gives us, Action within what we can influence, and Acceptance of what we cannot change. There are certain parts of the concrete box that you can smash with action while some walls of the box are outside your control, here awareness and acceptance are key. Unlike John Locke, the seventeenth-century philosopher who argued that the mind begins as a blank slate (tabula rasa), I believe the mind at birth is largely empty but not entirely blank, for genetics and biology have already left their watermark (see figure 3.1).

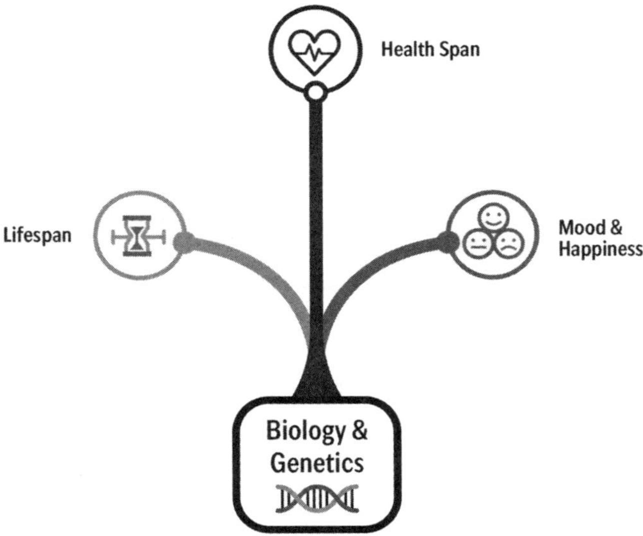

Figure 3.1: Genetics and biology exert powerful influences on behavior, potential, and life outcomes.

Genes and Limitations

It may feel un-American, even defeatist, to admit that you have limits. But ignoring biological constraints doesn't make them disappear. Understanding them, on the other hand, can free you. Unlike religion and politics, our control on biology and genetics may be limited.

Your genes don't determine everything, but they set the range within which you live. They shape your predisposition to disease, your physical traits, your emotional tendencies, and yes—even your capacity for happiness. As Michael Sandel writes in *The Tyranny of Merit*, "Even if we do 'work hard' or 'succeed on our own,' our natural talents—like intelligence, discipline, or athletic ability—are not things we earned. They are gifts."[1]

Recognizing the role of genetic luck is not meant to diminish personal responsibility. Instead, it adds humility and perspective to your narratives of success—and compassion for others who walk different biological paths.

YOUR EXPECTED LIFESPAN

Twin and family studies confirm that genetics account for 20–30 percent of lifespan variability, with the remainder driven by environment, behavior, and chance. For instance, a 2022 review in the *International Journal of Molecular Science* identified more than fifty genes linked to human longevity. The authors stated that "About 40% of human life expectancy is inherited among generations. Genetic mechanisms and pathways that influence lifespan have been demonstrated across decades of research."[2] A separate review published in *Immunity & Ageing* supports the finding that "Approximately 25% of the variation in human longevity is due to genetic factors."[3]

HAPPINESS AND HEREDITY

Now let's explore a more surprising (and perhaps unsettling) finding: Your genes influence happiness. A lot.

Aristotle famously wrote in *Nicomachean Ethics*: "Happiness depends on ourselves."[4] He argued that human flourishing (or *eudaimonia*) is cultivated through virtue. And to a degree, he was right. But modern positive psychology reveals a more nuanced picture (see figure 3.2):

- 50 percent of your happiness is determined by your genetic set point[5]
- 10 percent by your life circumstances[6]
- 40 percent by intentional activity (your mindset, habits, and relationships)[7]

WHAT DETERMINES HAPPINESS?

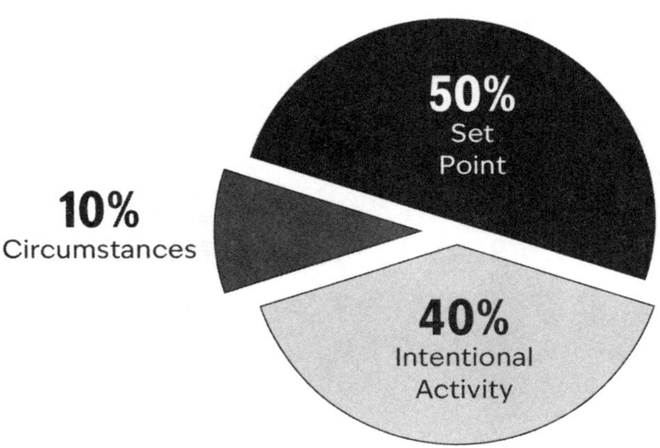

Figure 3.2: The surprising drivers of happiness.

This model, developed by psychologist Sonja Lyubomirsky in *The How of Happiness*, suggests that half of your emotional baseline is hardwired.[8] Some people simply win the happiness gene lottery.

Your wealth, career status, or educational level (life circumstances) account for only 10 percent of happiness. The biggest opportunity lies in the 40 percent—intentional choices that you make every day. *How you think. How you act. Who you love. How you move. What you pursue.*

You can't choose your parents. You can't rewrite your genetic code. You may not even be able to change your life circumstances quickly. But you can control the 40 percent. The intentional part. The effort part. The "how you live" part. This is where LIVING360 focuses its energy:

Not on selling false hope, but on building real agency through clarity, self-awareness, and practical action.

How you use your 40 percent determines whether you live as a victim of your genes or as the author of your own life. In the chapters ahead, we'll explore practical ways to use that 40 percent to elevate your happiness and well-being.

GENES AND DISEASE RISK

Beyond monogenic illnesses, even complex diseases like heart disease, kidney failure, and major depression are significantly influenced by genetic predisposition (see table 3.1):

TABLE 3.1: GENETIC INFLUENCE ON DISEASE

Disease	Estimated Genetic Influence
Heart Disease	40-60%[9]
Kidney Failure	30-50%[10]
Depression	35-40%[11]

Genetics interact with lifestyle and environment. Within the genetic framework behavior and personal choice contributes to lifespan and health span. Recognizing the influence of genetics and biology, can help you abandon blame and focus on early detection, personalized prevention, and emotional empathy.

To say that genes matter is not to say that effort doesn't. To acknowledge biological limits is not to surrender to them. It is to see the truth clearly—so we can respond wisely.[12] You may not control your starting point, but you can control your direction. You may inherit a predisposition to sadness, but you can train your brain for resilience.

You may face biological obstacles, but you can learn to navigate around them. You may not choose the story you were born into, but you can shape the chapters ahead.

This is the essence of LIVING360: honoring the parts of our life that are fixed, while fully embracing the parts we can influence.

Genetics gives us a frame. Biology sets some boundaries. But meaning, fulfillment, and peace? Those still lie in how we choose to live. Let's choose wisely. Let's move forward—intentionally, and with clarity.

Reflection Questions

1. What role do you think genetics and biology play in how long a person will live?
2. Do you agree with the research that genetics determine 50 percent of a person's happiness?
3. Has your life been influenced by your biology or genetics in any way?

CHAPTER 4

Free Will and Decision Making

You didn't choose your parents. You didn't choose your body. You didn't choose your first language, your culture, or the stories you grew up hearing. And yet, there is something in you that pauses, that questions, that dreams of different paths. But the question remains: Is your next decision truly yours or just a product of wiring, upbringing, and algorithmic nudges? In a world where neuroscience maps the brain like a machine and social media engineers your attention, the age-old debate intensifies: Do we genuinely possess free will, or are we passengers with the illusion of control?

From the determinism of Schopenhauer to the moral imperative of Kant, philosophers have wrestled with the idea of free will for centuries. Today, the advancement of modern technology begs a new question: If algorithms know us better than we know ourselves, and they accurately predict our actions can freedom still exist, or are our wills merely predetermined scripts running quietly in the background? As you bump and bounce against your concrete box, you need to know if you really choose your actions—or if you are simply following a path led by your genes, environment, and cosmic circumstances.

In my own personal life, I am quite certain that I am addicted to sugar and, more specifically, chocolate. While I am not obese, it's fifteen years that I have been trying to shed the fifteen additional pounds of fat I carry around. This has made me a pre-diabetic but every night, I feel an urge to have chocolate. Most nights I give in. I believe that this craving has come from my unique biology and my childhood. As a child, I only got to eat chocolate once a year when a distant relative visited us in Karachi from London and brought a Cadbury bar. My parents would give it to me, and I would eat it in five minutes. Then I had to wait an entire year or longer to taste chocolate again. This may have altered my brain chemistry for life, pushing me to want chocolate all the time. Do I freely eat chocolate every night or was it determined fifty years ago when I spent so long dreaming of chocolate? For me, it is chocolate: for others, it may be sex, pornography, alcohol, gambling, or arguing with the boss. Do you freely choose?

The question of free will versus determinism is not just an abstract philosophical puzzle. It's foundational to how you view responsibility, justice, personal identity, and the meaning of life itself. If your choices are not truly yours, what does that mean for morality, self-improvement, or accountability?

Free Will Versus Determinism

At its core, free will exists when a person can control their actions with intent, recognizes the availability of alternatives, and has the power to veto what they do not want. It assumes agency—that someone is a conscious author of their own choices.

The opposite of free will is determinism. *The Stanford Encyclopedia of Philosophy* defines causal determinism as "the idea that every event is necessitated by antecedent events and conditions together with the laws of nature."[1]

Under determinism, no matter how free your choice feels, you could not have chosen otherwise. Every decision is the inevitable endpoint of a vast chain of prior causes—your childhood, your biology, your neurons, the weather, the cosmos, and so on (see figure 4.1).

INFLUENCERS OR
DETERMINANTS OF CHOICES

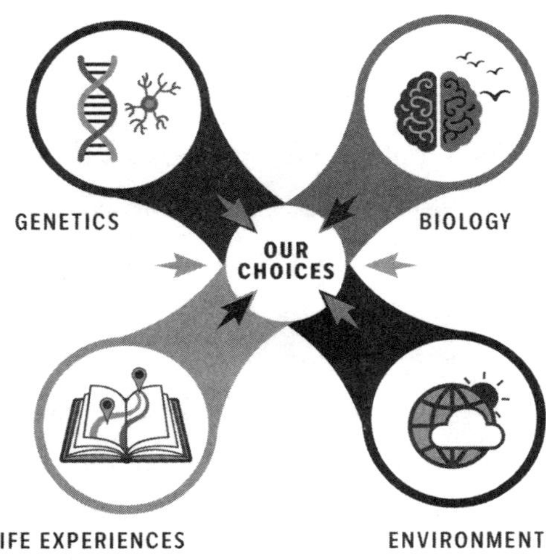

Figure 4.1: Our choices emerge from the interaction of genetics, biology, life experiences, and environment.

TWO THOUSAND YEARS OF PHILOSOPHICAL TRADITION

Philosophers of every age have found new reasons to doubt human freedom. If God controls everything, or if natural laws govern all outcomes, then what room remains for agency and choice? For Aristotle, moral responsibility required that people act knowingly and voluntarily: "We are the cause of our actions . . . it is up to us to act or not to act."[2]

Yet the Stoics, particularly Epictetus and Zeno, believed that while events are fated by a rational universe, human freedom lies in how we respond. True freedom, they argued, is inner freedom—not changing events but accepting them.

This debate extended into Christian theology as well. St. Augustine defended free will as essential to morality and salvation, writing that humans sin or obey by their own volition. Martin Luther, however, declared in *On the Bondage of the Will*: "Free will is a downright lie."[3] He argued that salvation and human conduct are entirely governed by divine grace.

During the Enlightenment, philosophers such as Immanuel Kant argued that freedom was not just compatible with morality—it was its precondition. Without autonomy, moral law would lose all force. "Freedom is the ground of the moral law," Kant wrote.[4]

In the twentieth century, Sigmund Freud introduced the idea of the unconscious mind, suggesting that much of what we do is shaped by hidden, irrational forces. Meanwhile, Albert Einstein famously said: "God does not play dice with the universe."[5] With this statement, Einstein aligned himself with a strictly causal view of reality. But dissent endured. Karl Popper, one of the great philosophers of science, pushed back: "The future is open. It is not predetermined and thus cannot be predicted, except by accident."[6]

THE MODERN SCIENTIFIC ASSAULT ON FREE WILL

Today, science offers a powerful challenge to the idea of free agency. Neuroscience, evolutionary biology, and physics increasingly suggest that free will might be an illusion. One of the most compelling arguments comes from Robert Sapolsky, professor of evolutionary biology at Stanford University. In his books *Behave* and *Determined*, Sapolsky argues that human behavior is entirely determined by biology and context. Free will, he says, is a comforting illusion.

Here are four of his most compelling points:[7]

1. "All we are is the history of our biology, over which we had no control, and its interaction with environments, over which we also had no control."
2. "Another relevant factor is the brain chemistry, of just how tempting the temptation is." He argues that even the belief "I have willpower and can choose to use it" is itself determined by biology, experience, environment—and thus not a free choice.
3. "Luck does not even out over time, and bad or good luck is further amplified over time."
4. "Free will is biology we do not understand."

Sapolsky also systematically dismantles popular arguments that attempt to salvage free will:[8]

- Chaos theory introduces unpredictability but not volition. It doesn't grant freedom—just makes outcomes harder to calculate.
- Emergent complexity adds layers to causality but doesn't break the chain. A more complex cause is still a cause.
- Quantum indeterminacy, where subatomic particles behave probabilistically, offers randomness—not conscious control. Chance is not choice.

Physicist Brian Greene, in his book, *Until the End of Time*, explains that "Our choices and thoughts arise from physical processes—the firing of neurons, governed by the laws of physics . . . and the absence of free will, as traditionally defined, seems to be the inescapable conclusion of scientific determinism."[9] To Greene, free will is a subjective experience—a psychological product of our brain's complexity and flexibility—but not something that truly exists in physical reality.

So What's the Truth?

Many philosophers and psychologists argue that thinkers such as Sapolsky and Greene conflate mechanism with meaning. Explaining how decisions happen doesn't render those decisions meaningless or automatic, in the same way that understanding respiration doesn't reduce the significance of breath. Understanding synaptic activity doesn't mean your reflections, dreams, or moral choices are illusions.

Human beings possess metacognition—we can reflect, imagine, delay, veto, and weigh alternatives. This may not break the chain of cause and effect, but it does introduce a layer of conscious participation. Maybe we are not entirely free—but maybe we are not entirely bound, either. Freedom may not mean absolute control—but rather the capacity to navigate, reflect, and resist.

WHY SOCIETY ASSUMES FREE WILL

Regardless of where the truth lies, modern civilization is built on the assumption of human agency:

- The Declaration of Independence speaks of "unalienable rights," implying a moral agent who can act upon them.
- The US Constitution presupposes rational choice: in voting, in lawmaking, in justice.
- Legal and moral systems rest on concepts of intent, consent, and culpability.

Even in economics, society assumes people can choose to work, save, invest, and innovate. If all decisions are determined, these systems become incoherent.

You must live *as if* you are free because this fiction—if it is one—provides meaning and creates moral order. Acknowledging the limits of free will doesn't undermine your life—it can deepen it. It can temper arrogance when you succeed. It can soften judgment when others fail. It can foster compassion both for others and yourself. Knowing the subtleties and debate around the good and bad choices and how to accept actions and outcomes that may appear unwise is Wisdom Wealth. Recognizing the debate around free will can, paradoxically, be liberating!

Maybe life is not about being the author of your story. Maybe it's about revising the story with awareness. The debate will continue. Maybe it should. Because freedom—real or not—is the most meaningful illusion you have. Psychological and cross-cultural evidence consistently shows that people who believe in free will report greater happiness, life satisfaction, and psychological wellness.[10] Welcome to the paradox!

How Bias Affects Your Decision Making

Aside from the existential implications of determinism versus free will, there is another force acting upon you—whether you're aware of it or not—exerting its powerful, invisible influence on every choice you make, insight you have, and opportunity you pursue. This force is, of course, your own unique personal bias. I have seen the undeniable effect of bias in action before.

It was July 2008. I sat in my Irvine, California, office, eyes fixed on the screen as Treasury Secretary Henry Paulson testified before Congress. He was asking lawmakers for what he called a "bazooka"—emergency authority to rescue Fannie Mae and Freddie Mac, the two mortgage giants teetering on the brink. Paulson explained that if markets believed he had the bazooka, he would never need to fire it. Confidence alone, he argued, would restore stability. Months later, that confidence proved misplaced: the US government stepped in and took control of both institutions. As this financial drama unfolded on my TV screen, a knock sounded at my door.

It was David, a name I use to represent a common situation I have seen many times. He was grinning like a man who had spotted treasure on a deserted beach. His navy blazer, gray pants, and crisp white shirt added to his personality and confidence. He sat down, leaning forward in the leather chair, and the words that followed were the kind that have preceded both great fortunes and great disasters.

"This is it," he said, his voice a low, confident hum. "The financial sector stocks are on sale, banks are dirt cheap. They'll bounce back in months—maybe six months but certainly within twelve months. I'm going in and big."

David wasn't a reckless man. He had built his wealth carefully, by investing in his company stock when it was small and private. When his company went public, his stock soared, and his little fortune turned into a big one. But on that day, something was different. His conviction wasn't the quiet kind that comes from sound reasoning; it was an electric, almost feverish certainty that bubbles up when the mind tells you it has found a once-in-a-lifetime opportunity. He was operating entirely inside his concrete box—the invisible space built from his personal history, successes, failures, and unquestioned assumptions.

Inside that box, the truth was a curated narrative. His past victories with big, contrarian bets formed one wall. The financial headlines and market chatter he had selectively absorbed formed another. His faith in his ability to read the market better than anyone else formed the ceiling. The reason these walls are so hard to see—and so difficult to challenge—is not a lack of intelligence, but the way the human mind works. To explain that, it helps to turn to one of the most influential psychologists of our time.

There Are Two Voices in Your Head

Years earlier, Nobel Prize–winning psychologist Daniel Kahneman gave the world the language for what we all experience but rarely notice.

He called them System 1 and System 2.[11] They describe two modes of thinking that, together, steer the course of your life.

- System 1: Fast, automatic, emotional. It's your mind's autopilot, handling routine tasks with incredible efficiency. It's the reflex that makes you brake when a car ahead stops suddenly or the gut feeling that lets you sense tension in someone's voice. Without System 1's split-second judgments, you couldn't survive.
- System 2: Slow, deliberate, analytical. It's the conscious pilot, the part of you that studies mortgage options, works through a difficult math problem, or debates a complex political question. It burns more mental energy than System 1, which is why you likely avoid engaging it unless you have no other choice.

Here's the trap: System 1 always wants to drive. Even when the road ahead is full of blind curves and hidden cliffs, it insists it knows the way. System 2, tired of arguing, often just lets it.

As I look back, David's System 1 was behind the wheel, pedal pressed to the floor. His mind wasn't calculating probabilities; it was narrating a story—one in which he, the savvy investor, bought the banks at the bottom and doubled his fortune. Kahneman called this "narrative coherence." Once a story makes sense in your head, your brain stops searching for other possibilities. This is where the walls of the concrete box begin to feel like an unshakeable truth.

Case Study: David's Biases at Work

The biases of System 1 aren't abstract philosophical concepts; they are the invisible materials that build the walls of our box. On that day in 2008, David's mind was a masterclass in their power.

- **Confirmation Bias:** David was an avid reader, but his mind was on a mission. He wasn't seeking truth; he was seeking confirmation. He was selectively focused on every headline or analyst report that supported his contrarian story, why bank stocks are a bargain, completely ignoring the risk of systemic failure. The information he was consuming wasn't a window to the world; it was a mirror reflecting his own belief.

- **Anchoring Bias:** The past price of the stocks was an irresistible anchor. A bank stock that once traded at $80 was now available for $30. David's System 1 saw this as an incredible discount, not a grim verdict on its true value. He fixated on that old price as a baseline, unable to see that the current price was still a disastrously bad deal given the new reality. That single piece of information, a number from the past, exerted a gravity he couldn't escape.
- **Overconfidence Bias:** David's past success during his company's IPO had become a ceiling on his thinking. His mind whispered, "You've been right before, and you'll be right again." This bias convinced him that his singular insight was superior to the collective anxiety of the market. It was a comfortable illusion of expertise that, in a matter of months, cost him dearly.

I see this powerful need for certainty play out in my MBA classroom every semester. When students ask me, "Where do you think the S&P 500 will be next year?" or "What's your forecast for interest rates?" they don't want an honest response; they want a confident answer, the kind that sounds like prophecy. When I tell them, "I don't know," and offer a range of probabilities, they often look at me with disappointment, convinced that I am simply keeping a secret, better opinion to myself. But that's the truth: The world is not certain, and pretending otherwise is the most dangerous form of self-deception.

Thinking in Probabilities

This is where renowned statistician Nate Silver's work offers a powerful solution. Silver, famous for his election forecasts, urges us to stop asking, "What will happen?" and start asking, "What is likely to happen, and by how much?"[12] This is probabilistic thinking—assigning odds instead of certainties (see figure 4.2). It's the disciplined art of confronting reality as it is, not as we wish it to be. Probabilistic thinking is a conscious mental tool that allows us to crack the walls of our concrete box. It replaces the comfort of a single story with the humility of a range of possibilities.

Imagine if David had engaged this tool. His thought process would have looked less like a monologue and more like a structured conversation:

- *Step 1: Assign Probabilities.* Instead of "I'm going all in," a probabilistic thinker might have said, "I assign a 40 percent chance the banks will recover in one year, a 30 percent chance they'll stay flat or fail, and a 30 percent chance of a quick bounce." This isn't a guess; it's an act of intellectual honesty that forces you to acknowledge uncertainty.
- *Step 2: Incorporate New Information.* As new data emerged—the collapse of Bear Stearns, the failure of Lehman Brothers, the government takeover of Freddie and Fannie—the probabilistic thinker would have adjusted those odds. The 40 percent chance of recovery might have quickly dropped to 30 percent, then 20 percent. This continuous updating, which statisticians call Bayesian updating, is like a GPS recalculating your route after every missed turn. It's the practice of opening your mind to reality, one new fact at a time.
- *Step 3: Track and Learn.* The final step is to keep a log of your decisions. What were your original probabilities? How did the situation evolve? Where did your assumptions go wrong?

> Tracking your decisions is how the conscious pilot (System 2) gets smarter over time. It's how you build a better compass for life's inevitable turbulence.

The problem is that most people don't update their narratives. Once a belief takes root, it becomes part of the box. And when the walls are painted with certainty, you can mistake them for truth.

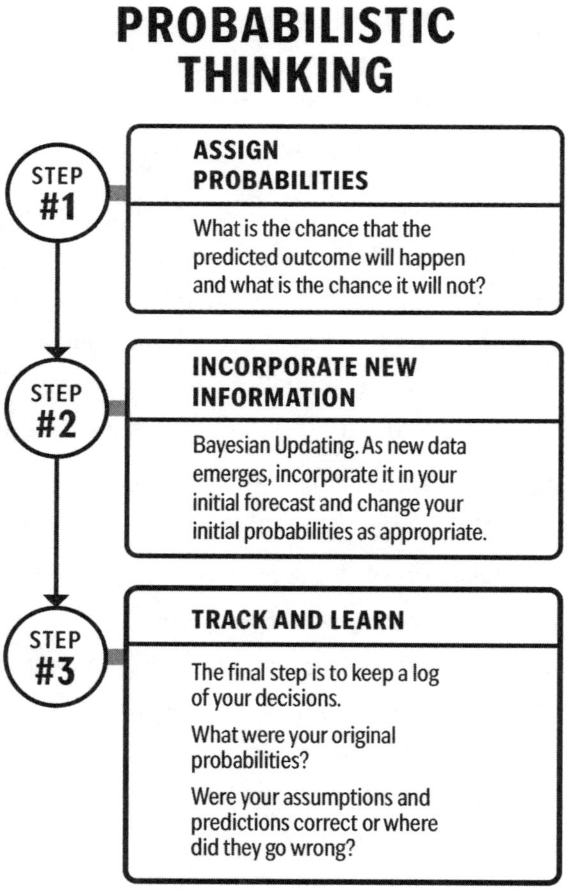

PROBABILISTIC THINKING

STEP #1

ASSIGN PROBABILITIES

What is the chance that the predicted outcome will happen and what is the chance it will not?

STEP #2

INCORPORATE NEW INFORMATION

Bayesian Updating. As new data emerges, incorporate it in your initial forecast and change your initial probabilities as appropriate.

STEP #3

TRACK AND LEARN

The final step is to keep a log of your decisions.

What were your original probabilities?

Were your assumptions and predictions correct or where did they go wrong?

Figure 4.2: This chart illustrates the three steps in probabilistic thinking.

David never adjusted. He held firm to his original story even as the headlines got worse and financial stocks continued declining. By the time he realized the narrative in his head didn't match reality, the damage was done. He didn't lose everything, but the setback cost him dearly. Even now, when he calls me with a "can't miss" idea, I remind him of that day. He laughs, but it's the rueful laugh of a man who has learned the hard way that certainty can be the most expensive emotion in finance.

How to Live with Bias

The goal is not to eliminate your biases. That's impossible. The objective is to recognize them and to allow System 2 to take control of deliberation when the stakes are high and decisions are complex.

This is the ultimate lesson of Wisdom Wealth. It's the humbling realization that the world is too complex to be certain. In embracing that uncertainty, you create Awareness. You don't lose power; you find new, more profound ways to take Action. It allows you to be honest with yourself and gain Acceptance of the outcome.

Predicting the future with certainty and accuracy is impossible. The goal is to prepare for it—intelligently, humbly, and with the awareness that wisdom grows not from being right all the time, but from being wrong less disastrously. This is the difference between a life lived on autopilot and a life lived with purpose. It is the very essence of LIVING360.

The debate about your free will may continue for eternity, but every time you catch a bias in your decision making, you reclaim your freedom from the iron fist of determinism.

Reflection Questions

1. How much free will do you believe you have? Circle below:

Total Determinism									Absolute Free Will
1	2	3	4	5	6	7	8	9	10

2. Can you think of a decision you made that didn't feel like a true choice?
3. Can you think of a time when you vetoed your initial choice and took a different direction freely?
4. Do you like it when people provide forecasts and answers with absolute confidence and certainty?
5. Do you tend to frame questions or decisions in a binary (yes/no) manner, or do you use a probabilistic approach?

PART II

Know the World

Stepping outside your concrete box is a transformative moment. Once you begin to understand yourself, the next challenge becomes unavoidable: you must understand the world that shapes you. You do not live in isolation. Your happiness, your opportunities, your career, your relationships, and even your financial security are deeply intertwined with forces far larger than any individual (see figure II.1).

The universe around us is driven by a thousand currents: the laws of nature, the sweep of history, shifting cultures, scientific breakthroughs, demographic changes, political power struggles, and global economic tides. Together, they form the environment in which every one of your decisions—personal, professional, emotional, and financial—will play out.

We will journey from the birth of the universe to the rise of modern society, from cosmic dust to cultural identity. Its purpose is to widen your sense of time, sharpen your understanding of change, and equip you to navigate an age of acceleration with both wisdom and wealth. The wider your field of vision, the better your decisions about money, work, health, purpose, and the future.

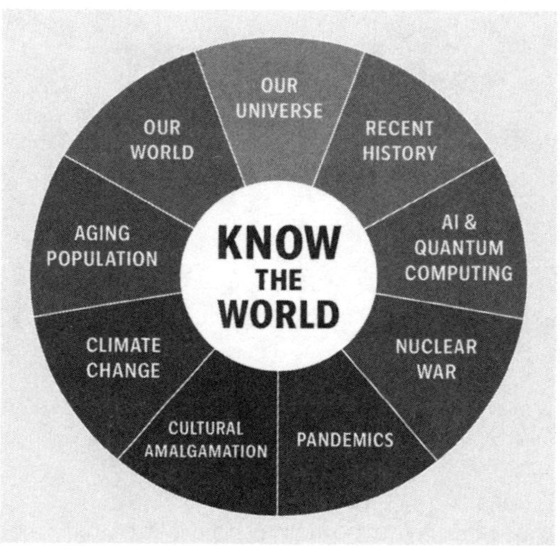

Figure II.1: The future is shaped by global forces spanning past and present.

Humanity now stands at the edge of profound transformation. The AI revolution is rewriting the rules of work, creativity, and even thinking. Longevity and health spans are altering markets and economies. Global power dynamics—especially the evolving relationship between the United States and China—will determine the direction of the next century. Meanwhile, cultural amalgamation is reshaping identities, blending traditions, and redefining belonging.

This section is intentionally expansive. It distills the most critical ideas, forces, and megatrends that will influence your life—your career, your sense of purpose, your community, your family, and your financial future.

My goal is not just to inform you, but to prepare you—to give you the foresight and clarity required to thrive in a world that is accelerating, integrating, and transforming. Understanding the world is not an intellectual luxury—it is a survival skill. The next few decades will redefine what it means to work, to age, to relate, to belong, and to plan for the future. Those who practice the 3As—Awareness of what is changing, Action aligned with reality, and Acceptance of uncertainty—are far more likely to adapt, seize opportunities, and build lasting relationships and financial security on the path toward LIVING360. Those who don't may find themselves overwhelmed by changes they never saw coming.

CHAPTER 5

The Big Picture

I want to take you back to a memory from my childhood, a rooftop in Karachi. The city's noise would fade and the lights would dim, allowing the sky to open up. I would lie on my back and stare into the endless, star-dusted darkness, trying to grasp the scale of it all. It felt like an ocean of silence, and I was just a single grain of sand.

Have you ever had a moment like that? A moment when you felt an overwhelming sense of smallness, and in that smallness, a strange, powerful sense of peace?

That feeling, that profound sense of wonder and humility, is where your journey into knowing the world must begin. You can't hope to understand your place in the universe until you first accept its scale and, more importantly, humanity's staggering ignorance of it. As Socrates once said, "The only true wisdom is in knowing you know nothing." This Socratic idea is to push you to continue learning by recognizing the limits of your knowledge. Albert Einstein also noted, "As our circle of knowledge expands, so does the circumference of darkness surrounding it."[1]

And yet, we wonder. Curiosity is the most human of traits, the force that pushes us to ask: What sparked the Big Bang? Could consciousness exist elsewhere in the universe? Am I just a flicker in cosmic time or part of something larger?

These are questions worth sitting with—not because you will find easy answers, but because the asking itself is an act of defiance against your own limited perceptions. These reflections will guide you deeper into your own journey of understanding and provide a sense of calm and peace through widening your perspective.

This isn't just an exercise in stargazing. LIVING360 is about living with both wisdom and financial security. Wisdom begins with awareness—seeing beyond your immediate concerns, beyond your cultural box, beyond even the Earth itself. When you hold a cosmic perspective, your daily anxieties shrink to their proper size. Financial setbacks, career disappointments, even personal conflicts—all look different when you remember that you are a speck in a galaxy among trillions, alive for a blink of cosmic time.

The Luck of a Billion-Dollar Lottery

Astrophysicists believe the universe began roughly 14 billion years ago with an event they call the Big Bang. From that explosive beginning, space and time emerged. But what came before it? What triggered it? Here, even the most brilliant minds go quiet. The universe begins after the miracle.

Over billions of years, matter cooled, particles clumped together, and stars and galaxies formed. Then, 4.5 billion years ago, our own solar system came into being. Think for a moment about the improbable perfection of our home. Earth is at a perfect distance from the Sun: not too far to be frozen, not too close that everything burns, but just right for life to thrive. This is a delicate, astronomical dance, a series of cosmic coincidences so vast it boggles the mind. We are in the right spot in a galaxy that is the right size, orbiting a star that is the right temperature.

The chances of this occurring are so infinitesimal that it's like buying a lottery ticket and not only winning the jackpot, but winning it again the next day, and the next week, and the next month—all with the same ticket, for every single day of your life. Divine intervention or a random event? Physicists or statisticians may say that when you increase the time period to billions of years, everything will happen. Things that have a very, very low chance of happening will inevitably happen because the time scale is so large. The human mind can't grasp what a billion years means, but it can grasp the wonder of such astronomical luck.

This cosmic perspective is a gift. It allows for a profound sense of acceptance that your existence is a beautiful, improbable accident. Whether divine or random, the result is the same. The only question that matters is what you will do with your cosmic jackpot?

Since the 1700s, human understanding of the cosmos has accelerated rapidly—thanks to Newton, Hubble, Hawking, and the minds behind modern physics. Yet despite satellites, telescopes, and quantum models, we are still barely scratching the surface. With more than two trillion galaxies and hundreds of sextillions of stars and planets, it's difficult to believe Earth is the only place with life. The numbers alone suggest we're probably not alone—though no confirmed evidence of extraterrestrial life has yet reached the public domain.

Greater knowledge leads not to arrogance, but to awe. And awe, once felt, changes the way you see everything that follows. Because the deeper you look into the universe, the more you realize that what you see may not be what's truly there.

A Useful Illusion

What if I told you that the very "reality" you see with your own eyes is a useful illusion? Close your eyes for a moment. What do you picture when I say the word "tree"? You likely see a brown trunk, green leaves, and branches reaching for the sky. You see a familiar, solid object. Now, what if I told you that this image is not a true representation of the tree, but a brilliant lie?

Professor Donald Hoffman's interface theory of perception (ITP) suggests that evolution did not equip us to see reality as it is, but rather as it helps us survive.[2] He likens our perception to a computer desktop. The folder icon on your screen doesn't show you the raw code of the files inside it; it's a simple, functional shortcut. In the same way, the image of a tree is a shortcut crafted by your brain. It tells you, "This is a stable thing to climb," or "This is a place to find fruit." It's a survival tool, not a truth-seeking device. Hoffman's evolutionary models suggest that creatures who see reality too accurately often go extinct, while those who see a simplified, functional version survive and reproduce. Your brain's deception is why you don't perceive a tiger as a complex web of quantum probabilities, but as a clear, immediate threat you must run from.

Over millennia, our senses as a species have evolved to help us dodge predators, not comprehend galaxies. Humanity's tools may have improved, but our biological limitations remain. Your brain is a brilliant liar, and it lies to keep you safe.

Understanding that your mind is an artist, not a camera, frees you from the illusion of certainty. It reminds you that seeing clearly isn't about adding more facts—it's about noticing your filters or the walls of the concrete box.

A Brief History of How You Got Here (1609–2025)

Now that you have witnessed the vastness of space and time, it is time to turn your gaze from the cosmic to the human. From stardust to society.

To continue on your path to Wisdom Wealth, you must now make a short leap, from the year 5 billion BCE to 1609 CE. While your journey through the stars was meant to awaken awe, this brief history of the modern world is the story of humanity's continuous cycle of awareness, action, and acceptance. It is a story of how we became aware of our power to reason, how we took action to build a new world with that power, and how we were forced to accept the consequences of both our greatest triumphs and our most devastating mistakes. This is the framework you will use to understand your world.

Humans, as a species, have walked this Earth for roughly three hundred thousand years. For the vast majority of that time, we lived as nomadic hunter-gatherers in tight-knit bands of one hundred to two hundred people, moving constantly in search of food, water, and shelter. Then, around ten thousand to twelve thousand years ago, everything changed. In a quiet revolution, wheat was sown, animals were domesticated, and humans began to settle.[3] Yuval Noah Harari famously posed the question: "Did humans domesticate wheat, or did wheat domesticate humans?"[4]

With agriculture came permanent settlements, rigid social hierarchies, property ownership, population booms—and with them, new forms of anxiety, monotony, and inequality. Life expectancy improved, but did the quality of life follow suit?

For nearly ten thousand years after agriculture took root, human progress in knowledge and lifestyle remained relatively slow. The story of civilization is long and layered, and while we could linger in the philosophical depths of Ancient Greece or witness the profound rise of spiritual traditions like Christianity and Islam, this chapter will focus on a more immediate arc: from the early 1600s to today. This is the era that birthed the modern world we inhabit—the institutions we rely on, the technologies we wield, the ideologies we debate, and the systems that now shape our global destiny. It's the recent past, but its impact is nothing short of revolutionary.

THE NIGHT GALILEO LOOKED THROUGH THE GLASS

On a cold winter night in 1609, Galileo Galilei stood on a rooftop in Padua, Italy, peering through a strange new contraption: a telescope he had built himself. What he saw that night would shatter the intellectual order of Europe.

The moon was not a perfect heavenly sphere, but a rugged world of craters and mountains. Jupiter had moons of its own, orbiting not the Earth, but another planet entirely. And the stars? There were far more than the naked eye could see—countless points of light stretching endlessly into darkness.

Galileo's discoveries didn't just challenge astronomy; they challenged the belief, deeply rooted in both religion and tradition, that Earth was the fixed center of the universe and humanity the focus of all creation. He wrote, "All truths are easy to understand once they are discovered; the point is to discover them."[5]

For his daring to look beyond the accepted frame—to step outside the concrete box of his time—Galileo was threatened with imprisonment and forced to recant under the glare of the Inquisition. He had seen farther than his society was ready to accept. The lesson was clear: Every leap forward begins with someone willing to see past the walls others cannot.

ENLIGHTENMENT THINKING

A new current of thought had begun coursing through Europe by the eighteenth century. In salons, coffeehouses, and lecture halls, people debated radical ideas about governance, human rights, and the nature of knowledge itself.

What if rulers were not chosen by divine will? What if ordinary citizens had the right—and the capacity—to govern themselves? What if reason, evidence, and the scientific method could illuminate truth more reliably than tradition?

John Locke championed the idea that the government derived its legitimacy from the consent of the governed.[6] Immanuel Kant urged, "Dare to know! Have the courage to use your own reason."[7] Mary Wollstonecraft argued for the equal rights of women in education and society.[8]

These ideas erupted into action. In 1776, the American colonies declared independence from Britain. In 1789, revolution swept through France, toppling the monarchy and spreading the cry of *Liberté, Égalité, Fraternité.* These movements did not merely alter governments; they rewired humanity's sense of what was possible.

MACHINES AND MOMENTUM

In the late eighteenth century, another revolution transformed the human experience—this one forged in iron and driven by steam. James Watt's improved steam engine, mechanized looms, and coal-fueled factories unleashed a wave of productivity previously unimaginable.

For centuries, human labor had been bound by the limits of muscle—human or animal. Now, machines could do the work of hundreds. Cities swelled with workers drawn from the countryside. Time itself seemed to change as factory whistles replaced sunrise as the signal to begin the day.

The Industrial Revolution created immense wealth, but also vast inequality. Adam Smith's *Wealth of Nations* celebrated free markets,[9] while Karl Marx warned that unchecked capitalism would produce exploitation and social unrest. It was a period of breathtaking progress and deep social cost, proof that every leap forward has its shadows.

THE SCIENTIFIC REVOLUTION'S SECOND WAVE

Alongside the ideological and industrial upheavals, science and technology made breathtaking advances. Einstein redefined time and space with his theory of relativity. Antibiotics revolutionized medicine, saving millions. The Manhattan Project introduced the atomic age. Watson, Crick, and Franklin revealed the structure of DNA, unlocking the code of life. And the internet—born out of Cold War defense research—reshaped communication, commerce, and culture.

This wave of discovery stretched from infinitely large galaxies and black holes to infinitely small atoms, genes, and particles. Each breakthrough shattered old assumptions, expanding humanity's power to understand and shape the world.

CONFLICT AND COOPERATION IN THE TWENTIETH CENTURY

The twentieth century was a proving ground for both human ingenuity and our darkest capacities. World War I (1914–1918) ended empires and shattered the optimism of a world that believed war could be short and decisive. Two decades later, World War II (1939–1945) revealed humanity's capacity for both brutality and heroism: fascism, genocide, and atomic destruction on one hand; courage, resistance, and eventual rebuilding on the other. In its aftermath, the United Nations was created to prevent future wars, while the European Union began binding former enemies together through economic and political ties.

Then came the Cold War—a decades-long standoff between capitalism, led by the United States, and communism, led by the Soviet Union. Nuclear weapons deterred direct conflict but fueled proxy wars in Korea, Vietnam, and Afghanistan. The world often felt one miscalculation away from annihilation. Leaders like Roosevelt, Churchill, Stalin, Reagan, and Gorbachev shaped not only geopolitics but the modern psyche.

OUR NEW REALITY

By the late twentieth century, the digital age was in full swing. Computers shrank from room-sized machines to devices that fit in our pockets. The internet linked billions of people. Artificial intelligence (AI) emerged, promising breakthroughs—and disruptions—that rival those of the Industrial Revolution.

This new world is borderless yet divided, overflowing with information yet plagued by misinformation. It offers unprecedented opportunity, but also deep uncertainty about how technology will shape human identity, work, and relationships.

From Galileo's telescope to quantum computing, the story of the modern world is the story of breaking through walls—political, scientific, technological, and cultural. Each era expanded what humanity could see, understand, and achieve. And yet, every breakthrough brought new boundaries, new assumptions, and new blind spots.

LIVING360 is about developing the awareness to recognize those walls in our own time—the courage to question them, and the wisdom to step beyond them when they hold us back from a richer, more meaningful life.

The Digital World of the Twenty-First Century

It's early morning. You scroll through your phone before even getting out of bed—headline after headline flashes past: a war zone in the Middle East, planes falling from skies, a market crash in Asia, a political scandal in the West. Social media amplifies every alarm. Tragedy trends. Outrage travels faster than facts. The old newsroom adage, "If it bleeds, it leads," now reigns supreme in our algorithm-driven world. No wonder it feels like everything is falling apart.

Our daily news feed is a powerful lens, showing us every detail of the chaos and tragedy. But our Wisdom Wealth encourages us to use a different tool: a cognitive telescope. A wider view doesn't dismiss suffering; it contextualizes it. Wisdom doesn't ignore what's wrong—it remembers what's right, too.

Imagine you're looking at the human story not through today's news feed, but through the lens of centuries. What you'll find may surprise you. Contrary to the chaos we consume daily, we are—by almost every major measure—living in an era of unprecedented peace, progress, and possibility.

The twenty-first century didn't just usher in a new calendar—it triggered a revolution on par with the discovery of fire or the invention of the printing press. The digital age didn't just change how we communicate; it reshaped who has access to knowledge and how fast that knowledge travels. For most of human history, information was a luxury, hoarded by the powerful. Scholars debated in ivory towers while the rest of humanity toiled in ignorance. But then came the internet—a force as disruptive as the wheel.

In 2025, more than 68 percent of humanity was connected to the web, unlocking access to information once unimaginable.[10] A young woman in a village in Kenya can now watch lectures from Harvard. A teenager in Mumbai can study classical art or quantum physics on YouTube. A farmer in rural Brazil can access weather forecasts, crop prices, and financial services on a $50 smartphone. This is no small feat. It is one of the greatest redistributions of power and possibility in human history—and yet, our news feeds rarely reflect it.

It's easy to assume that the world is spinning out of control because of the propensity of your mind to focus on bad news. Your mind is designed to focus on information that can impact your chance of survival. This evolutionary capability amplifies what is wrong, but this noise often drowns out a quieter, more powerful truth: Humanity is making remarkable progress.

HUMANITY BY THE NUMBERS

Numbers can feel cold until you remember they are true stories of real lives transformed. Despite the pessimism that often dominates your screen, the facts paint a more hopeful picture about the human condition.

- Global life expectancy has increased from 66.8 years in 2000 to 73.13 years in 2023.[11]
- The global under-five mortality rate has dropped by 52 percent, from seventy-seven deaths per one thousand live births in 2000 to thirty-seven per one thousand in 2023.[12]
- The percentage of people living in extreme poverty (less than $2.15/day) has fallen from 29.3 percent in 2000 to just 8.5 percent in 2024.[13]
- Global trade has surged from $6.6 trillion in 2000 to over $33 trillion in 2024—a fivefold increase.[14]
- Per capita income in developing countries (adjusted for purchasing power) has nearly tripled, from $2,800 to $8,000 between 2000 and 2024.[15]

These numbers aren't just statistics—they represent millions of lives saved, educated, and lifted out of poverty. They reflect growing global opportunity and the rising tide of human capability for LIVING360.

RELATIVE PEACE AND PROSPERITY

Violence still exists and always will. But the idea that we live in the most violent period in human history is a myth. In fact, based on population-adjusted death rates, violence has dramatically declined both in absolute and relative terms (see table 5.1).

TABLE 5.1: GLOBAL CONFLICT FATALITIES COMPARISON, 1900-2025[16]

Period	Estimated Deaths (millions)	Estimated World Population (billions)	Major Contributors	% of World Population
1900–1925	35	1.7	WWI, Russian Civil War, Armenian Genocide, Mexican Revolution	2.06%
1925–1950	90	2.4	WWII, Holocaust, Chinese Civil War, Indian Partition	3.75%
1950–1975	25	3.7	Korean & Vietnam Wars, Great Leap Famine, Biafra, Bangladesh War	0.65%
1975–2000	18	5.3	Cambodia Genocide, Afghan, Iran, Iraq Wars, Rwanda, Congo	0.34%
2000–2025	4	7.7	Iraq & Afghan Wars, Syria, Yemen, Tigray, Terrorism	0.05%

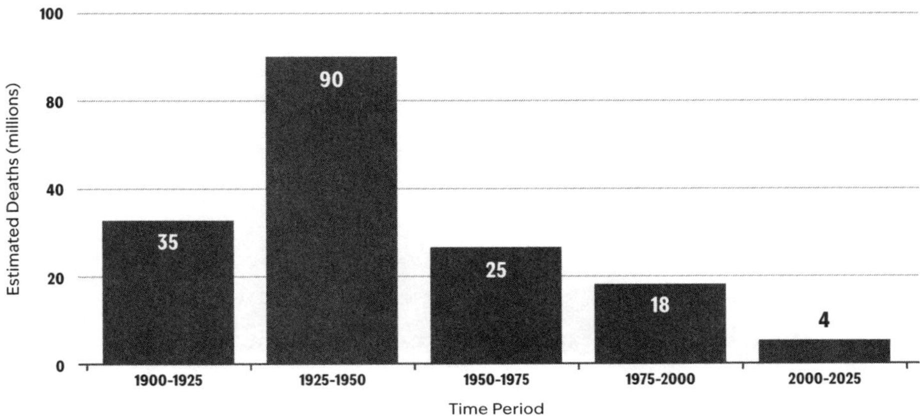

Figure 5.1: Estimated global conflict deaths by historical era (millions).[17]

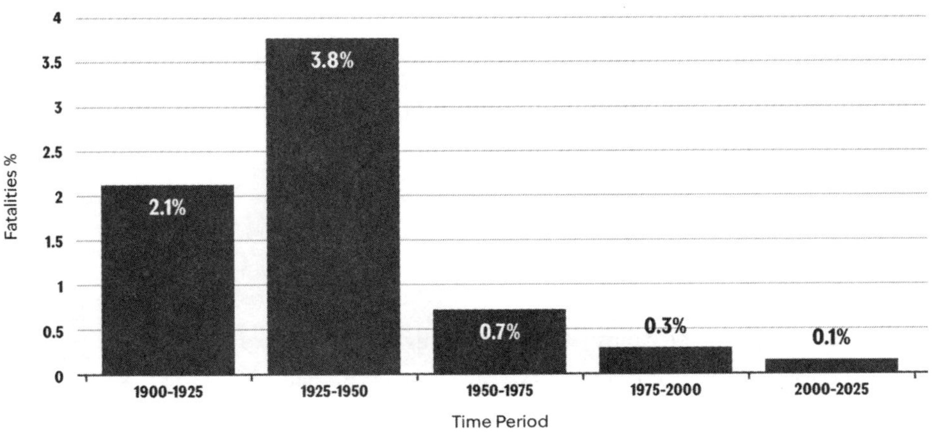

Figure 5.2: Global conflict fatalities as a share of world population (1900–2025).[18]

As table 5.1 and figures 5.1 and 5.2 show, the percentage of the global population lost to war has fallen dramatically over the past century. From the devastating world wars of the early twentieth century to more recent conflicts, we've progressed—slowly but surely—toward a world where peace is increasingly the norm.

This is the central argument in Steven Pinker's powerful book, *The Better Angels of Our Nature*. Pinker argues that the long arc of history is bending toward less violence, not more. He attributes this decline to both internal and external forces:

- Internally, we are guided by our empathy, self-control, moral sense, and capacity for reason—what he calls our "better angels."
- Externally, we are shaped by historical developments such as:
    - The rise of centralized states with a monopoly on force
    - The spread of manners and social norms that encourage restraint
    - The rise of human rights and individual dignity
    - The long peace following World War II
    - Increasing respect for the rights of women, minorities, and vulnerable groups

While Pinker does not deny the brutality humans are capable of, he reminds us that we must also recognize our progress. Violence is no longer the default state of civilization—it is increasingly the exception.[19]

Human Nature and Digital Dilemmas

Of course, progress doesn't mean perfection. Human nature is complex. Are we fundamentally a tournament species, where competition and dominance—especially among males—drives behavior? Or are we pair-bonding creatures, wired for connection, cooperation, and care? The truth lies somewhere in between, influenced by genetic variation, cultural conditioning, and even hormones like oxytocin that shape our tendency toward trust and empathy.

In a hyperconnected digital age, our ancient instincts—for status, belonging, fear—can be amplified in unhealthy ways. Social media often fuels tribalism, outrage, and misinformation. Algorithms prioritize emotion over accuracy. And yet, this same digital world offers tools for connection, learning, and solidarity across borders.

It's a paradox of our time: We have more power to build than ever before—and more power to destroy. Which direction we choose depends on whether we nurture our better angels or surrender to our inner demons. We can leverage the digital age opportunities: relative peace and prosperity to design a life that encompasses all four drivers of LIVING360: Know Yourself, Know the World, Know Your Purpose, and Build Financial Security.

Immortality, Longevity, and Health Span

Can you imagine blowing out one hundred candles on your birthday cake—and still hiking, reading, working, or mentoring others with clarity and energy? It may sound like science fiction, but it could soon be science fact.

When I ask my graduate students how many of them expect to live to one hundred, nearly half raise their hands. But when I ask the follow-up, "What kind of life do you expect at ninety-five?" their enthusiasm fades. Many worry not about living longer but living well. That's the crux of this chapter: not just quantity of years (lifespan), but quality as well (health span).

The modern longevity movement is fueled by a remarkable convergence of biotechnology, medicine, and AI. For the first time in history, human beings may have a realistic chance of significantly extending their lifespans—and their health spans. In fact, if you're fewer than fifty years old today, there's a good chance you'll make it to ninety, and quite a few will pass one hundred.

But could we go even further? Could we become . . . immortal?

As of this writing, no verified case of human biological immortality exists. The longest confirmed human lifespan belongs to Jeanne Calment, a French woman who lived to the age of 122 years and 164 days.[20] Calment smoked for most of her life, drank wine daily, and lived through both world wars. Her longevity baffled scientists. But she also lived in a walkable town, had strong social connections, and kept mentally active—factors we now know are crucial for long life. But while true immortality remains the realm of myth and science fiction, the boundaries of longevity are being stretched further than ever before.

In both scientific and speculative circles—especially in the fields of biogerontology and transhumanism—there's growing optimism that dramatic life extension may soon be within reach.

ESCAPING AGING

Ray Kurzweil, futurist, author, and Google's Director of Engineering, predicts that by 2045 we could reach what he calls "longevity escape velocity."[21] This is the point at which medical advances extend life faster than we age, meaning that for every year you live, science buys you more than a year of additional life. In Kurzweil's vision, this could lead to a form of practical immortality—if technology continues advancing at an exponential pace.

Another bold voice is Aubrey de Grey, a Cambridge-educated biomedical gerontologist. De Grey argues that aging is not inevitable, but rather a treatable condition—a disease, or more precisely, a collection of biological processes that can be slowed, stopped, or even reversed. His framework, known as SENS (strategies for engineered negligible senescence), targets the cellular and molecular damage that accumulates over time. He believes that with regenerative therapies, the first person to live to one thousand years may already be alive today.[22]

Speculative ideas such as cryonics—freezing the body after death with the hope of future revival—have long fascinated people. There's also the radical concept of mind uploading; transferring human consciousness into a digital or mechanical medium, potentially leading to a kind of digital immortality. While both remain highly controversial and technically out of reach, the rapid progress in neuroscience and AI continues to blur the line between science, imagination, and consciousness.

While the futurists are dreaming of longevity escape velocity, the rest of us are building the foundation of our health span portfolio right here, right now. Based on current research in biotech, bioengineering, and drug development, a more reasonable projection is that most healthy fifty-year-olds today have a good chance of reaching one hundred, and those younger than forty can hope to celebrate their 105th birthday. One key reason: medical innovation.[23]

GLP-1 receptor agonists—a class of drugs originally designed for diabetes and now used for weight management—are showing promise in reducing the risks of heart disease, stroke, and kidney failure. These drugs may not only extend lifespan but also health span: the number of years we live free from chronic disease and disability.

THE ECONOMICS OF AGING

We're not just living longer—we're working longer, thinking sharper, and remaining productive well into what used to be considered old age. My clients are healthier and working much, much longer. One particular client, Mr. D, is ninety-four and works four days a week as a buying consultant for one of the largest Southern California dental practices. He recently shared his routine, which includes eight hours of sleep; a balanced diet; six days of exercise; and most importantly, lots of time spent with family, friends, and grandkids. During the last two years, he saved his client over $1.0 million through negotiations with suppliers, with his share of the savings being 25 percent. A cool $250,000 for two years of work while keeping his mind active and engaged.

According to a recent report by Goldman Sachs, the global population is aging due to longer lifespans and declining fertility rates. In developed economies, the share of the population aged fifteen to sixty-four had already dropped from 67 percent in 2000 to 63 percent in 2025 and is projected to fall to 57 percent by 2075.[24] Emerging economies are not far behind.

This demographic shift has often been described as a "time bomb"—a looming crisis of too many elderly people and too few workers. But the data tell a more nuanced story.

Despite a shrinking working-age ratio:

- Life expectancy in developed nations has risen from seventy-eight to eighty-two years since 2000.
- Effective working life has increased even faster—from thirty-four to thirty-eight years.
- The share of the total population in employment has grown from 46.0 percent to 48.3 percent.[25]

In other words, older people are staying healthier and working longer, even in countries that have made minimal changes to retirement laws. One remarkable study found that a person who was seventy in 2022 had, on average, the same cognitive ability as a fifty-three-year-old in 2000. Seventy is truly the new fifty-three.[26]

Figure 5.3 illustrates humanity's remarkable journey from survival to thriving. Each curve represents an era—from the early 1800s, when the average human life ended around age thirty-five, to projections for those born in 2100, expected to live past one hundred. The x-axis measures lifespan—the number of years lived—while the y-axis represents health span, a measure of how long those years remain healthy, active, and free of disease.

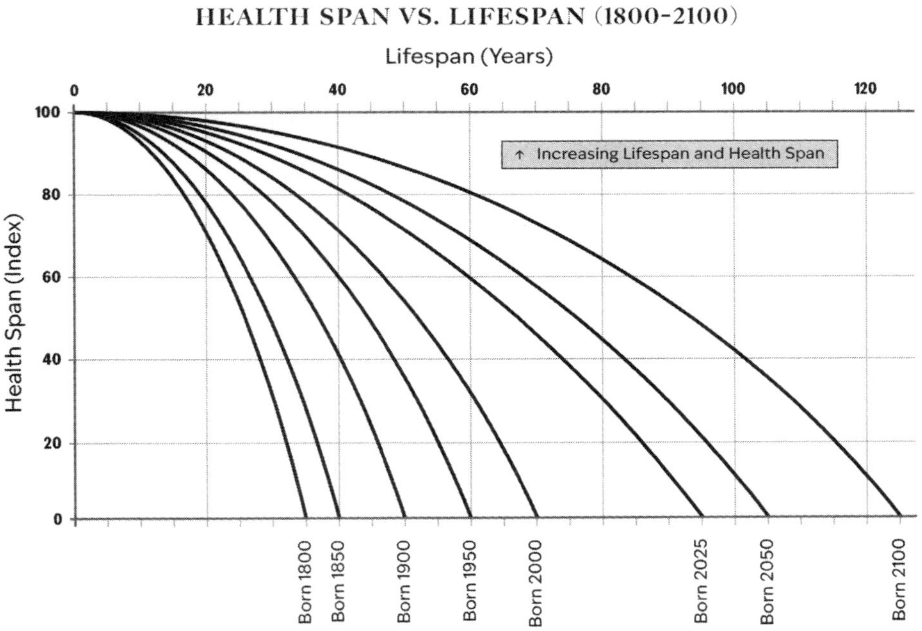

HEALTH SPAN VS. LIFESPAN (1800-2100)

Figure 5.3: The evolving shape of human aging—longer lives, later decline.

Over time, the curves stretch outward and flatten, showing that we are not only living longer but staying healthier for a greater portion of our lives. In the nineteenth century, life was short and often burdened by illness; today, medical advances, sanitation, nutrition, and social progress have added decades of vigor. The trajectory of these curves tells the story of human ingenuity—how science, policy, and collective wisdom have nearly doubled both our years and the quality of those years.

Lifespan Versus Health Span

A longer, healthier life for humanity is one of the most impactful global trends we can frame as a positive transformation. But every new opportunity comes with profound questions. It's one thing to reach 95 or 105. It's another to dance at your great-grandchild's wedding when you get there. The narrative of aging as decline is giving way to a new story, one of active longevity. Longer lives will force us to rethink everything from retirement savings and social services to how we pass on jobs, wisdom, and leadership to the next generation. In a world full of challenges—climate change, wealth and income inequality, and political disruption—we continue to push human longevity.

Take Warren Buffett, for example. As of this writing, he is ninety-five years old and remains the CEO of Berkshire Hathaway, overseeing a portfolio worth hundreds of billions of dollars. He reads more than six hours a day, speaks with clarity and wit, and continues to make high-stakes investment decisions that influence global markets. His longtime partner, Charlie Munger, worked actively until his death at age ninety-nine. Buffett famously quipped, "I tap dance to work every day,"[27] and that attitude—curiosity, engagement, joy in purpose—is perhaps the most powerful longevity drug of all. People such as Warren Buffet and my client, Mr. D, are living proof that wisdom doesn't expire, and that our most productive years don't have to end at sixty-five. In fact, with the right mindset and habits, they may be just beginning.

In the coming decades, you may live far longer than your ancestors ever imagined. But living longer is not the goal—living *wiser* is. The true gift of longevity is the chance to contribute more, love deeper, and grow stronger across more chapters of life. That's what LIVING360 is about: not just extending time but elevating it.

Living longer can mean living better—if you plan for it wisely with Wisdom Wealth. Your concrete box today is unlike any in history. Its walls are transparent screens. Sunlight pours in from every time zone.

You can see the best and worst of humanity on demand. But if you forget that the view is curated—and skewed—you'll live as though the world is doomed, even as it quietly improves.

The choice is yours: Stay inside, reacting to every shadow on the wall, or step outside, measure the whole horizon, and act with clarity and purpose. History has given you one of the most peaceful, connected, opportunity-rich boxes ever built. Wisdom Wealth means using it not as a prison—but as a launch pad. That is the starting point for a rich, meaningful life. That is the essence of LIVING360.

When I look up at the night sky, my childhood rooftop memory returns. I remember feeling small, but somehow now at peace, as if the vastness above made everything below make sense.

The boy who once looked up searching for answers has learned that understanding the world isn't about control; it's about contentment and acceptance. Those qualities are what move you from prosperity without peace to LIVING360. To see life clearly is to realize that uncertainty is part of its beauty, and impermanence is part of its grace.

So pause once in a while. Step outside. Look up. Let the stars remind you how brief, fragile, and extraordinary this moment truly is.

That awareness is the beginning of wisdom.

That is *the big picture.*

Reflection Questions

1. How confident are you about the Big Bang theory? And is there intelligent life on other planets?
2. In your opinion, is the world safer, healthier, and more just today compared to the 1960s and 1970s?
3. Is your city and community safer and more inclusive today than it was in previous generations?

4. Do you think you will live to age one hundred?
5. What kind of life do you want to lead in your nineties? What are you doing now to prepare for it?

CHAPTER 6

The Next Horizon

It is November 30, 2022. There is no countdown clock, no global press conference—just a quiet link on a website: *ChatGPT*.

In a dorm room at Princeton, a philosophy major slouched in his chair, nursing a coffee that had gone cold. His final paper loomed—a two-thousand-word essay on Kant's categorical imperative. Out of curiosity, he typed the prompt into this strange new AI chat box and hit *enter*. Twelve seconds later, paragraphs rolled across his screen: clear, cogent, and footnoted. He leaned back, staring, half laughing and half alarmed.

Across the country in San Francisco, a software engineer hunched over his laptop. A spreadsheet error had cost him hours. Out of desperation, he pasted the data into ChatGPT and asked it to write code to fix the problem. Seconds later, a neatly formatted, bug-free script appeared—complete with explanations. It worked perfectly on the first try.

In a Texas suburb, an exhausted mom sat cross-legged on her son's bed, trying to summon the energy to invent a bedtime story. She typed a request into her phone: "Tell me a bedtime story about a dragon who doesn't like fire." The AI responded with a charming tale of a gentle dragon who preferred painting sunsets to breathing flames. Her son listened wide-eyed, then drifted to sleep.

Within seventy-two hours, a million people were using this odd, uncanny conversational engine. In classrooms, corporate Slack channels, Reddit threads, and at kitchen tables, the same realization echoed: *Something fundamental has shifted.*

As of that moment, AI was no longer a distant laboratory project. It was now in everyone's hands. LIVING360 calls you to use this powerful force to enhance your life experience. It is here—in your pocket, on your screens—ready to write essays, debug code, tell stories, translate languages, and answer almost any question. A Silicon Valley founder compared it to the launch of the iPhone, calling it "the iPhone moment of intelligence."[1]

Artificial intelligence is triggering a magnitude-8 earthquake in human civilization—and most people are still asleep. The ground beneath human civilization has shifted. Technology has become intelligent and merged with humanity.

From Rule Books to Reasoners

For decades, AI meant rigid, rule-based systems. Programmers would handcraft instructions: if *x*, then *y*. Early AI could play chess, sort emails, or detect spam, but it could not surprise us. These systems didn't "think"—they followed recipes.

Then came the leap: deep learning. And from that leap, the most transformative AI systems yet—large language models (LLMs). Based on a breakthrough transformer architecture first described by Google in 2017, these models ingested vast amounts of text—books, articles, code, conversations—learning patterns in how words and ideas connect (see figure 6.1).

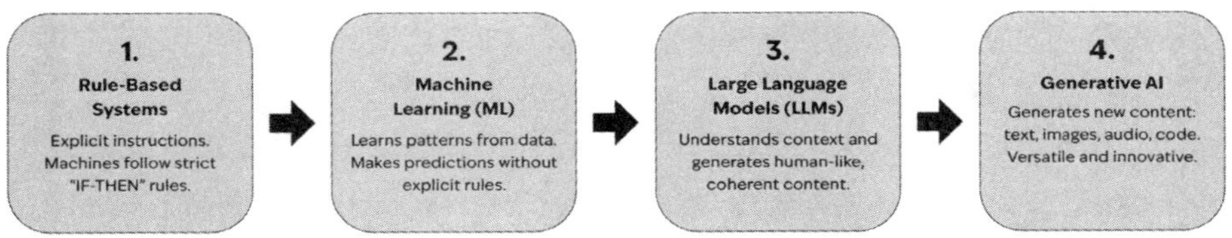

Figure 6.1: The evolution of AI: the progression from explicit instructions to creative generation.

Unlike their rule-bound ancestors, LLMs could *generate* new content. They could produce an original poem in the style of Shakespeare, draft a legal contract, write a functioning Python script, create videos, or explain quantum physics at a ten-year-old's level.

They don't "think" as we do. They don't feel. But they can generate responses with a fluency, versatility, and contextual grasp that narrows the gap between machine output and human cognition. And they are improving at a pace that feels less like progress and more like acceleration.

A Near Future, Reimagined

Over the next decade, AI will seep into every sector: education, healthcare, law, journalism, customer service, marketing, finance, and creative work.

Picture a student in rural Kenya using AI to tutor her in calculus at no cost. A small-town lawyer using AI to instantly scan decades of case law before stepping into court. A farmer in India consulting AI to diagnose crop disease and optimize irrigation.

Some jobs will prove resistant, at least in the short term—roles that demand muscle, dexterity, or deep in-person human connection:

plumbers, electricians, nurses, special education teachers, and surgeons. But many others—especially those heavy on data manipulation, routine problem-solving, or predictable workflows—will be disrupted or redefined entirely.

Already, AI models have outscored physicians on medical board exams, ranked in the top 10 percent of bar exam takers, and posted eightieth percentile or higher on the SAT, GRE, and GMAT. These feats are not endpoints—they are warm-ups. As AI gains new senses,[2] it may soon match, or surpass, humans in most cognitive domains.

Power Without Guardrails

Artificial intelligence's power is its speed and scale. It can read millions of documents in minutes, integrate feedback instantly, and generate solutions humans would never think of. This makes it an unprecedented engine for progress—and a potential accelerant for catastrophe.

On an individual level, over-reliance on AI risks diminishing human agency, critical thinking, and creativity. Consider a world where physicians blindly trust AI for diagnoses, judges use AI to determine prison sentences, or military generals rely on AI to determine who lives or dies during combat. Is AI a true thinker, or simply a stochastic parrot, repeating words based on probability, without understanding them, making their answers sophisticated mimicry? Imagine AI generating art, music, literature, and poetry without emotion. "With great power comes great responsibility," said Spider-Man's Uncle Ben. The trouble is, the AI race is sprinting toward capability, not responsibility.

Some of the brightest minds in the field are raising alarms:

- Geoffrey Hinton, the "Godfather of AI": "It's not inconceivable that AI could wipe out humanity."[3]
- Sam Altman, CEO of OpenAI: "An AI that could design novel biological pathogens . . . these are real and scary risks."[4]

- Yoshua Bengio, Turing Award winner: "The risk of catastrophe is real enough that action is needed now."[5]
- Elon Musk: "AI is a fundamental risk to the existence of human civilization."[6]
- Stephen Hawking: "Success in creating AI would be the biggest event in human history. It might also be the last, unless we learn how to avoid the risks."[7]

What makes AI unsettling is its opacity. Even its creators often can't explain why a model makes a given decision. As these systems begin writing code, designing drugs, and influencing military strategy, this "black box" problem becomes a global risk. We can see the brilliance of what comes out—the beautiful code, the flawless essay, the medical diagnosis—but we can't see inside. We don't know why it chose that word, or that line of code, or that medical conclusion. It's like having a brilliant oracle that gives you the right answer every time but refuses to explain its reasoning. And as we give this black box more and more control over our lives—from our finances to our defense systems—the stakes of that opacity become terrifyingly high.

THE 3As IN A WORLD OF AI

In LIVING360, our approach to AI is simple: Awareness, Action, and Acceptance.

- Awareness: Learn how it works and what it can (and can't) do. Try ChatGPT, Gemini, Claude, or Perplexity. Ask questions. Explore.
- Action: Integrate AI into your daily life. Use it to brainstorm, analyze, plan, and problem-solve.
- Acceptance: AI is here to stay. The sooner you learn to collaborate with it, the more empowered you will be.

The Unknown Disruptor

Unlike the internet or electricity, AI is not just a tool—it is becoming a mind-like presence woven into the fabric of global systems. And yet we have few rules, no global treaties, and little public understanding. Governments scramble to regulate systems they barely comprehend. Ethical guidelines are drafted in real time, even as AI becomes more autonomous and integrated. We are not just building tools. We are building something that reasons, adapts, and—within its own parameters—creates.

We are the first generation to build a form of intelligence that may one day surpass us. The question is not whether it will change the world—it already has. The question is whether we will guide it or be swept along by it. The fear is real, but so is the potential. In the coming years, AI will test not just our ingenuity, but our values. It will challenge us to define what is uniquely human. And it will force us to collectively decide whether we will approach it with ignorance and fear, or the wisdom and courage to make it serve life, not replace it.

For the first time in history, we are shaping an intelligence not bound by biology, emotion, or mortality. It will not get tired. It will not forget. It will not die. In the next ten to twenty years, AI will not replace humanity outright—but it will reshape it profoundly. Those who ignore it risk irrelevance. Those who fear it risk paralysis. But those who engage with it—wisely, curiously, ethically—can use it to amplify their own capabilities and improve their lives. As AI pushes the boundaries of intelligence, it exposes a paradox: our tools evolve faster than our wisdom. We can build systems that learn but struggle to build guardrails that protect. And that's where the deeper challenge begins—not in machines outsmarting us, but in humans outpacing their own moral maturity. Even as technology propels us forward, three powerful forces still threaten to pull us back (see figure 6.2).

Figure 6.2: The asymmetry of risk in modern civilization.

Three Storms on the Horizon: Nuclear War, Pandemics, and Climate Change

We are the most advanced generation in history yet never have we had so many ways to end our own story. As Daniel Quinn wrote in *Ishmael*: "You're captives of a civilizational story that tells you that you are the pinnacle of creation and that the world was made for you."[8]

This quote captures a powerful truth: Modern civilization has been built on the belief that we are separate from, and superior to, nature. We have mastered fire, split the atom, decoded DNA, and built machines that think. But the same tools that mark our genius also carry the seeds of our undoing. We stand on a cliff's edge with three storms gathering behind us: one that could strike in an instant, one that moves invisibly, and one that rises slowly but relentlessly.

Understanding the risks is not about fear. It's about foresight. It's about cultivating Wisdom Wealth that helps us walk the narrow path between peril and possibility.

NUCLEAR WAR

In 1983, a Soviet early-warning system detected what it believed were multiple incoming US missiles. An officer, Stanislav Petrov, correctly identified it as a system malfunction—the satellite had misinterpreted sunlight reflecting off high-altitude clouds. His calm decision prevented a retaliatory strike that would have certainly ended the world as we know it.

In the twentieth century, humans split the atom and unlocked terrifying potential. Today, the world's nine nuclear-armed nations collectively hold over 12,500 nuclear warheads. While this is down from a peak of over 60,000 during the Cold War, even a small fraction of that arsenal could lead to global catastrophe.

A regional conflict using just one hundred to two hundred nuclear weapons—for example, between India and Pakistan—could kill tens of millions in immediate blasts and radiation and trigger a nuclear winter where smoke and soot block sunlight, disrupting global agriculture and threatening mass famine.

Though major powers like the United States, Russia, and China adhere to deterrence doctrines, the increasing tensions in regions such as the Korean Peninsula, the Middle East, and Eastern Europe add to the risks. Countries such as Iran have flirted with nuclear ambitions, and others, like Japan or South Korea, could theoretically build weapons within months if they chose to. The danger isn't only from malice—it could arise from miscalculation, false alarm, or overconfidence.

Wisdom Wealth in an age of nuclear risk means resisting the impulse to retaliate and cultivating the foresight to pause. It is the wisdom to understand the cascade of consequences that follow a single, irrevocable decision. We build this wealth by studying history, understanding the mechanisms of miscalculation, and supporting leaders who prioritize diplomacy and de-escalation over brinkmanship. The second storm doesn't explode—it seeps. Where nuclear danger is loud and immediate, the next threat whispers its arrival.

PANDEMICS

The second storm is silent at first. It begins in a crowded market, a remote village, or perhaps a research lab. It slips quietly from one person to another until, like a tide, it begins to rise. Until 2020, pandemics were something that happened in history books. They were images of masks from a century ago, or a plot device in a Hollywood thriller. We lived in our concrete box, believing we were immune.

It started quietly. In late 2019, a few cases of pneumonia were reported in Wuhan, China. By March 2020, the world was on lockdown. Airplanes were grounded. Hospitals were overwhelmed. Cities fell silent. Schoolyards emptied. Within eighteen months, COVID-19 resulted in over six million deaths. Economies stalled. Families were separated. Life, everywhere, was reshaped.[9]

COVID-19 was likely not the worst-case scenario—it was relatively mild compared to how the virus could have mutated to become more transmissible and virulent. But it proved that a new virus could emerge suddenly, spread rapidly through a connected world, and upend global stability.

Future pandemics may come from zoonotic spillovers (pathogens jumping from animals to humans), laboratory accidents, or even engineered bio-threats. With rising deforestation, intensive animal farming, and massive urbanization, the chances of novel viruses emerging have increased.

Building Wisdom Wealth against pandemic risk means fostering a spirit of global cooperation, supporting scientific research, and understanding the fragility of our healthcare systems. It is the foresight to proactively invest in genomic surveillance, supply chain resilience, and public trust before the next crisis, not just in the chaotic aftermath. Pandemics expose our fragility. Climate change tests our endurance. One arrives in waves; the other in decades. Both ask the same question: Can human cooperation outpace human denial and isolationism?

CLIMATE CHANGE

The third storm is not sudden, nor silent. It is slow, heavy, and patient—creeping higher year by year. In 2023, the skies over New York City turned a surreal, apocalyptic orange. It wasn't from a movie set. The smoke had drifted thousands of miles from wildfires raging in Canada. My friend in Greece described stepping out of her air-conditioned home and feeling a physical assault from the 113°F heat—a heat so intense it buckled pavement and killed thousands.

In Pakistan, historic monsoon floods displaced more than thirty million people and submerged one-third of the country.[10] Meanwhile, glaciers in the Alps and Himalayas melted at record speeds, entire coral reefs bleached into ghostly white, and rivers such as the Yangtze and Colorado shrank under relentless drought.

Daniel Quinn's book, *Ishmael,* captures the interdependence of humanity with nature and other species: "With man gone, will there be hope for gorilla? With gorilla gone, will there be hope for man?"[11]

Climate change doesn't announce itself; it accumulates one

degree, one storm, one vanished coastline at a time. According to the Intergovernmental Panel on Climate Change (IPCC), Earth has warmed by approximately +1.2°C since 1900.[12] Most of that has occurred since the mid-1970s, and 2023 was the hottest year ever recorded.

According to most climate scientists, the causes are well established: the burning of fossil fuels, industrial activity, and land-use changes. The effects—rising seas, extreme weather, disrupted ecosystems—are accelerating and already visible across the globe. The climate models referenced by the Intergovernmental Panel on Climate Change (IPCC), have mapped a number of potential pathways for the increase in global temperature:

Climate Futures by 2100 (IPCC Scenarios)

1. Low-Emissions Pathway (+1.5°C to +2.0°C)

   Requires rapid clean energy transition, net-zero emissions by mid-century, and unprecedented global coordination.

2. Intermediate Pathway (+2.5°C to +3.0°C)

   Reflects current national policies and modest improvements—significant but manageable risks.

3. High-Emissions Pathway (+4.0°C or more)

   Business-as-usual scenario. Devastating outcomes: widespread displacement, food crises, and uninhabitable regions.

Not all scientists agree on the precision of these forecasts. In *Unsettled*, physicist and former Caltech provost Dr. Steven Koonin argues that climate models struggle to replicate past climate accurately and often disagree with one another.[13] He holds that many key conclusions in IPCC reports contain acknowledged uncertainties that are often downplayed in media summaries. Koonin posits that short-term regional forecasts are highly speculative, and much of the policy debate exaggerates certainty about long-term impacts.

He emphasizes that while the human role in warming is real, the magnitude and impact of future changes remain deeply complex and, in many areas, unsettled. He warns against politicizing science and urges policymakers and the public to embrace nuanced, evidence-based conversations.

Koonin's critics argue that he underplays the urgency of climate action. Still, his contribution reminds us that truth is often layered, and certainty in complex systems is rare. Responsible action, after all, requires both awareness of risk and openness to complexity. Indeed, consensus seems to be robust on direction and risk, but uncertainty persists with respect to timing and magnitude.

Building Wisdom Wealth against climate change means thinking in generations, not just election cycles. It is the foresight to understand that our actions today will have consequences for our children and grandchildren. We build it by embracing sustainable innovation, holding our leaders accountable for long-term policy, and recognizing that our individual choices—from what we consume to how we vote—are acts of stewardship for the future.

No other species has reshaped the planet like we have. No other species has the power to destroy it—or to save it. Elephants, whales, wolves, and birds live instinctively, driven by evolution and survival. Humans alone possess conscious foresight. We can map the consequences of our actions. We can imagine the future. And we can change course.

That is both our gift and our burden.

Today, we face three monumental risks: nuclear conflict, pandemics, and climate change. These are serious problems, but they are also solvable by our own ingenuity, collaboration, and willpower. The same tools that threaten to undo us—science, technology, and political power—can also be harnessed to build resilience, peace, and sustainability.

The main idea of this section is to be aware of the most pressing threats and how they can affect us and the world. Awareness and information is key to understanding risks, their potential impact, and their probability of actually happening. As you navigate your life's decisions and evaluate risk, spend time acquiring factual and relevant information to evaluate your choices and always be open to revising your opinions based on new facts.

In the end, the question is not whether humanity has power. The real question is: Do we have the wisdom—and the courage—to use it wisely?

As the planet warms, pandemics breed isolationism, and more countries have access to nuclear weapons, global influence shifts. Climate change may reshape coastlines, but geopolitical tides are redrawing maps of power. The next chapter of human destiny may not be written by nature alone, but by nations and militaries competing to assert control.

The Rise of China

In early 2020, as COVID-19 swept through Wuhan and Chinese factories shut down, American retailers started noticing delays. Walmart couldn't restock children's bikes. Home Depot ran low on power tools. Amazon sellers warned of inventory "backorders until further notice." At first, people blamed the virus. But behind the headlines, a deeper truth emerged: The United States had outsourced its supply chain—and most of its manufacturing muscle—to China.

Walk through a typical American home. The lamp in the living room? Made in Guangdong. The iPhone on the kitchen counter?

Assembled in Zhengzhou. The fridge motor? Likely from Suzhou. Your vitamins? Labeled "USA," but the active ingredients likely shipped from Shenzhen.

By 2023, nearly one in every seven goods purchased by American consumers came from China.[14] Not counting the hidden parts: the electronics inside your car, the textiles in your favorite jacket, the batteries in your cordless drill.

Now imagine this: What if trade stopped—not for a month, but for a year? Not due to a pandemic, but a geopolitical standoff. No ships from Shanghai. No containers from Ningbo. No microchips, no medicines, no microwaves.

The shelves would empty in weeks. Prices would soar. US factories couldn't just "restart." The machinery's gone. The labor isn't trained. The suppliers are on the other side of the Pacific. This isn't science fiction. It's a real vulnerability. And in an era of rising tensions between Washington and Beijing, it poses one of the greatest economic and strategic risks of our time. Because in today's world, conflict doesn't need missiles. A shipping halt can be just as devastating for LIVING360.

In 2017, Harvard scholar Graham Allison published *Destined for War*, a sobering examination of what happens when a rising power threatens to overtake a ruling one.[15] Drawing on the lessons of ancient history, he revives the concept of the Thucydides Trap, based on the Peloponnesian War between Athens and Sparta—where fear of displacement made conflict nearly inevitable. Allison identified sixteen historical power transitions. In twelve of those cases during the past five hundred years, the result was war.

Allison does not claim that a US–China war is inevitable, but he does argue that the structural tension is real and dangerous. China's rise—economically, militarily, and technologically—is challenging the US's long-standing global leadership. At the same time, the

US views its role as the custodian of international order—making retreat politically and strategically difficult. Unless both sides act with extraordinary foresight, history suggests that conflict is more likely than we want to believe.

A SHIFT IN GLOBAL POWER

After the collapse of the Soviet Union in 1991, the US emerged as the world's sole superpower. For more than thirty years, it enjoyed unparalleled economic, technological, and military dominance. But the last three decades have seen the greatest economic growth story in human history—China.

A few highlights:

- China's GDP (nominal) grew from $360 billion in 1990 to over $17.8 trillion in 2024—a more than forty-eight-fold increase.[16]
- Exports surged from just $62 billion in 1990 to over $3.5 trillion in 2024—making China the largest exporter in the world.[17]
- Over eight hundred million people have been lifted out of poverty in China in the past thirty-five years—an unprecedented feat in modern history.[18]
- In 2024 China published 878,307 journal articles and reviews, compared with 509,485 produced by the United States.[19]

A side-by-side snapshot comparing US and China in 1990 and 2024 is depicted in table 6.1.

When compared to Europe and Japan, the US has performed exceptionally well since 1990. Still, China's ascent is a paradigm-shifting phenomenon.

TABLE 6.1: US VS. CHINA[20]

Indicator	Country	1990	2024	% Change
GDP (Nominal, USD)	United States	$5.96T	$27.72T	365%
	China	$0.36T	$17.80T	4844%
GDP (PPP, Intl $)	United States	$5.96T	$27.72T	365%
	China	$1.12T	$33.0T	2,846%
GDP per Capita (Nominal, USD)	United States	$23,954	$81,695	241%
	China	$318	$12,614	3865%
Military Spending (USD)*	United States	$299B	$910B	204%
	China	$10B	$471B	4610%
Exports (USD)	United States	$394B	$2.995T	660%
	China	$62B	$3.513T	5566%
Research Papers Published	United States	~265,000	~422,800	59%
	China	~20,000	~528,300	2541%

*China's military expenditure is at purchasing power parity (PPP).

THE ECONOMIC INTERDEPENDENCE DILEMMA

Despite the rhetoric of rivalry, the US and China are economically intertwined at every level. Here are five powerful reasons why outright war may be avoided:

1. China is the world's factory. Around 60 percent of Walmart's products are made in China. Roughly 22 percent of all US consumer goods originate from China, not counting intermediate goods used in other countries' manufacturing.[21]

2. China supplies critical materials. From rare earth minerals to solar panels, chemical components, medical equipment, and electric vehicle batteries, the US depends on Chinese exports for essential industries.
3. Trade is a lifeline for both. China exports $422+ billion worth of goods to the US annually. A trade freeze would shock China's economy—and disrupt the American consumer market.[22]
4. China holds US debt. As of 2025, China owns about $700 billion in US Treasury bonds. A war or breakdown in relations could freeze or destroy these assets.[23]
5. China imports high-value goods. The US is a major supplier of agricultural products, commercial aircraft, semiconductors, and advanced medical equipment to China. Beijing cannot easily replace these inputs without severe consequences.

This is what makes the US–China relationship fundamentally different from the Cold War between the US and the Soviet Union. The USSR was isolated from global markets. China is integrated into them. While the US and USSR were ideological enemies with little trade, the US and China are economic rivals and trading partners locked in mutual dependence.

THE TAIWAN FLASHPOINT

If anything could spark a true "hot war" between the US and China, it is Taiwan. Beijing views Taiwan as a breakaway province that must be reunited with mainland China—by force if necessary. Washington, on the other hand, maintains a policy of "strategic ambiguity"—recognizing the One China policy but also pledging to help Taiwan defend itself.

A Chinese military invasion of Taiwan could pull the US and its allies into a full-blown conflict, disrupt the global semiconductor supply chain (Taiwan produces over 60 percent of the world's advanced chips), and trigger sanctions and economic collapse on both sides. This would be a lose-lose scenario for everyone, including the rest of the world.

HIGHER SPENDING DOESN'T EQUAL A SUPERIOR MILITARY

As of 2025, the US spends $997 billion on defense. China spends about $544 billion (PPP-adjusted), the second largest in the world. These figures are misleading. Military dominance is not just about spending. It's about capability, efficiency, doctrine, and regional reach. China is catching up fast. The Chinese military-industrial complex, once dependent on Russian hardware, now designs and exports competitive fighter jets, drones, missile systems, and warships.

The brief 2025 war between India and Pakistan, in which Pakistan used Chinese-made systems to impressive effect, served as a global showcase for China's military technology. China is also investing heavily in space warfare, hypersonic weapons, and AI-driven battlefield systems. While the US remains the dominant global military power, the gap is narrowing—and with it, the certainty of deterrence.

The road ahead will be bumpy. A long-term trade war is possible, but likely unsustainable. Both sides stand to lose too much. As the economic cost rises, rational actors in both countries may eventually pull back from the brink.

But competition will intensify—in AI, quantum computing, energy technology, and geopolitical influence. This contest is not just about economics or ideology. It's about who sets the rules for the twenty-first century. Geopolitics, wars, and trade impact our professional and personal lives. Being aware of the risks and opportunities that come from US–China competition is important for LIVING360.

While nations divide through boundaries and compete for dominance through power, something subtle and perhaps more revolutionary is happening at the human level.

Global Cultural Amalgamation

You're sitting cross-legged on a yoga mat in a boutique studio in Los Angeles. The lights are dim. Soft Indian sitar music hums through the speakers. The instructor begins with a Sanskrit mantra. You don't know exactly what it means—but you hum along anyway. After class, you stop by the café next door and order a steaming cup of herbal green tea—marketed for its metabolism-boosting and fat-burning properties. The barista recommends adding a splash of turmeric and ginger "for anti-inflammatory benefits." You nod approvingly, vaguely recalling something you read about Ayurvedic healing.

Later, you scroll through Instagram and see a Swedish wellness influencer doing breathwork in Bali, a tech CEO quoting a Zen koan[24] about stillness, a Brazilian chef posting a fusion recipe that mixes Japanese miso with Peruvian ceviche. Somewhere in the feed, you spot a meme that reads: "Be like water."—Bruce Lee.

You smile and keep scrolling.

What's striking isn't how unusual any of this is—but how utterly *normal* it has become. Eastern traditions and global ideas have seeped into Western daily life so subtly, so completely, that most people don't even question their origins. Meditation apps shaped by Tibetan Buddhism. Intermittent fasting rooted in ancient Islamic and Vedic practices. Mindfulness retreats inspired by Japanese Zen. Korean skincare. Lebanese hummus. Nigerian Afrobeats. TikTok dances born in Ghana. Everything, everywhere, all the time.

Today global culture is no longer imported—it's embedded. Ideas, rituals, values, and aesthetics from every corner of the planet are blending into the everyday fabric of modern life. But in this remixing of culture, what are we gaining—and what might we be losing? Is this rapid amalgamation of cultures accretive for LIVING360 or are we losing our connection to our identity, roots, and meaning?

When Thomas Friedman published *The World Is Flat* in 2005, he introduced the idea that globalization—driven by technology, supply chains, and geopolitics—was leveling the economic playing field.[25] Two decades later, we are witnessing a similar flattening of culture. But this time, it's not happening in factories or boardrooms—it's unfolding on screens, in earbuds, and across social media feeds.

Throughout history, civilizations have exchanged language, rituals, music, and philosophy through trade, conquest, and migration. But the digital revolution has accelerated cultural exchange to warp speed. In today's interconnected world, a teenager in Jakarta grooves to a TikTok trend from Los Angeles; a Nairobi entrepreneur finds branding inspiration in the quotes of New York-based self-help authors; a software engineer in Mumbai lives by the ethos of Silicon Valley—not as a place, but as a mindset.

What we're seeing is not a simple Westernization of the world, but a two-way cultural flow—a remixing of global values, practices, and aesthetics. Western values such as individualism, personal freedom, consumerism, and the nuclear family have spread far beyond their original contexts, largely through movies, music, tech platforms, and online education. At the same time, South American traditions have swept across the West in surprising ways. Psychedelic rituals once reserved for Amazonian shamans—for example, Ayahuasca—have been reinterpreted as tools for spiritual awakening in Silicon Valley and among global elites. Traditional South American cuisines like tacos, burritos, salsa, ceviche, and empanadas are now ubiquitous in the Western culinary landscape, and Latin American dance styles, such as salsa, tango, and samba, have been widely embraced in North America and Europe.

Even language is blending: In the West, English remains dominant, but it's increasingly peppered with Arabic greetings, Japanese expressions, Hindi mantras, and African proverbs. In many urban centers around the world, multilingual vocab has become the new native tongue.

BLENDING OR LOSING?

This cultural amalgamation offers both liberation and disruption. On one hand, it frees us from rigid cultural confines, allowing us to sample, adopt, and integrate global ideas that resonate personally—be it in fashion, wellness, spirituality, or career. A person in São Paulo can now meditate like a Tibetan monk, eat like a Korean chef, and think like a Californian entrepreneur—all in a single day.

On the other hand, this fusion risks flattening depth and tradition. As global values of autonomy and self-expression rise, community-based structures, oral traditions, rituals, and local languages are declining in influence. Cultural homogenization, often accelerated by global capitalism and algorithmic reinforcement, can erode the richness of local identities—leaving people more connected than ever, but less rooted and more isolated.

Children who grow up on global platforms may feel more kinship with influencers thousands of miles away than with the elders in their own neighborhoods. Traditional celebrations, once a lifeblood of community, may now compete with—or be replaced by—global entertainment culture.

WHAT COMES NEXT?

The future challenge is not whether cultures will blend—they already are—but whether we can preserve depth, diversity, and meaning in a converging world. Can we build a global society where plurality thrives rather than fades?

Or as one could ask provocatively: Does it really matter? Perhaps we should let the most useful, meaningful, and productive norms win, regardless of where they originated. Just as genes evolve through selection, maybe cultures do too. The question is: What are we selecting for—efficiency or meaning, connection or belonging? Being aware that what we do and how we think stems from cross-pollination of culture and values will make us more open-minded and accepting, helping with LIVING360.

In the end, Wisdom Wealth is not about choosing one culture over another—it's about choosing consciously. To blend without losing yourself. To be global without becoming hollow.

From Awareness to Action

We stand at a turning point. Machines can now write, reason, and learn. Nations rise, fall, and realign. Cultures blend, blur, and flourish. Yet beneath all the noise, one question remains: will our wisdom grow as fast as our power?

LIVING360 isn't about predicting the future—it's about preparing the mind and heart to meet it. Technology, wealth, and globalization have changed what we can do. Wisdom changes *why* we do it.

The world will keep accelerating, but wisdom will always move at the pace of reflection. The ability to pause, to choose with awareness, and to live with meaning is your edge.

Reflection Questions

1. Should AI be treated as a public utility—like electricity—or as a force requiring strict control, like nuclear technology?

2. Do you expect another global pandemic in your lifetime?
3. What is your assessment of the impact of climate change on humanity by the year 2050 and 2100?
4. How might the rise of China affect your profession, your investments, or your quality of life?
5. Do you believe that incorporating ideas from other cultures has enriched your life? If so, how?

PART III

Know Your Purpose

You can understand yourself. You can understand the world. But until you understand why you are here, your life will never feel whole. Purpose is the force that turns wisdom into action, clarity into direction, and financial security into a meaningful life rather than a well-funded existence.

In Part I, you explored the inner architecture of your mind—your beliefs, your biology, your biases. In Part II, you stepped into the vastness of the world—its systems, its history, its accelerating change. Now we arrive at the heart of the journey: meaning and purpose, the third pillar of Wisdom Wealth and the bridge that carries you toward lasting financial and emotional security.

This section is about what gives life its richness—purpose, relationships, career, gratitude (see figure III.1). These are not luxuries reserved for philosophers or monks. They are the essential ingredients of a life well-lived, and the foundation on which every wise financial and life decision rests.

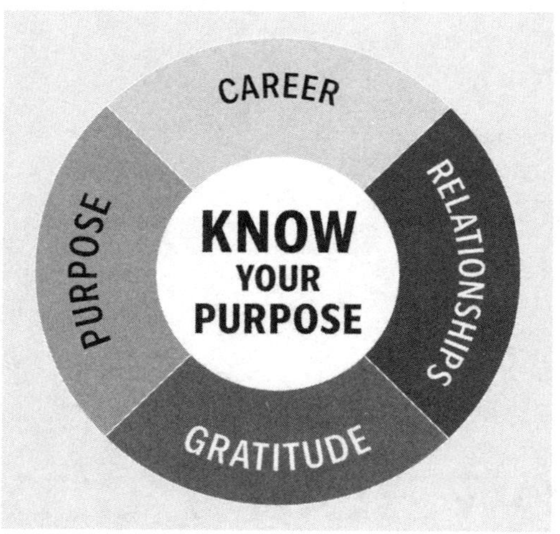

Figure III.1: The architecture of a meaningful life.

For the past fifteen years, I've been obsessed with a question that transcends income brackets, job titles, age, and geography: What actually makes people happy?

As a wealth advisor to thousands of families, I have witnessed something profound: financial security without purpose leads to quiet dissatisfaction. Purpose without financial clarity leads to anxiety and instability. True flourishing requires both.

This realization led me to develop a structured framework inspired by happiness and positive psychology research. I've shared it with CEOs and teachers, retirees and students, families building legacies, and young adults searching for direction. I've seen it transform perspectives across cultures, communities, and generations.

This section distills that journey into practical wisdom. It is a synthesis of data, insight, and lived experience—all designed to help you build a life anchored in meaning and sustained by financial clarity.

And it begins where all great lives begin—not with how much we earn, but why we live. Because once you understand your purpose, the decisions in the next section—Financial Security—are no longer about numbers. They become a reflection of who you are, and who you aspire to be.

CHAPTER 7

Your Life's Purpose

Is it possible to find life's purpose while living inside a concrete box, surrounded by routines, deadlines, and walls that lie outside our awareness? Before we can answer that, we must confront deeper questions: *Why am I here? What is the purpose of my existence?* These are not riddles for philosophers alone; they are the oldest and most intimate of human longings.

From the first handprints pressed on the cave walls of Sulawesi, Indonesia, painted some forty-five thousand years ago, to the stone pillars of Göbekli Tepe in Turkey, built nearly twelve thousand years ago, humanity has searched for meaning. Every culture, every age, and every heart has whispered the same questions: Is life a cosmic accident or a sacred assignment? Does my existence matter?

Across time, people have offered different answers. Some see life as part of an epic struggle between light and darkness, between good and evil, where every virtuous act tips the balance toward order or equilibrium. Others look closer to home, finding purpose in love, family, work, and community. Whether you believe in a divine plan or in the significance of human connection, one truth remains: your life carries meaning, cosmic or earthly, transcendent or tangible.

Consider the odds of your very existence. Among billions of galaxies and septillions of planets, *you* emerged, a conscious being capable of reflection, wonder, and choice. That alone borders on the miraculous. If one morning you discovered a billion dollars in your account and the bank confirmed it was no mistake, would you spend your life trying to trace its origin, or would you use it to enhance your life experience and uplift others? Your existence is that improbable windfall. Whether you view it as a divine gift or a cosmic accident, the only fitting response is awe, gratitude, and a responsibility to make the most of it.

To live with purpose, then, is to honor that gift. It is to step beyond your concrete box, to see the world as it truly is, and to live your authentic LIVING360—a life guided by wisdom, justice, and courage. Meaning is not something handed to you; it is something you create, through how you love, how you serve, and how fully you live.

Think of the last time you stood in a quiet chapel, listening to people speak about someone they loved. No one measured her life in résumés or possessions. They spoke of small, luminous moments; her delicious turkey with the special yams at the Thanksgiving dinner; her hand wrapped around a cousin's during chemotherapy; her habit of sharing what little she had. In that stillness, you understood something words rarely capture: That purpose isn't something we find at the end of life. It's what we live, every day, in the choices that touch others and give our existence meaning. Is life about more? More money, more power, more pleasure? Or is it about enough, being whole, being at peace, being of service? We begin this section not with tools or tactics, but with reflection. The answers we find will be shaped by our beliefs, values, and worldview.

Human Consciousness Confers Cosmic Meaning

The awareness of existence—the ability to experience sensations, thoughts, emotions, and perceptions—is what makes this question of meaning possible.

As Carl Sagan famously put it: "The cosmos is within us. We are a way for the universe to know itself."[1]

We are not passive spectators of a meaningless universe. We are the storytellers, the interpreters, the witnesses. If the universe matters to us, it is because we have made it matter. This view offers dignity: our awareness confers relevance. Without us, the stars shine in vain.

At the start of this book, we examined the roots of religion—why it arose, why it remains, and how it can shape the boundaries of your concrete box. Now, we shift our lens to another truth: for the majority of the world's population, religion is not a barrier but a foundation, offering a deep well of meaning and purpose. Religious traditions add cosmic value to our lives, and they give purpose to what we do and how we do it. In the next few pages, we will briefly review the tenets of numerous traditions that focus on the meaning and purpose of our lives. If you are someone who does not subscribe to a traditional religion, we will end by diving deep into Confucius' Concentric Circles, which can provide a key source of terrestrial meaning.

ABRAHAMIC FAITHS

In Judaism, life's purpose is deeply intertwined with covenant and community. The Torah frames humanity as a divine creation—fashioned in the image of God (Genesis 1:27), with a responsibility to uphold justice, kindness, and humility (Micah 6:8). Observing commandments and ethical living are not simply religious duties; they are how one sanctifies everyday life. The meaning of life is to partner with God in perfecting the world (*tikkun olam*). Picture a Jewish grandmother lighting Shabbat candles on a Friday evening. She's teaching her granddaughter not just a ritual, but a worldview: that ordinary acts can be sacred, and that to be just and kind is to fulfill one's reason for being.

In Christianity, life is a sacred gift. Jesus's teachings emphasize love, grace, and self-sacrifice. The highest human purpose is to love God and love one's neighbor (Mark 12:30–31). The story of Christ's resurrection offers a narrative of redemption—that suffering is not the end, and that life has eternal value. Meaning is not just found in faith but in acts of compassion, forgiveness, and service

In Islam, life is a test (Qur'an 67:2). Humans are God's stewards (*khalifah*) on Earth (Qur'an 2:30), entrusted with agency and moral responsibility. Worship, charity, honesty, and fulfilling one's obligations are central to living out this purpose. The Prophet Muhammad (PBUH) emphasized accountability, teaching: "Every one of you is a shepherd, and every one of you will be questioned about his flock"[2] He also highlighted service to humanity, saying: "Whoever relieves a believer's distress of this world, Allah will relieve his distress on the Day of Resurrection."[3] Islam teaches that meaning is found in surrendering to God's will, living with integrity, fostering justice, serving others, and preparing for the eternal life to come.

INDIAN TRADITIONS

In Hinduism, the human birth is rare and precious—it's a chance to break free from the cycle of birth and death (*samsara*). Life's purpose is to attain *moksha*, or spiritual liberation. This is achieved by fulfilling one's *dharma* (duty), accumulating good *karma* through ethical actions, and pursuing *jnana* (wisdom) and *bhakti* (devotion). The Bhagavad Gita teaches that one must act with righteousness without attachment to outcomes.[4]

In Buddhism, there is no creator god, but a clear path to end suffering. Life's meaning is not found in external achievements but in awakening—seeing reality clearly, letting go of ego and desire, and cultivating compassion. The Buddha taught the Four Noble Truths and the Eightfold Path, emphasizing mindfulness, ethical living, and wisdom. Meaning is liberation from delusion, arriving at nirvana, a state of peace beyond suffering.[5]

In Jainism, nonviolence (*ahimsa*), truth, and renunciation form the foundation of a meaningful life. The soul's journey is understood as a process of gradually shedding karma through ethical conduct, self-discipline, and inner purification. Unlike Hinduism, where karma is primarily an invisible moral law, Jainism teaches that karma is made of extremely subtle particles that cling to the soul whenever a person acts with passion, ignorance, violence, or desire. These karmic particles obscure the soul's innate purity and luminosity. Jainism emphasizes that even the smallest actions carry moral weight, and that spiritual liberation requires both inner purity and deep compassion for all living beings.[6]

TAOISM AND SHINTOISM

In Taoism, life's purpose is to live in accordance with the Tao, the natural flow of the universe. Forced striving is discouraged; instead, the wise embrace spontaneity, simplicity, and humility. Laozi writes, "Knowing others is intelligence; knowing yourself is true wisdom." Meaning is found in balance, not ambition.[7]

In Shinto, indigenous to Japan, meaning arises through reverence for nature, ancestors, and rituals. Purity, gratitude, and connection to one's land and heritage are central. While less doctrinal than other religions, Shinto offers a deep sense of identity and belonging.

Confucianism as a Source of Terrestrial Meaning for All

Confucianism emphasizes relationships, duty, and virtue. Confucius gives us a map everyone can practice today. Confucius' concentric circles (see figure 7.1) begin with the self and widen toward the world. A well-lived life is deeply rooted in family, respect, and ethical action. He stated, "To put the world right in order, we must first put the nation in order; to put the nation in order, we must first put the family in order; to put the family in order, we must first cultivate our personal life; we must first set our hearts right."[8]

CONFUCIUS'S CONCENTRIC CIRCLES

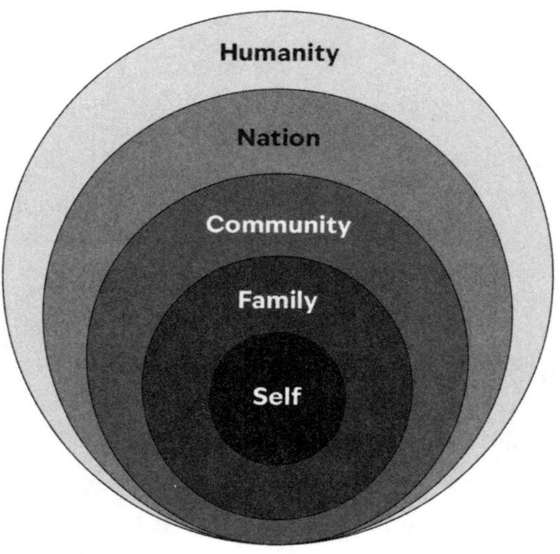

Figure 7.1: Purpose expands outward from self-cultivation to universal concern.

Imagine these concentric circles expanding from your personal core:

- Self: The innermost circle starts with personal integrity and self-cultivation. Confucius taught that meaningful living begins with refining one's own character, moral discipline, and self-awareness. He stated, "From the Son of Heaven down to the common people, all without exception must regard the cultivation of the person as the root."[9]

- Family: The second circle expands to family, the foundational unit of society. Filial piety (*xiao*)—respect and care for parents and elders—is paramount. Confucius emphasized that respect for parents is not just an obligation, but a reflection of character and humanity. He declared, "Filial piety and brotherly love are the root of humanity."[10] Relationships within the family nurture and anchor us, serving as the first proving ground of ethics, compassion, and responsibility.
- Community: The third circle includes your local community, neighbors, and colleagues. Confucius taught that one's ethical duties extend beyond family, influencing how we treat our neighbors, colleagues, and acquaintances. Meaning emerges as we actively contribute to community welfare, harmony, and shared prosperity. Confucius advised, "The superior person helps others to realize their good and does not help them to do wrong."[11] Within this circle, personal virtues become public virtues.
- Nation: The fourth circle expands to the nation or state. Citizens hold responsibilities to uphold social order, justice, and governance through active participation and ethical conduct. Confucius stressed loyalty and integrity as civic duties, advocating for righteous leadership and responsible citizenship. He believed a noble individual contributes positively to a virtuous society: "When rulers are virtuous, the people respond with loyalty; when leaders set good examples, harmony prevails."[12]

- Humanity: The outermost circle encompasses all humankind. Confucius's ultimate vision was universal harmony (*Datong*), an ideal state of collective well-being and moral interconnectedness. He recognized the shared humanity that binds everyone: "All within the Four Seas are brothers and sisters." Meaning at this level is about acknowledging our interconnectedness, transcending national and cultural barriers, and actively contributing to global compassion, peace, and understanding.[13]

These concentric circles are interconnected: the care you practice at each inner level strengthens your capacity at the outer levels. Reflect on where you stand today in these circles: How well have you cultivated your inner virtues? How does your family embody your values? How do your actions uplift your community, your country, and beyond?

Confucius has provided a framework to guide your efforts. Most of my clients and students are not aware of the concentric circles, but a large number of them structure their lives around this philosophy unintentionally. In my opinion, Confucius's concentric circles align with human psyche and biology.

Over the years working with countless clients, I've seen how a neglected friendship or missed opportunity to be there for a family member can haunt more than any financial misstep. Real meaning is a mosaic—built day by day in the choices we make within our circles.

In this structure lies a powerful blueprint for living purposefully, ethically, and harmoniously. It encourages us to build meaning not just vertically, achieving personal success, but also horizontally, by enriching relationships and embracing our shared humanity. In figure 7.2, starting with self, write inside the circle what action you have taken recently to develop, deepen, and strengthen your contribution to each.

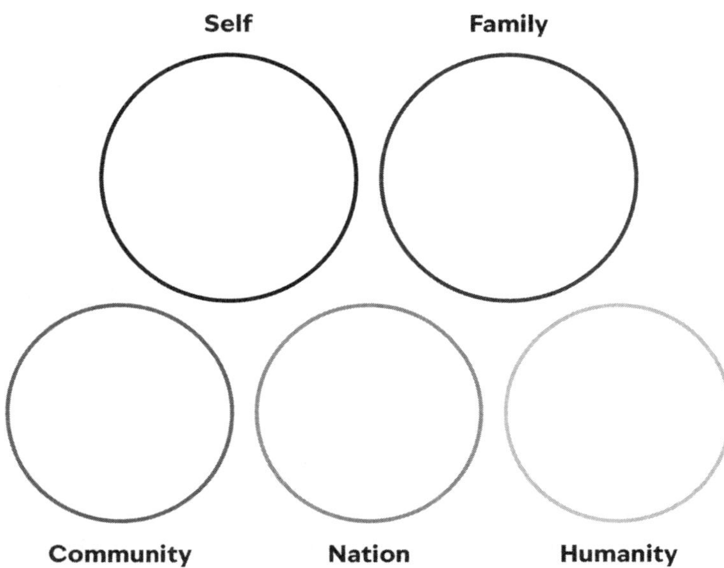

Figure 7.2: From awareness to action, align behavior with responsibility.

Agnostics, Atheists, and Terrestrial Meaning

What about those who do not believe in God or an afterlife? For agnostics, who remain unsure about the existence of a higher power, meaning is often shaped by a sense of awe at the mystery of life and an appreciation of beauty, love, and knowledge. They may find comfort in spirituality without religion, exploring practices like meditation, nature walks, or contemplative reading.

Atheists, meanwhile, often build meaning on more humanistic grounds. Life has no predefined purpose, they argue—but this is liberating. It means you get to create your own meaning. Legacy, contribution, relationships, creativity, and joy become their compass. As philosopher Albert Camus put it, "The struggle itself toward the heights is enough to fill a man's heart. One must imagine Sisyphus happy."[14]

Psychologist Viktor Frankl, a Holocaust survivor and founder of logotherapy, wrote: "Life is never made unbearable by circumstances, but only by lack of meaning and purpose."[15] He argued that meaning can be found even in suffering, through love, courage, and responsibility. For many non-theists, this insight offers profound inspiration: You may not control everything, but you can control your response.

THE VALUE OF YOUR LIFE, HERE AND NOW

Belief in a greater force is not the only source of meaning. Terrestrial meaning—the grounded sense of purpose you create in this life, on this Earth—is just as real, just as powerful, and often more immediate. You don't have to believe in heaven to make someone's life feel like a slice of it. You don't need to imagine reincarnation to recognize the impact you leave behind.

Think about your place in the lives of others. To your child, your parents, your friends, your colleagues, you may be irreplaceable. You are a source of love, safety, humor, advice, and meaning. You may not be in the history books, but you're in someone's heart, and that may be the most important record of all.

Your profession, too, is a profound source of meaning. A carpenter who builds homes leaves behind shelters that hold generations. A nurse eases suffering in moments of vulnerability. A teacher helps a child believe in themselves. These are not small things. These are the sacred tasks of everyday life.

We often idolize the famous or the extraordinary, but the truth is this: A life of consistency, kindness, and reliability is heroic. Being a good parent, a loyal partner, a dependable friend—that is a purpose-filled life. You don't need a divine mandate to live a meaningful life. All you need is to care, and to show up.

As discussed earlier, Confucius's model of concentric circles offers a strong ethical and existential framework for everyone—theist, agnostic, and atheist individuals.

Confucianism is fundamentally ethical and human-centered with a focus on cultivating virtue, harmony, and relational ethics rather than divine revelation. As modern interpreters note, the tradition resists the idea of an ultimate divine personality exerting control, preferring to root ethics and purpose in the natural and social order rather than in theology. For agnostics or atheists, Confucian thought provides a moral cosmos without doctrine, purpose through cultivation, and belonging through community.

The Role of Family and Individualism in the West

Culture plays a silent, yet powerful role in shaping how we see relationship, responsibility, and purpose. In much of our Western society, especially the United States, adulthood often means leaving home at eighteen—becoming self-sufficient, moving out, "making it on your own." It's a cultural rite of passage. Parents may feel their role is done once the child is "off the payroll." Children, in turn, are conditioned to value independence and personal success above all else.

But independence can come with a cost—emotional distance, generational disconnection, and loneliness. In countries like Japan, India, China, or Mexico, the idea of family is far more interwoven. Multigenerational households are common. Elders are cared for. Adult children stay connected—emotionally, physically, even financially. These bonds may limit some freedoms, but they foster depth, continuity, community, and purpose.

In a time when more people in the West report feeling isolated than ever before, perhaps the ancient model of extended kinship has wisdom worth reclaiming.

ASSESSMENT: INTERPERSONAL CONNECTION

Ask yourself:

1. Do I feel deeply connected to my family and close friends?
2. Do they feel connected to me?
3. What can I do to strengthen that circle—for their sake and mine?

Meaning is not one-size-fits-all. Whether you believe in God, karma, or only in what's observable—what you give still matters. So does what you stand for.

Meaning doesn't need to be cosmic to be real. It can be found in the sweat of your labor, the joy in your child's face, the peace of doing the right thing when no one is watching. It isn't a single destination—it's a map that helps you navigate the valleys and mountains of life. Sometimes it leads you upward, toward transcendence; other times inward, toward stillness and self-reflection.

Whether your compass points to God, to dharma, to awakening, to civic virtue, to duty, or to love itself—what matters most is that you have a compass. That you live on purpose. The philosopher Friedrich Nietzsche once said: "He who has a why to live can bear almost any how."

In this fast-moving, tech-driven world, it is important to take time and sit with your why. Life is short, but it can be rich. The world may be vast, but you are not small. You are the carrier of meaning, the author of purpose, and the witness to wonder. This recognition is Wisdom Wealth.

Reflection Questions

1. What is your life's purpose?
2. Do you draw more meaning from cosmic beliefs or terrestrial roles?
3. How do you show up in the concentric circles of Confucian care—self, family, community, nation, humanity?
4. How can you deepen your connections and expand your impact?

CHAPTER 8

The Power of Relationships

At 8:30 a.m., Jack walked into his office. A chorus of polite greetings echoed around him. "How are you?" his coworkers asked mechanically, eyes barely lifting from their screens. Jack hesitated briefly, feeling the weight of his true answer pressing heavily on him. His wife had recently been diagnosed with breast cancer, and his son had just dropped out of school. Inside, Jack felt utterly shattered. He wanted to scream, "I feel miserable. I'm depressed. I'm lost." But instead, he offered a forced smile and responded, "Doing great," his voice showing nothing of his inner turmoil.

Throughout the day, surrounded by colleagues who spoke easily but superficially, Jack felt profoundly alone and deeply stressed. Conversations rarely moved beyond small talk, leaving him craving something deeper, something real.

That evening, exhausted from the façade he'd maintained, Jack arrived home. He found his wife in the kitchen, her brave eyes masking her own fears. Without a word, he held her tightly. Together, they dialed their son's number. His voice was hesitant, unsure, filled with shame for his decision to leave school. Softly, Jack assured him, "It's okay. Come home. Take the time you need. We're here for you." After hanging up, Jack felt immense relief. Jack's story plays out millions of times every day and across the world. I can recall numerous times when I was in his shoes. According to one estimate, "How are you?"—the most widely used and perhaps most meaningless sentence in the English language—is spoken more than one billion times each day. Almost invariably, it demands no genuine answer.

Science confirms Jack's intuitive need for authentic relationships. Neuroscientists highlight mirror neurons—brain cells activated both when experiencing emotions and observing others experiencing them. These neurons facilitate empathy and genuine emotional connections—vital aspects of meaningful relationships that superficial interactions never engage.

True joy and comfort come not from polite yet empty inquiries at the office, but from genuine connection, empathy, and love within his real relationships. Jack understood clearly: Wisdom Wealth and authentic bonds are foundational for a fulfilling life.

What Are Human Relationships?

Take a moment to reflect on your life's most meaningful memories. Chances are, they're not about the things you owned, the titles you earned, or the places you visited—but about the people who were there with you. The laughter shared over a simple meal. The silent support during your darkest hour. The hand you held when words weren't enough.

It is nearly impossible to live a joyful, fulfilling life without at least one deep, authentic relationship. No amount of success, wealth, or achievement can replace the emotional nourishment we receive from true connection. In fact, the quality, depth, and number of your relationships may be the single most important predictor of meaning, purpose, and long-term well-being.

In the pages ahead, we'll explore why relationships matter so profoundly, drawing from anthropology, psychology, biology, and even evolutionary theory. Most importantly, we'll uncover what you can do to build and nurture the kinds of relationships that make life not just livable—but deeply worthwhile.

"SURVIVAL OF THE FRIENDLIEST"

Humans underwent a kind of "self-domestication" to become more friendly and cooperative. Researchers Brian Hare and Vanessa Woods argue that sometime in the past two hundred thousand years, individuals who were less aggressively competitive and more socially tolerant were preferred as mates and allies, leading our species to evolve "to be friendly, gregarious organisms."[1] This "self-domestication" hypothesis posits that we as humans gradually bred ourselves to be more playful and trusting, which enabled larger, more complex social groups to form.

Notably, even Darwin had foreshadowed this idea. He observed that animals (including humans) who "took the greatest pleasure in society would best escape various dangers; whilst those that cared least for their comrades . . . would perish in greater numbers."[2] In essence, evolution favored those who enjoyed each other's company and formed strong social bonds—truly a "survival of the friendliest." Hence, you value and appreciate friendship!

So yes, being social, cooperative, and emotionally connected is not just a nice idea—it's a survival strategy genetically embedded into us. Building deep, supportive relationships doesn't just help us endure life; it helps us truly experience it. But this raises an important question: How many relationships do we actually need—and what kind of relationships matter most?

HOW MANY FRIENDS CAN YOU HANDLE?

Humans are profoundly social—but we're not limitless in our capacity to connect. Despite modern technology giving us thousands of "friends" and followers at our fingertips, our brains are wired with a natural boundary. British anthropologist Robin Dunbar famously explored this and proposed a cognitive limit to the number of stable, meaningful social relationships we can maintain at any one time. That number? Roughly 150.

Dunbar arrived at this figure by studying primates.[3] He found that species with larger neocortex sizes—the thinking, social part of the brain—could maintain larger social groups. When applied to humans, the result was revealing: We can manage about 150 meaningful connections. Go much beyond that, and it becomes hard to remember who's who, let alone track the subtle dynamics between everyone in the group.

But it's not just about the number—it's also about depth. Dunbar's research showed that our relationships naturally fall into layers, like Confucius's concentric circles radiating out from our most intimate core:

- **5 People in Your Innermost Circle:** Your ride-or-die relationships. These are the people you trust with your life: your closest family, your dearest friends.
- **15 Close Family Members and Friends:** People you care about deeply and see or speak with regularly.
- **50 Good Friends:** Those you know well and genuinely enjoy being around.
- **150 Meaningful Connections:** The outer edge of Dunbar's number. People you'd invite to a large gathering or holiday party.
- **500 Acquaintances:** People you recognize, know casually, or might make small talk with.
- **1,500 Faces:** Individuals you can recognize by sight or name but with whom you have no real relationship.

While our brains might allow for hundreds of shallow connections, true intimacy is reserved for the precious few. And in today's hyperconnected world, many people are struggling to fill even their innermost circle. While all relationships are valuable, Wisdom Wealth and LIVING360 emphasize strengthening the core relationships.

A 2006 American Sociological Review study found that the number of confidants (people you can discuss important matters with) had declined from three in 1985 to about two in more recent surveys.[4] According to a 2021 report by the Survey Center on American Life, 12 percent of US adults reported having no close friends, an increase from 3 percent in 1990. Since 1990, there has been a massive decline in the number of deep relationships among Americans (see figure 8.1).[5]

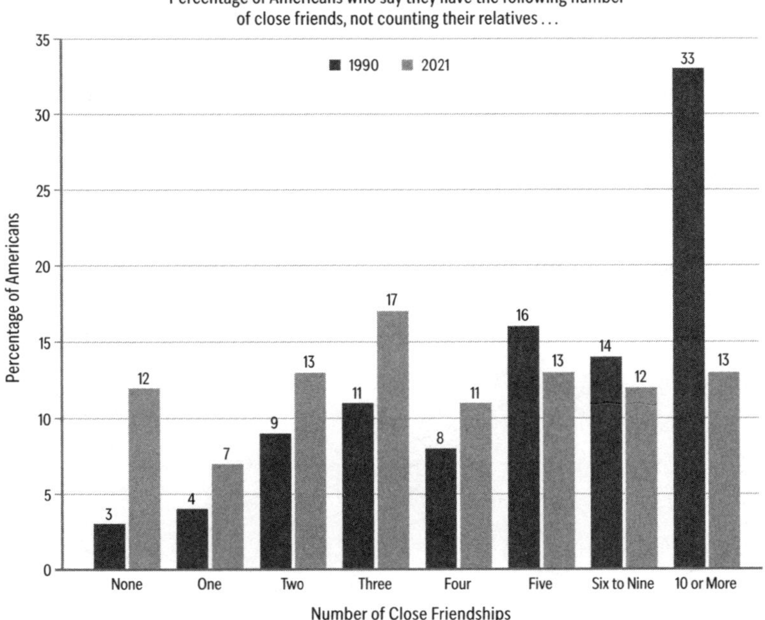

Figure 8.1: This chart illustrates the growing problem of loneliness in the US.

Loneliness is a serious problem. According to the US Census Bureau:

- In 2022, non-family households (which include one-person households) accounted for about 36 percent. In 1970 this number was only 19 percent. Doubling in six decades![6]
- In 2022, among adults age sixty-five or older, roughly three in ten lived alone. This number was one in seven back in 1960![7]

These are not just statistics—it's a reflection of a deeper loneliness in our modern lives. Dunbar's number reminds us that while acquaintances are many, the people who truly know you, support you, and walk beside you through life are rare and irreplaceable.

While our cognitive ability allows us to have five deep and fifteen close friends in our circle, with social media we are challenged by a large number of superficial connections. Dunbar's number underscores the value of those inner circles: we reserve our deepest attention and care for a relatively small number of close relationships. Social media distracts us from developing and deepening our core relationships. In the following box, write the names of the people you feel closest to:

1. ______________________________

2. ______________________________

3. ______________________________

4. ______________________________

5. ______________________________

In the next box, write the names of the people you consider close family and friends and with whom you meet regularly:

1. ______________________________

2. ______________________________

3. ______________________________

4. ______________________________

5. ______________________________

Now compare how many people are in your inner circle and how many are close family and friends you meet regularly. The more people you have in your inner circle with whom you share a deep bond, the higher your probability of LIVING360.

Relationships and Stress

Modern life is stressful, and comparison on social media adds to our existential anxiety. The strength and depth of our relationships have a direct impact on how we deal with stress and anxiety. We often think of stress as a purely individual reaction—a racing heart, sweaty palms, worry in the mind. But a wealth of research shows that our relationships profoundly affect how we experience and manage stress.

Psychologists Shelley Taylor and Gonzalo (Al) Gonzaga have proposed the social shaping hypothesis to explain this dynamic.[8] In essence, it suggests that throughout evolution, humans "outsourced" part of our stress regulation to our social relationships. From childbirth, our stress system is calibrated through the support and care we receive from family during difficult circumstances. Our reaction to stressful situations is regulated by supportive relationships, and the people in our network who are able to provide information about the dangers in our environment.[9]

What does this mean for our daily lives? It's a powerful reminder that we need a community of our own. Our loved ones can be literal lifesavers in times of stress—lowering our blood pressure with a reassuring word or motivating us to persevere. On the other hand, chronic loneliness or toxic relationships can take a severe toll on our health. Some believe that interaction on social media (likes, thumbs up) is not the solution to loneliness and is actually a key cause of isolation.

Priya, one of my students, was unraveling under the pressure of finals. Far from home, cut off from her usual support system, and drowning in coursework, she began experiencing full-blown panic attacks. But just as the stress threatened to completely overwhelm her, Jane, her roommate, quietly stepped in—not with grand gestures, but with small acts of genuine care. A gentle conversation. A quiet walk through the quad under the trees. Each interaction helped Priya breathe a little easier.

After the semester ended, she told me, "I studied hard, but it was Jane's presence that truly got me through. I don't think I could've managed without her."

It wasn't a social media "like" or a distant online friend that made the difference. It was a real, in-the-moment human connection—someone who noticed, who cared, and who showed up. And sometimes, that's all we really need.

Across all ages, rich and positive relationships are among the strongest predictors of happiness, health, and even longevity. This isn't just feel-good wisdom; it's backed by extensive research. The field of positive psychology—the study of what makes life most worth living—has repeatedly revealed that other people matter immensely when it comes to our well-being.

Relationships and Lifelong Well-Being

Perhaps the most compelling evidence for the importance of relationships comes from the Harvard Study of Adult Development, one of the longest-running studies on happiness. Launched in the late 1930s, it has followed hundreds of men (and later, their spouses and children) over eight decades, tracking their life trajectories in health, work, and relationships. The overarching message from this eighty-five-year study can be summed up simply: good relationships keep us happier and healthier, period.[10] As the current director, Robert Waldinger, puts it, "The most consistent finding we've learned through eighty-five years of study is: Positive relationships keep us happier, healthier, and help us live longer."[11]

This study has yielded some other eye-opening specific findings. For instance, the quality of people's relationships at age fifty was a better predictor of their physical health at age eighty than their cholesterol levels. In other words, having satisfying relationships is a stronger indicator of long-term health than traditional medical risk factors! Participants who were most satisfied in their relationships in midlife were the healthiest (and often happiest) octogenarians. By contrast, those who were lonely or had chronic conflict in their relationships showed earlier declines in health and brain functioning. Indeed, the study found that socially isolated people or those in unhealthy relationships often died younger, while "those who kept warm relationships got to live longer and happier."[12]

One striking finding was that marital happiness in one's eighties buffered physical pain: elders in happy marriages reported that on days when they had physical aches and pains, their mood stayed high, whereas those in unhappy marriages felt both more emotional and physical pain. This illustrates how a loving relationship can literally act as a pain reliver, softening the hardships of aging. The Harvard researchers have remarked that "good relationships don't just protect our bodies; they protect our brains."[13] In the study, those with strong social support in old age experienced less memory decline, whereas those who were socially isolated experienced earlier cognitive decline.

It's important to note that "good relationships" don't mean they are perfect or free of conflict. As Waldinger noted in his TED Talk, some of the happiest older couples "could bicker with each other day in and day out," but what mattered was that "they felt they could really count on the other when the going got tough."[14] In those relationships, occasional arguments didn't erode their deep bond. The strength and security of the connection were key, not the absence of minor squabbles. This is a heartening lesson: what counts is having people you can truly rely on, not having a flawless, storybook relationship.

The Harvard Study's former director, George Vaillant, after decades of observing the participants, summed it up with a memorable conclusion: "The key to healthy aging is relationships, relationships, relationships."[15]

Science and stories converge on the same insight: human relationships are the bedrock of your well-being. You are biologically wired for connection, psychologically nourished by love and friendship, and our bodies thrive when supported by others. From the evolutionary need to belong and cooperate, to the way a child's first attachments shape their world, to the protective effect of friendship and love against life's stresses, relationships form our shelter and our meaning. In the words of an old proverb, "A joy shared is doubled, a sorrow shared is halved." Modern research confirms this wisdom: sharing joys amplifies them and sharing struggles lightens our load.

Life's Two Most Important Choices: #1 Your Life Partner

There is a moment in every life when the gravity of certain choices becomes clear, and few choices shape your life more profoundly than who you choose as your life partner.

You may think you are immune to your environment, but neuroscience and psychology say otherwise. Studies in emotional contagion show we unconsciously pick up the moods, speech patterns, and even the *physiology* of those with whom we spend the most time. Mirror neurons fire, habits sync, and values merge quietly but steadily. Over time, your partner's dreams, frustrations, and patterns of handling life's ups and downs will shape your own.

THE MOST IMPORTANT DECISION, HIDDEN IN PLAIN SIGHT

When I ask my MBA students what the most important decision of their lives will be, they often say, "career choice" or "investing early." Both matter, of course. But eventually, someone will pause and say quietly, "Who I choose to marry." They are correct.

Your partner will influence:

- **Your Daily Emotional Climate:** Studies show that having a supportive partner can significantly lower cortisol levels (stress hormone) and reduce cardiovascular risk.[16]
- **Your Financial Future:** The University of Michigan's Health and Retirement Study found that couples who share similar money values and communicate about finances are more likely to build wealth.[17]
- **Your Health and Habits:** Research published in *JAMA Internal Medicine* shows that when one spouse adopts healthier behaviors (like exercising or quitting smoking), the other is significantly more likely to follow.[18]
- **Your Dreams and Goals:** Whether they flourish or wither often depends on the environment you create together.

Marriage and long-term relationships are not just a romantic commitment; they are strategic partnerships that impact every dimension of your life.

WHEN THE WRONG PARTNERSHIP BECOMES A LIFE SENTENCE

Imagine spending your days with someone who is chronically negative, addicted to alcohol or gambling, or financially reckless. You wake up every day carrying the weight of their decisions on your shoulders. Their choices become your crises. Their chaos becomes your daily environment.

Even less dramatic issues—a partner who resents your ambitions, spends beyond your means, or refuses to grow emotionally—can insidiously drain your energy and confidence over years.

The stakes are high. According to the American Psychological Association, about 40–50 percent of marriages in the United States end in divorce,[19] and divorce is ranked among the top three most stressful life events, often resulting in:

- Financial losses that can set you back for decades
- Emotional scars that affect your self-esteem and mental health
- Long-term impacts on children, including higher risks of anxiety, depression, and academic difficulties

Over years of advising clients on their financial futures, I have found that our conversations inevitably move far beyond numbers and investment returns. As trust grows, clients come to share not only their financial goals but also their deepest fears, personal challenges, and relationship struggles. Again and again, I have witnessed that—short of a life-altering diagnosis or unexpected death—nothing erodes a family's Total Wealth more profoundly than toxic relationships and divorce.

In my practice, I have seen couples spend years entangled in costly legal battles—fighting over assets, custody of children, even family heirlooms or beloved pets. For some, the courtroom becomes a battleground for infidelity, betrayal, or abuse, turning what was once a partnership rooted in love and meaning into a source of grief, trauma, and lasting resentment. The emotional and financial costs are immeasurable.

This is why choosing a life partner stands among the few decisions where getting it right or wrong can alter your happiness, legacy, and prosperity for decades to come.

WHAT THE RIGHT PARTNERSHIP FEELS LIKE

Imagine sharing your life with someone who cheers for your dreams while pursuing their own, creating a partnership rooted in mutual growth rather than silent resentment. You wake up each day beside someone who shares your values around family, financial priorities, and the commitment to keep evolving. Conversations about challenges and differences happen with honesty and kindness, even when emotions run high, because you both believe in protecting the emotional safety of your connection.

In this kind of partnership, you feel encouraged to become your best self—not out of fear or obligation, but from a place of warmth and inspiration that comes from love rooted in respect. You feel seen, valued, and supported as you take on the world, while your partner knows you are in their corner as they strive for their own goals.

CHOOSING WITH CLARITY AND COURAGE

Many people find themselves drifting into lifelong partnerships without truly pausing to consider whether the relationship aligns with their values and life vision. Fear of loneliness often whispers that "someone is better than no one." Family expectations and cultural pressures can nudge us forward, while the momentum of a long relationship can carry us past red flags we don't want to see. Sometimes, physical attraction clouds the quiet discomfort of fundamental misalignments.

But the reality is that loneliness within a misaligned relationship can feel far more isolating than being alone.

Compatibility doesn't mean finding someone perfect; it means finding someone whose values align with yours on the things that matter most. It is alignment on family goals and the role of extended family in your lives. It is shared perspectives on money, saving, spending, and long-term financial aspirations. It is having a clear and mutual understanding about children, parenting philosophies, and lifestyle choices. It is feeling connected on personal growth, faith, or spirituality, and being able to handle conflict with emotional intelligence and respect.

Choosing your life partner should be one of the most deliberate, thoughtful decisions you ever make, approached with the same care you would give to building your life's foundation.

ASSESSMENT: RELATIONSHIPS

Take a quiet moment to sit with these questions as you shape your LIVING360 journey:

- Do I feel emotionally safe, respected, and seen in this relationship?
- Are we aligned on the big issues of life that matter most?
- Do we share the same vision and does this partnership energize me?
- Can I see us growing together through the inevitable changes that life will bring?

Your partner will influence your mornings and nights, setting the emotional tone for how you start and end each day. They will shape your stress levels, determining whether you face challenges together or feel alone in your struggles. They will impact your financial trajectory through their spending, saving, and investing habits, helping you build or destroy your financial future. Your dreams will either be encouraged or quietly stifled, depending on the support you receive. Even your ability to find joy in life's simplest moments will be colored by the partnership you share.

In many ways, your life partner will either add momentum to your journey toward a fully lived, purpose-driven life or become the largest roadblock you will face to LIVING360.

Life's Two Most Important Choices: #2 Having Children

There are few decisions in life as *consequential and irreversible* as choosing to have children. For most of human history, this was not even seen as a decision—it was nature's design, driven by our deeply embedded desire to leave copies of our DNA and to find intimacy through connection. Even today, about half of pregnancies worldwide are unplanned, often arising simply from our natural desire for sex, as reported by the United Nations.[20]

I have two sons, now twenty-three and twenty-six, and I can say without hesitation that they have been among the greatest sources of meaning, growth, and joy in my life. While I have yet to experience the joy of grandchildren, every grandparent I know describes it as a *next-level happiness*. For many, children provide a sense of purpose and enduring love that no career achievement or financial success can replicate. Parenting is hard work and a lifelong commitment, but for many, it becomes a cornerstone of their LIVING360 journey.

A DIFFERENT PERSPECTIVE: ANTINATALISM

Several years ago, I came across the works of South African philosopher David Benatar, including *Better Never to Have Been*[21] and *The Human Predicament*.[22] His philosophy of antinatalism challenges the default assumption that bringing new life into the world is a positive moral act.

Benatar argues that coming into existence is always a harm. His reasoning is built on what he calls the asymmetry between pleasure and pain:

- The presence of pain is bad.
- The presence of pleasure is good.
- The absence of pain (by never existing) is good, even if there is no one to experience it.
- The absence of pleasure (by never existing) is not bad, unless someone exists to be deprived of it.

From this, Benatar concludes that since nonexistence prevents harm without depriving anyone, it is better never to have come into existence.

He further argues that life inevitably includes suffering—illness, frustration, anxiety, aging, and death—and that people underestimate how bad life can be due to psychological biases like optimism, adaptation, and comparisons with worse scenarios. Because bringing a child into the world exposes them to suffering without their consent, Benatar views procreation as morally problematic.

While Benatar's perspective is worth considering, it is not without strong criticisms:

- Critics question why the absence of pain should be considered "good" if there is no subject to experience it, arguing that Benatar's asymmetry is arbitrary.

- Others point out the nonidentity problem: Before existence, there is no person to harm or to deprive of pleasure, making the claim that existence "harms" someone incoherent.
- Finally, Benatar's pessimistic evaluation of life may not reflect the lived experiences of many people who, despite suffering, find life meaningful and worth living.

Antinatalism also highlights an uncomfortable but essential question: Is it ethical to bring a life into the world knowing that suffering is inevitable? What about the risk of serious disabilities, disease, addiction, or tragedy that can bring chronic suffering to children and their parents?

These are not easy questions, and they force us to look deeply at what it means to live a good life and to make choices aligned with our values. While most people would not agree with Benatar, I believe keeping an open mind and exploring ideas outside our concrete box is essential for Wisdom Wealth.

For those of us committed to LIVING360, the question is not simply whether to have children, but how we can create a life where suffering is minimized, and joy and purpose are amplified. Parenting with intentionality, emotional maturity, and financial preparedness can help us raise children in a way that equips them to find meaning and navigate the inevitable challenges of existence.

ASSESSMENT: HAVING CHILDREN

Take a moment to consider these questions as you reflect on this consequential life choice:

- Why do I want (or not want) to have children?
- Am I prepared emotionally, financially, and relationally to take on the lifelong commitment of parenting?

continued

- How will having children impact my LIVING360 journey of living fully, bravely, and intentionally?
- If I choose to have children, how can I parent in a way that minimizes unnecessary suffering and helps them lead a purposeful life?

Bringing a child into the world is one of the most profound acts of hope, love, and responsibility. It requires us to look beyond our desires and to deeply consider the life we can provide for another human being. For many, it becomes a path to living fully and leaving a legacy of love. For others, the choice to remain child-free can be a conscious, values-driven decision aligned with their vision of a meaningful life.

Whatever choice you make, may it be made intentionally, courageously, and with the wisdom that your journey deserves.

Happiness Solution: Deep Relationships

Spouse, children, family, friends, and colleagues are all potential sources of deep relationships and happiness. Here are six actionable ways to strengthen the relationships in your life:

1. Celebrate Each Other
    - Share good news and take joy in each other's successes. Be genuinely happy for your friends, family, and partners. Your response to someone's joy is just as important as your support during hard times.

2. Give Compliments and Appreciation
    - Don't assume people know how much they mean to you. Say it. Write it. Show it. A kind word or a thoughtful thank-you can build connection and trust.
3. Listen and Be Curious
    - Ask questions. Put your phone down. Make eye contact. When someone speaks, listen not just to respond, but to understand.
4. Make Time
    - Schedule calls, dinners, walks, and game nights. Relationships need time to grow. Even small, regular touchpoints can go a long way.
5. Do Things Together (Play Together)
    - Shared experiences create shared meaning. Cook a meal, take a trip, volunteer together—do anything that builds memories.
6. Repair and Resolve Conflict
    - No relationship is perfect. Disagreements happen. What matters is showing up, apologizing when needed, and working through problems together.

At the end of the day, relationships are not a luxury. They are one of the most important elements of LIVING360. They are where we find meaning, joy, resilience, and strength. No success, no possession, no achievement can replace the comfort of being seen, understood, and loved. So invest in your relationships. Reach out. Forgive. Celebrate. Listen. Make time. Because in the end, it's not what you've accomplished that matters most—it's who walked the journey with you.

Make a list of people you would like to deepen your relationship with:

1. ____________________
2. ____________________
3. ____________________
4. ____________________

From the preceding list, what steps are you going to take to deepen your relationship with the people who are really important to you:

Step 1: ____________________

Step 2: ____________________

Step 3: ____________________

Reflection Questions

1. How important are relationships to human health and happiness?
2. Think of a person you believe has a good life. How are this person's relationships with friends and family?
3. How important are relationships in your life?

CHAPTER 9

The Meaning of Work

Your career deserves a special place in this book because it bridges both Financial Wealth and Wisdom Wealth. For most of us, work is necessary to sustain our lifestyle—but a career is never *just* a paycheck. It is also a source of identity, community, purpose, and relationships.

Think about how much of life is shaped by work. If you live to eighty, you'll spend about one-third of your time asleep and nearly another third working. That means most of your waking adult life will be spent on the job. It's no wonder careers have inspired countless reflections. Steve Jobs, the co-founder of Apple, was famously credited as saying, "Stay hungry, stay foolish." Beautiful words. Inspiring. Perfect for commencement speeches. But the reality for most people is more complicated. Opportunities, skills, economic trade-offs, and personal desires all shape what our careers look like. Just as "financial security" means different things to different families, the idea that *everyone* must chase their passion, climb the highest mountain, or "stay hungry" isn't realistic—or even desirable—for all.

A career is one of the most important determinants of Total Wealth. Your Financial Wealth is closely tied to the profession you choose—it's very hard to become a multimillionaire as a park ranger or elementary school teacher. At the same time, some of the highest-paying careers—investment banking, transactional law, surgery—can consume so many hours and create so much stress that family, leisure, and health suffer. Many of my clients in high-paying, high-pressure fields admit, "I don't like my job . . . but I want the money." On the other hand, some of my clients who maintain work-life balance in jobs—such as teachers, clergy, and electricians—describe their work as joyful. Too often, the echo inside our concrete boxes—the voices of status, expectation, and comparison—pushes people toward careers misaligned with their true skills, temperament, and calling. The choice is yours!

Long hours, high stakes, and big paychecks don't automatically rob life of joy, nor do shorter, simpler jobs guarantee peace. Some people come alive under pressure; others wither under the same heat. Routine can be grounding for one person and suffocating for another. The difference isn't the job; it's the fit.

Knowing yourself, your biology, temperament, and values is the foundation of choosing work that sustains rather than consumes you. True satisfaction comes not from ease or intensity, but from alignment: between what you do, what you value, and who you are becoming. The tension between money, meaning, time, and stress sits at the heart of career choice. Work can be deeply fulfilling, or it can drain joy and create anxiety. For most people, work will always feel like work. The key is not to chase perfection but to avoid the trap of a toxic environment where your career erodes your health, happiness, and sense of purpose. One of my engineer clients in Silicon Valley told me, "I don't need to love my job. I just need to love what my job allows me to do after six p.m."

The Four Pillars of Career Choice

To find a career that supports both your Financial Wealth and your Wisdom Wealth, you need to think beyond the paycheck. Four core pillars shape career decisions:

1. Financial Aspirations

   How much money do you want to make—and what are you willing to sacrifice for it? Are you comfortable working forty hours a week, or would you commit to sixty, eighty, or even one hundred hours a week in pursuit of higher earnings?

2. Skills and Abilities

   How well do your talents match what the marketplace rewards? Can you honestly assess your skill set, and do you understand the long-term prospects of your profession? Some careers rise with technology and globalization; others shrink.

3. Risk Appetite

   Are you comfortable betting on yourself, even if that means a failed start-up or a business venture that goes belly-up? Or do you prefer the predictability of a nine-to-five job with a steady paycheck?

4. Health and Biology

   What are your limits? Some jobs demand long hours, high stress, and constant travel. Others are physically taxing. Your career choice has to align not just with ambition but with the reality of your mind and body.

These four pillars don't exist in a vacuum. They are shaped by the opportunities around you, the economy you live in, and the biology you inherited—with all its strengths and limitations.

Ambition, Culture, and *Amor Fati* (Love Your Fate)

In Western meritocracies, children grow up hearing, "You can be whatever you want to be." Parents beam when their child declares they want to be president. Positive thinking is valuable, and ambition should be encouraged. Ambition is a spark; *amor fati* is the hearth that contains it. Loving your fate doesn't mean surrender—it means finding grace in the cards you're dealt while still playing them to the best of your ability. It's the wisdom to optimize within your reality.

The truth is that the world shapes careers and success as much as individual choice. During the last thirty years, globalization has lifted over a billion people out of poverty. Factories moved to Asia, providing jobs and dignity for workers who once lived in extreme poverty. At the same time, Western blue-collar workers lost jobs, income, and pride as manufacturing shifted overseas.

When Foxconn opened a factory in Shenzhen, millions of rural families gained steady wages for the first time. The same shift that lifted them out of poverty closed plants in Detroit and Cleveland. One family's promotion became another's layoff.

The winners of this global shift were those at the top of the innovation pyramid—entrepreneurs and companies who could scale unique ideas to millions of customers. Your career is not only about your skills and effort but also about how global tides of technology, geopolitics, and economics reshape what is possible.

To arrive at a career that enhances your Total Wealth, you must balance both inputs: meaning and money.

Total Wealth	=	**Wisdom Wealth**	+	**Financial Wealth**
		(career as a source of meaning, relationships, community, and identity)		(career as a source of income to achieve your financial security)

The Evolution of Work in the Age of AI

Compared to any earlier era, work in the modern Western world has undergone a profound transformation. At the dawn of the Industrial Age, in 1890, the average American worker earned the equivalent of about $15,593 a year (in today's dollars) and labored nearly fifty-nine hours a week, often in harsh, unsafe conditions. By contrast, the median salary in 2023 reached $63,914, with the average workweek reduced to about thirty-four hours.[1] The shift from factory floors and farms to offices, studios, and digital workspaces represents not just a change in occupation, but a revolution in how we define labor itself.

It's easy to believe that work has become more stressful and precarious, especially amid layoffs, automation, and the rise of the gig economy. Yet the truth is more nuanced and far more hopeful. Today, most workers enjoy unprecedented flexibility, autonomy, and opportunity. The gig economy that feels uncertain to some also offers new forms of independence and creative freedom. Across much of the developed world, the conditions of work such as safety, wages, access, rights, and choice have improved more dramatically in the last fifty years than in the previous five hundred.

The next great transformation is already underway. Get ready, because automation and AI are reshaping the landscape of work, altering not just what we do but how we think, learn, and create value. Algorithms can now analyze data, draft reports, design buildings, and even diagnose diseases. Yet the one thing machines cannot replicate is wisdom, our uniquely human ability to reason ethically, imagine new possibilities, and connect meaningfully with others. In this age of intelligent tools, success will depend less on what you know and more on how you apply your knowledge with judgment, creativity, empathy, and adaptability.

Work is far more than labor exchanged for pay. It reflects who you are, who you might become, and the mark you leave on the world.

A fulfilling career may not be one that perfectly blends passion and paycheck. Few achieve that ideal. Instead, it's one that supports your broader life: enough income to feel financially secure and enough meaning to maintain health, deepen relationships, and attain joy. The goal is not simply to "make a living." The goal is LIVING360!

Reflection Questions

1. Describe your ideal career.
2. How does your current job compare with your ideal career?
3. What three steps can you take today to make your career more meaningful? List them here:

1. ______________________________
2. ______________________________
3. ______________________________

CHAPTER 10

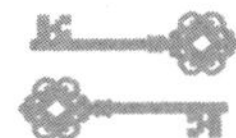

The Value of Gratitude

After a LIVING360 presentation, one of the participants, Alex, shared how his fiftieth birthday celebration had gone. First, Alex came home to a cake he didn't feel he'd earned. Fifty had promised him milestones: corner office, kids at elite schools, a house paid off, a number in a retirement account that would make his father proud. Instead, he carried a modest title, a stubborn mortgage, and children who were choosing beautifully unpredictable lives. He set his briefcase down and felt the old equation rise in his throat: *Happiness equals reality minus expectations.* He did the subtraction and came up short.

Then the lights went out.

For a moment, the kitchen felt like failure embodied—unfinished cabinets, a blinking microwave now blank, the cake's candles the only light. His daughter laughed from the hallway, the sound bright as a bell. "Maybe the universe is saving us on electricity," she said, striking a lighter. His wife placed the flickering candles in the middle of the table and the room softened: edges blurred, shadows warmed, faces glowed.

Alex's phone buzzed with a message from an old college friend: a picture of a Tuscan villa and a line, "Promotion to partner today. *Saluti!*" The old tug of comparison tightened his chest. Then another notification: a photo from his son of a greasy engine block and two hands streaked with oil. "First paycheck from the shop. Feels good," the text read.

In the darkness, his cell phone rang. His mother called from three time zones away, her voice thin but steady. "On your birthday," she said, "we always thank God for you." She recited, as she had since he was a boy, a short prayer of gratitude. When she finished, the room was still. While Alex was cutting his birthday cake, three thoughts ran through his mind:

Today I had a kitchen full of candlelight.

My son's hands know honest work.

Someone thanked God that I exist.

His daughter flipped the switch, and lights returned with a pop, blooming harsh and white. For a second, he missed the dark. That night, before going to bed, Alex started writing everything that was good in his life, and he was surprised that the list kept getting longer and longer. He looked down at the page and understood, dimly but truly, what he had just done: He hadn't changed his life; he'd changed how he was letting it in.

What follows in this chapter is the art and science of that shift—why the mind shrinks our frame by default, how ancient wisdom and modern psychology point to the same practice, how the voice in your head can be trained to notice light, and how a handful of small rituals can turn gratitude from a mood into a way of living.

This question cuts deeper than metrics. It invites you to examine not just what life gave you, but how you've learned to see it. Because how you feel about your life is not just about your reality. It's about your expectations, your mindset, and most powerfully, your sense of gratitude. This chapter is about reclaiming peace, not by changing your life, but by changing how you live within it.

Gratitude is not about pretending everything is perfect. It's about recognizing what is good—even when life looks different from the script you once wrote. Imagine waking up tomorrow not with a sense of lack, but with a quiet appreciation for the fact that you're here, breathing, and surrounded by moments of beauty and meaning, however small. Psychologists define gratitude as a "thankful appreciation for what an individual receives, whether tangible or intangible"—an intentional act of noticing the good and acknowledging that much of it comes from beyond yourself.

The Roman philosopher Cicero called gratitude the parent of all virtues.[1] Poet Maya Angelou echoed this truth, advising us to "be present in all things and thankful for all things."[2] Whether spoken in scripture, philosophy, or science, the message is clear: gratitude doesn't just make life *feel* better—it actually *makes life better*. And as you'll discover in the pages ahead, it may be one of the most powerful tools for reclaiming peace, joy, and meaning in a world that constantly tells us we're falling short.

The 40 Percent of Happiness We Can Control

Two friends from college reunite after twenty-five years. One lives in a luxurious home, runs a tech firm, and vacations in Europe. The other lives modestly, works as a schoolteacher, and spends weekends gardening. Surprisingly, it's the second friend who seems lighter, warmer, and more at peace. What's his secret? "Every Saturday or Sunday morning I start by writing down three things I'm grateful for," he says. "It resets everything." That simple ritual—backed by science—is one way we can intentionally steer the 40 percent of happiness within our control.[3]

As we explored in Chapter 3, one of the most surprising insights from positive psychology research is that only a small portion of our happiness is determined by our circumstances. We might assume that things like wealth, social status, or education level would make or break our joy. Yet studies show that life circumstances account for only about 10 percent of our long-term happiness, while a much larger chunk—around 40 percent—comes from our intentional activities and daily choices. The remaining 50 percent is attributed to our genetic predisposition or personality set point for happiness (see figure 3.2).[4]

WHAT DETERMINES HAPPINESS?

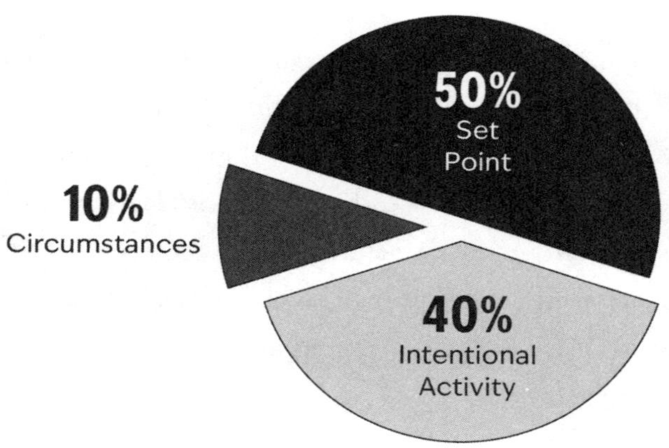

Figure 3.2: The surprising drivers of happiness.

Among those intentional habits, practicing gratitude stands out as especially potent. Researchers have found that gratitude is "strongly and consistently associated with greater happiness."[5] People who regularly take time to appreciate the good in their lives tend to experience more positive emotions, less stress, and closer relationships. In one famous study, two psychologists asked participants to jot down a few sentences each week—one group wrote about things they were grateful for, while others wrote about hassles or neutral events. After ten weeks, the gratitude group was not only more optimistic but also felt better about their lives and even had fewer physical complaints.[6]

Gratitude works its magic through multiple pathways. Psychologically, it shifts our focus from what's lacking to what's already present and good. Biologically, neuroscience has shown that gratitude activates brain regions associated with reward and positive emotion, triggering the release of "feel-good" neurotransmitters like dopamine. Regularly practicing gratitude can even lead to long-term changes in the brain, reinforcing neural pathways for contentment and resilience.

Why We Get Used to Good Things

Evolution designed us to adapt quickly—for survival. But that same strength, while shielding us from prolonged pain, also mutes our joy. We become numb to blessings as they become routine. When we experience negative, unhappy, or even tragic events, we become temporarily sad, but some time passes, we move on, adapt, and even forget. This is key to avoiding depression and surviving.

When we acquire or experience something we have been wanting, it initially enhances our life experience, we feel happy and elated but after some time we adjust to the new circumstance and the new is not new, it's not fun, there is no excitement, and we get back to our baseline happiness level. Like a person on a treadmill, we rapidly get used to improvements, so we end up no happier than before. Research has shown, for example, that lottery winners experience a spike in happiness shortly after their win, but within a year or two they often revert to their previous happiness level. The same goes for many positive life changes—a dream job, a new romance, a fancy gadget. At first, we're thrilled, but as the extraordinary becomes ordinary, its ability to boost our mood fades.[7]

Research has shown that

- when most people buy a new car, they do get a bump in happiness, but it lasts only three weeks;
- when most people buy a new home, they do get a bump in happiness, but it lasts only nine months; and
- when most people get married, they do get a bump in happiness, but it lasts only two years (no eternal bliss for most people, actually over 40 percent of marriages end up in divorce).[8]

Why does this happen? How does special become ordinary? One major mechanism is that our expectations and desires increase along with our circumstances. Get a pay raise, and soon you start expecting that level of income; find a wonderful partner, and before long you might focus on minor imperfections. Our minds continually "shift the goalposts."

So, is there a way off the treadmill? Gratitude may be the answer. Deliberately practicing gratitude helps us *slow down* hedonic adaptation by keeping our blessings in the foreground of our minds. When we are grateful, we resist the urge to take good things for granted. We savor them. In fact, experts call gratitude "perhaps the most powerful antidote to hedonic adaptation."[9]

ANCIENT WISDOM MEETS MODERN SCIENCE

The Stoic philosopher Marcus Aurelius advised: "Take full account of what excellencies you possess, and in gratitude remember how you would hanker after them, if you had them not."[10] This is a profound exercise in fighting adaptation: frequently imagine life *without* the comforts, abilities, and loved ones you currently enjoy. By doing so, you renew your appreciation for them instead of letting them blend into the background.

Prophets and saints know the power of gratitude much before positive psychologists. In Christianity, gratitude is central to a spiritual life: "Give thanks in all circumstances; for this is God's will for you in Christ Jesus."[11] It is a way of living that acknowledges grace and encourages humility.

Islam emphasizes contentment and thankfulness. The Qur'an repeatedly instructs believers to be grateful, stating: "If you are grateful, I will surely increase you [in favor]."[12] Gratitude, in Islamic teaching, is both a form of worship and a pathway to abundance. Prophet Mohammad is quoted as saying: "Look at those below you and do not look at those above you, for that is more likely to keep you from belittling the favors Allah has bestowed upon you."[13]

In Hindu philosophy, the idea of *santosha* (contentment) is one of the key tenets of a fulfilling life. Santosha is about accepting what we have and appreciating life as it is. The Bhagavad Gita also speaks of detaching from outcomes and finding peace in the present moment, which aligns deeply with the mindset of gratitude.[14]

HAPPINESS = REALITY - SHIFTING EXPECTATIONS

A friend of mine called on the day he got promoted to vice president. I thought he'd be celebrating. Instead, he was sulking. He had just discovered a peer had landed a C-suite role at another firm. His joy had already turned to envy. Why? Because our expectations, like shadows, grow as we move forward. It wasn't about reality—it was about comparison.

There's a popular equation:

Happiness = Reality - Shifting Expectations

But what makes this equation dynamic is the fact that expectations shift. They're shaped by what we've had in the past, what others around us have, and what we choose to compare our lives to. For instance, someone who gets a promotion may feel proud initially, but that new position becomes the new normal. Soon they may compare themselves to a peer who's further ahead or expect even more recognition. This happens because a closed concrete box creates echoes of rising expectation, which diminishes reality causing happiness to decline.

This shifting nature of expectations is what makes contentment so elusive. If we constantly move the bar higher, reality will always feel behind, even if it's objectively improved. Gratitude, however, can interrupt this cycle by anchoring our expectations to a more realistic, appreciative baseline. It reminds us that what we have now was once only hoped for.

Gratitude also fosters acceptance. Acceptance does not mean passivity or settling for less; it means making peace with outcomes we can't control while increasing our awareness and continuing to strive for growth. When reality doesn't meet expectations, gratitude can help us embrace "what is" without bitterness. As Confucius put it, "He who is contented is rich."[15]

By learning to manage expectations and accept outcomes with grace, we free ourselves from chronic dissatisfaction. This balance of ambition and acceptance, this ability to find contentment while moving forward, is where you will thrive.

Managing Your Internal Conversation

Think of your internal voice as the narrator of your life's documentary. If that narrator is critical, cynical, or anxious, the whole film feels darker. But if it's encouraging, hopeful, and kind, even the hard scenes have warmth.

In my graduate class at the University of California–Irvine, I always start with a simple but revealing question:

"Who do you talk to the most every day?"

The room lights up with answers—"My spouse," "my best friend," "my mom," "my therapist," "my team at work."

Then, from the back row, a more insightful answer cuts through the noise:

"Myself."

And they're right. You talk to yourself more than anyone else ever will. This silent, constant voice—the internal narrator—is one of the most powerful forces shaping your entire life experience. It colors how you feel about yourself, how you interpret the world, and how you respond to challenges and opportunities. Yet for most people, this inner dialogue is almost completely unconscious. Like background music in a movie, it sets the emotional tone for everything—but unless you pause to listen, you may not realize it's even playing.

THE GOLF GURU WHO "BULLSHITS" HIS BRAIN

Sometimes wisdom doesn't come from textbooks or TED Talks—it comes from someone who's lived long, learned often, and figured out how to hack their own mindset. Recently, I had a conversation with one of my clients—an eighty-year-old man who is, in every sense, thriving. He's lean, strong, and sharp. He spends six months of the year traveling the world, plays golf like a pro, and just published a book about improving your golf game. He laughed as he told me his metabolic age is fifty-six. I asked him, "What's the secret?" Without hesitation, he answered, "I learned to bullshit my brain. I kept telling myself, over and over, that I'm healthy, vibrant, strong, grateful, and happy. And over time, my brain believed it—and my body followed. It works!"

He didn't mean that he was lying to himself. What he meant is that your brain listens—and the more often it hears something, the more it starts to treat it as truth. It may sound like magic, but it's backed by neuroscience. The brain believes what it hears most often—especially from you.

RESHAPE YOUR INNER VOICE

It begins with awareness. Most of us don't realize how much we generalize, catastrophize, or shame ourselves in our inner monologue. You might say things like:

"I always mess up." "Everyone's better than me." "This will never work." Pay attention to these moments. Catch them. Because the first step to change is noticing.

Once you recognize the negative voice, flip the narrative, tell your mind about all your successes and how you were able to manage through difficult situations. Show compassion to yourself. It quiets fear. It helps you think more clearly, act more decisively, and feel more whole.

This internal dialogue matters because the way you talk to yourself affects how you handle pressure, how you show up in your relationships, whether you bounce back from setbacks or spiral, and the overall shape and feel of your life. In the end, the most important relationship in your life—the one that shapes all others—is the relationship you have with yourself, and managing your internal conversation is part of Wisdom Wealth.

Because when your inner conversation changes, everything else follows.

Five Simple Ways to Practice Gratitude

1. **Write down three good things.** At least once a week, jot down or seriously reflect on three things that went well or made you smile. Do it in a notebook or notes app. Keep it simple and consistent.
2. **Appreciate people more.** Spend time recognizing, thanking, and appreciating people more. Express your love, do it genuinely

and frequently. Make it a point to tell them how important they are to you and what joy and happiness they bring to you. Express to your family members how important they are to you and how much you care for them. Reach out to your friends and especially your real good friends and say everything you have in your heart for them. Take time to sit next to your parents, hold their hand, and tell them how grateful you are to them. Recognize your boss or colleagues and be open about how they make your life good and special and how they help you day in and day out.

3. **Celebrate good fortune.** Use each and every opportunity to celebrate all good things that happen in your life or the life of people who are important to you. Birthdays, anniversaries, promotions, retirements, good grades for kids, graduations, winning a sporting event—leverage good things for goodness!
4. **Share what is important.** Talk to people around you and share what is important to you, what you value, what is good in your life, and ask them to do the same. This is how you continue to appreciate what is good.
5. **Notice small pleasures.** Take a few moments each day to enjoy simple things such as sunlight, a good meal, laughter, clean sheets. Mentally say, "I'm thankful for this."

Gratitude is not a miracle cure, but it's close. It won't eliminate problems, but it will expand your capacity for joy, peace, and connection. Practiced regularly, it becomes a lens that clarifies what matters most, helping you live not just reactively, but with presence, perspective, purpose, and 360 degrees of appreciation for life.

Reflection Questions

1. Would you consider spending five to ten minutes every week writing or thinking about all the positives in your life?
2. Do you feel that hedonic adaptation is the main reason why you stop appreciating the good things in your life?
3. Do you feel that the following equation captures your happiness formula?
    - Happiness = Reality – Shifting Expectation
    - Reflect on your reality. Which of your expectations come from your concrete box?

PART IV

Build Financial Security

There is a painful irony in modern life: You can know who you are, understand the world, and have a clear sense of purpose—and still feel trapped by money.

You've come a long way. You've reflected deeply on who you are. You've examined how the world works and how it may change in the coming decades. You've explored what brings true meaning, peace, and connection into your life. But none of it—not self-awareness, not purpose, not even gratitude—can fully flourish if you are living under the constant weight of financial stress.

For general and specific disclosures, please refer to Appendix 7.

People with good careers and good income can be unsure about their true financial situation. Many people feel the pressure of financial anxiety. High expenses, a large mortgage, school tuitions, aging parents, lifestyle expectations—all of it can require a constant level of income that makes changing jobs, taking a sabbatical, or even pursuing a passion project feel like a reckless gamble.

That feeling of being tethered to the hamster wheel of your life is a concrete box. And the key to that box is not simply "more money." It is financial security—a resilient foundation that gives you the ultimate luxury in life: options.

That's why financial independence is the final piece of your LIVING360 plan. We did not begin your journey here because money is not the meaning of life. But it is what allows you to live the life you have thoughtfully designed in the earlier parts of this book—with dignity, agency, and peace of mind. Financial security is the structure that protects your purpose, your relationships, your health, and your time.

Whether your vision includes retiring earlier, scaling back work, traveling the world, helping your community, supporting your children, or simply sleeping soundly at night, the principles ahead will show you how to move toward that life with clarity, discipline, and confidence.

Financial stability is not a single destination; it is a series of clear, controllable steps that gradually insulate your personal freedom from the inevitable volatility of markets and of life. It is the difference between feeling required to work and feeling free to work on what matters most to you.

In the chapters ahead, we will focus on the core principles, behaviors, and strategies that form a solid financial foundation (see figure IV.1). If, after this section, you want to go deeper into the specifics of investment planning—asset allocation, stocks and bonds, ETFs, bond ladders, real estate, and more—you'll find the Comprehensive Investment Guide, which serves as your detailed toolbox.

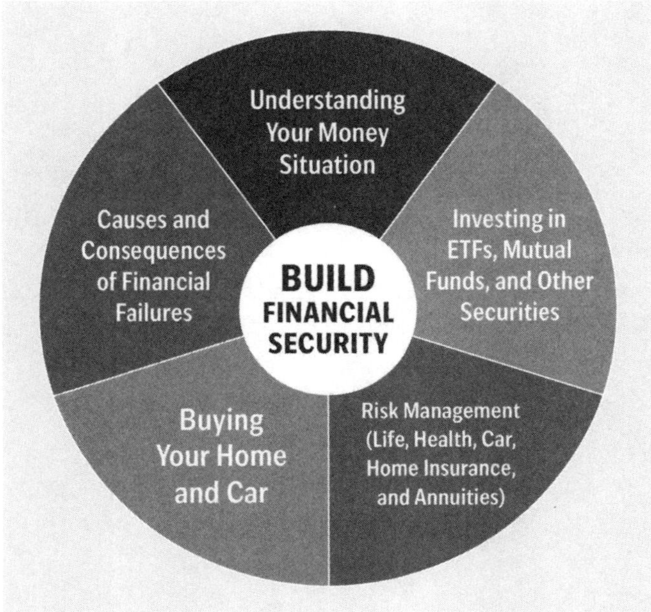

Figure IV.1: The why and how of financial security.
(See Appendix 7 for important disclosures.)

For now, our goal is simple and profound: to align your money with your meaning, and to build the financial security that lets your Wisdom Wealth truly come alive.

CHAPTER 11

Financial Security Is Freedom

You've examined your beliefs, your biases, your dreams, and the world you live in. You've stepped outside your concrete box to see yourself—and your possibilities—with new eyes. Now, I invite you to pause for a moment. Take a breath, close your eyes, and ask yourself: "What does financial security mean to me?"

For me, as an immigrant building a new life, financial security meant achieving the American dream: a nice house, a good car, freedom to travel, and good education for my two boys. For you, it might mean something very different. Close your eyes and ask yourself: Is it the ability to sleep well at night, knowing bills are covered? Is it the freedom to travel, to give generously, to pursue your passions without fear? Or is it simply the confidence that you will not be a burden to anyone you love?

Throughout history, a small fraction of humanity has pursued spiritual fulfillment through paths such as nirvana, asceticism, monasticism, or Sufism. However, the vast majority of us—perhaps as many as 99.9 percent—seek life's tangible comforts and pleasures. As we highlighted earlier, genuine happiness becomes elusive when basic necessities such as food, shelter, and safety remain uncertain. Financial security is not about having a high number in a bank account. It's about maximizing your freedom of choice.

True security means you can choose what you do with your time, whom you work with, and what risks you are willing to take in the pursuit of fulfillment. It is the ultimate antidote to the "golden handcuffs" of a high-stress, high-paying career or "iron shackles" struggling to just pay for the basic necessities of life. This financial independence is essential for LIVING360 because it significantly reduces stress, elevates happiness, and provides the freedom to truly enjoy life.

Picture two sixty-eight-year-olds, Samantha and Arthur, born in the same year, now standing at very different doorways to retirement. Samantha wakes up in a modest coastal home, pours her coffee slowly, feeling content and free to spend her day filled with yoga, volunteering, and time with grandchildren. She's not wealthy in a flashy sense, but she's free versus Arthur, waking up with a pit in his stomach as he rechecks his bank balance, heart pounding over the rent due. He checks his phone anxiously, worried whether the next Social Security check will cover rent and prescriptions. His dreams—travel, time, dignity have silently expired under the weight of financial strain.

The only real difference between them? How they saved, spent, and invested, not how smart they were, how much they earned, or even how hard they worked. One was financially savvy and followed a plan; the other floated on hope. Financial independence isn't about greed or luxury. It's about freedom from fear. The freedom to say yes to what matters, and no to what doesn't. It's the ability to age with dignity, to support those you love, and to live life on your terms—whether that means adventure, security, creativity, or service.

LIVING360 aims to equip you with the knowledge, discipline, and strategies to avoid the pitfalls of financial insecurity. This includes applying our trusted 3As framework to your pursuit of financial stability. Awareness, Action, and Acceptance are essential tools that will give you the clarity, control, and discipline you need to succeed in your endeavor.

- Awareness: First, acknowledge that financial stress robs you of your health, relationships, and peace of mind. With that clarity in mind, you will always understand the importance of your goal as you learn to master the time-tested, research-based principles of saving and investing.
- Action: Put your goals into motion by creating and executing a detailed plan for impactful saving, wise investing, and strategic risk management.
- Acceptance: True financial independence requires emotional discipline—the patience to ride the market's inevitable ups and downs and the courage to trust the long-term journey. This is where you learn that lasting success is built not on luck, but on consistent, unwavering effort.

Engaging thoughtfully with this section and following some simple yet powerful guidelines may dramatically reshape your financial trajectory, turning dreams of financial freedom into reality. Imagine the difference between retiring with financial security versus fear of running out of money. I will help you clearly map out this path, but ultimately, the choice, and responsibility, lie with you.

Why Financial Independence Matters

Contrary to popular belief, achieving financial security has far less to do with sheer intelligence and far more with behavior, discipline, patience, and managing emotions. Financial independence ensures a baseline of stability, upon which genuine happiness can grow. This chapter is about unpacking why you must take the reins of your financial destiny and move beyond mere safety into the realm of intentional choice.

And this move is backed by science. Here's what research tells us about why financial security is fundamentally important to quality of life:

- The richest 1 percent of men in the US live approximately fourteen years longer than the poorest 1 percent. For women, this gap is around ten years.[1] Financial insecurity doesn't just drain wallets; it shortens lives.
- Approximately one in five US adults experience mental illness annually, with financial stress as a significant contributing factor. Chronic financial anxiety can lead to anxiety disorders, depression, and insomnia.[2]
- Individuals earning at least twice the federal poverty level are significantly more likely to meet physical activity guidelines, directly improving their overall health and longevity.[3]
- Families experiencing poverty are three times more likely to face child maltreatment and neglect, often directly tied to financial hardship.[4]

Financial Insecurity in America

Ironically, even in the United States—the richest nation in history—financial insecurity remains alarmingly prevalent.

As of 2022, Americans aged sixty-five to seventy-four have an average net worth of about $1.79 million. But this number is misleading because wealth in the United States is not evenly distributed. A small percentage of households hold a very large share of Financial Wealth.

A better way to understand the financial reality of most older Americans is to look at the median, which represents the midpoint of the wealth distribution. For sixty-five to seventy-four-year-olds, the median ($410k) is roughly one-fourth of the mean ($1.79 million), revealing a dramatic gap (see figure 11.1).[5] This four-to-one difference shows how a relatively small number of highly wealthy households skew the average far above what most retirees actually possess.

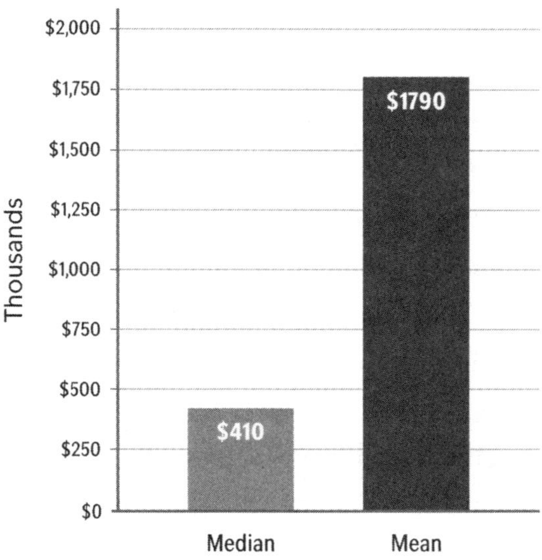

Figure 11.1: Median vs. mean wealth of Americans at age sixty-five.

Many factors contribute to this disparity—income inequality, home ownership patterns, market participation, inheritance, and generational advantages. But one of the most consistent and controllable drivers is a lack of financial literacy. Without the knowledge to save, invest, and make financially sound decisions, millions of Americans enter retirement with less security than they could have achieved.

- As of the second quarter of 2025, the share of net worth held by the bottom 50 percent of US population was only 2.5 percent, while the top 50 percent, owned 97.50 percent of all net worth. More surprisingly, the top 1 percent owned about 30 percent of household net worth in the US.[6]

- In 2024 alone, nearly half a million personal bankruptcy filings occurred, significantly impairing individuals' abilities to secure housing, credit, and even employment for years.[7] Behind every bankruptcy statistic is someone's broken dreams and sleepless nights.
- More than one million eviction filings in 2024 highlight the harsh reality faced by millions of renters, leading to profound emotional trauma and long-term financial setbacks.[8] That's not just a number; it represents families packing their lives into boxes because rent outpaced their paychecks.
- About 30 percent of Americans (seventy-one million people) have overdue debt collections, severely impacting their credit scores and mental health through relentless collection efforts.[9]
- Approximately eight hundred thousand people in the US experienced homelessness at the end of 2024, sleeping on streets and in shelters. This is evidence of profound systemic financial instability.[10]

These sobering figures raise a question: with so much opportunity (especially in wealthy countries like the US), why do so many people still end up financially insecure?

Why Do People Fail Financially?

In underdeveloped economies, resources and opportunities may be limited, but seeking financial security in the US is different. Financial distress can sometimes be attributed to systemic or macroeconomic conditions in the US, but more often it arises from individual circumstances or choices. Common reasons include:

- Medical emergencies and large medical bills
- Addiction and substance abuse
- Job loss or prolonged unemployment
- Divorce and the resulting financial burdens
- Poor budgeting habits, overspending, and excessive consumer debt
- Lack of financial education and literacy
- Failed businesses or entrepreneurial ventures

Understanding these risks underscores why financial literacy, planning, and discipline are crucial.

Financial independence doesn't merely enable comfort; it grants you control and dignity. In the chapter ahead, we will start mapping your personal path to financial security beginning with a lesson I give every one of my students why choices are more important than circumstances.

As we delve deeper, we will equip you with practical tools, strategies, and knowledge necessary to strive for a life marked by financial security. Your financial journey starts now. Every choice you make, every dollar you save, every habit you build is a step toward your freedom.

Reflection Questions

1. Do you believe that financial insecurity negatively impacts lifespan and health span?
2. In your opinion, should everyone learn financial literacy in high school or college?
3. Why is financial insecurity and stress so common in the US?

CHAPTER 12

Craft Your Personal Financial Security

At the start of my wealth management course at the University of California–Irvine, I project a bell curve of the approximate net worth of MBAs in the US at age sixty-five, and the room of graduate students falls silent. Eyes widen as they see the $4 million average. Then I tell them the twist: statistically, one of them could retire with over $25 million. And one will rely solely on Social Security just to buy groceries. Heads snap up. They're wondering, *Which one will I be?*

Figure 12.1 illustrates this spectrum. The average sixty-five-year-old American has a net worth of around $2 million. But as the curve shows, outcomes vary dramatically.

Please refer to Appendixes 7A and 7B for general and investment-related disclosures.

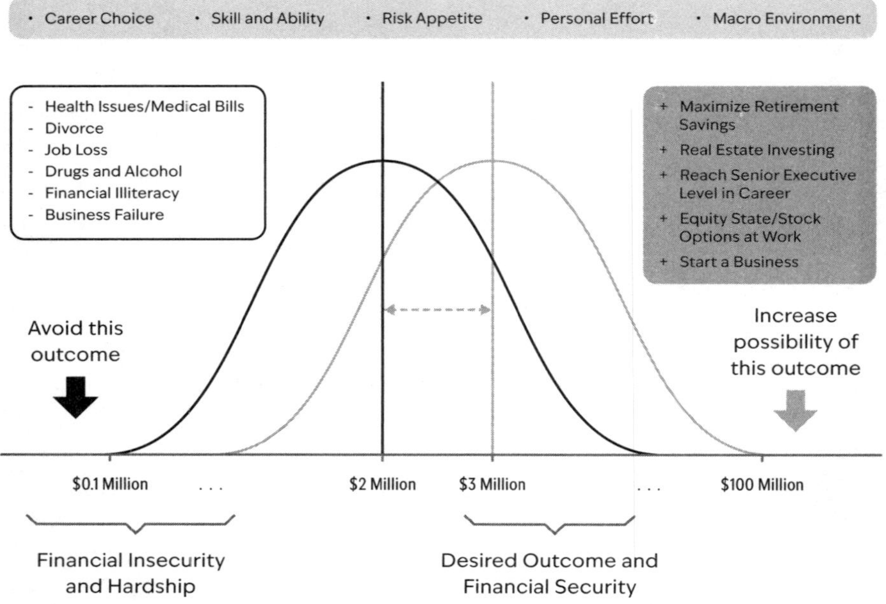

Figure 12.1: The wide dispersion of financial outcomes reflects both chance and choice.

Ending up on the wrong side of this bell curve can be the result of poor planning or of circumstances beyond a person's control. Starting your own business, for example, can be a source of immense wealth creation but also risks bankruptcy. To make uber wealth, a person must not only be talented and hardworking, but also in the right place at the right time.

Consider this: An incredibly talented chef diligently saved for twenty years to launch his dream restaurant in Scottsdale, Arizona. With great excitement, he opened in December 2019, only to face the devastating impact of COVID-19. By September 2020, he was bankrupt, sitting in his shuttered dream restaurant, feeling utterly crushed and asking, "Why me?" Sometimes, despite doing everything right, external circumstances—such as a recession—can overwhelm even the best plans. Acceptance and resilience become key in these challenging moments, embodying the LIVING360 philosophy.

It took two tough years and many sleepless nights, but he refused to give up. He launched a smaller bistro, pouring all his talent and wisdom into it. Today, that humble bistro has flourished into two thriving locations, with a third on the way, a testament to grit and resilience.

History shows that even doing everything "right" can be derailed by fate, which is why acceptance (the third "A" of our 3As framework) and resilience are so crucial. Yet there's a lot within your control: by reading this book you've equipped yourself with the tools to land on the right side of that curve. Still, effort isn't everything; chance and context play a big role.

Smart decisions such as maxing out retirement accounts, investing in real estate, and working for companies that offer stock options can push your net worth far above the mean. But setbacks including illness, divorce, job loss, and poor money habits can pull you downward, even if you did many things right. In wealth, as in life, you control your *path*, not the *outcome*. But if you walk it wisely, the destination you arrive at can be extraordinary.

THE SIMPLE SOLUTION FOR FINANCIAL SECURITY

What is that destination, exactly? There is no "one-size-fits-all" answer here. Your vision of financial security will be shaped by your aspirations, your values, and the life you wish to live—all guided by the wisdom you have gained on your LIVING360 journey.

To share some basic financial statistics, in low-cost US states income between $60,000 and $80,000 can cover most essential living expenses and in high-cost US states this number can be from $70,000 to $100,000. Most couples will get about $45,000 to $55,000 in Social Security retirement income. To cover your basic retirement expenses, you only need $5,000 to $55,000 per year in additional income beyond Social Security, depending on where you live. Once you get to this income, everything you "need" is really a "want." It is extra and luxury! Here is a mathematical explanation:

Basic Financial Security = Access to Money in an Emergency + Having a Clean and Safe Place to Live + Money to Buy Things You Need (Today and in the Future)

Personal Financial Security = Access to Money in an Emergency + A Place to Live Where You Desire + Money to Consume Things You Want + Legacy Goals (Must Leave Money to Heirs)

What You Need to Live Joyfully

If you had wisdom, meaning, and purpose in abundance . . . could you be truly happy living simply? The answer is yes—you absolutely could. But in LIVING360, that's not the only path. Your definition of a fulfilling life might involve a cozy cottage and a frugal budget. Or it might include an oceanfront mansion, first-class getaways, a collection of designer bags, and the thrill of fast cars. In my view, there's no "right" or "wrong" lifestyle.

In fact, I believe there is only one crucial truth about the nature of your end goal: Once you've secured enough money to cover the essentials, the relentless pursuit of more must never cost you your relationships. The hunger for wealth must never blind you to the treasures you already have.

Consider two entrepreneurs: One worked sixteen-hour days and grew his net worth to eight figures by fifty, but found himself attending his birthday dinner alone, his family long estranged. Another built his wealth more slowly, always home for family dinner, and by fifty had a modest nest egg and a house filled with laughter. Who was truly richer? Money can't buy back lost time.

Gratitude and contentment are not the enemies of ambition—they are the anchors that keep your ambitions from pulling you out to the sea of loneliness. For most people, "wants" are "needs." It is only through Wisdom Wealth that you can contemplate and arrive at a meaningful definition of your personal financial security.

With a modest level of effort and consistent discipline, you can develop a financial strategy that sets you firmly on the path to success. You might even outperform professional money managers, as approximately 85–90 percent of mutual fund managers underperform the market over the long run, according to the S&P Dow Jones SPIVA Scorecard.[1]

This section is dedicated to providing simple solutions to help you craft your own personal financial security. The goal here is to give you a road map to get started, while reserving more detailed explanations of the design and engineering for the Comprehensive Investment Guide. While the following recommendations are grounded in financial research and my professional experience, please note they might not align with your personal circumstances, and you should always seek professional advice when in doubt. What you are reading here is not financial advice specific to your situation but well-considered personal finance and investing ideas you can use to tailor a plan to achieve your life goals (see figure 12.2). With that in mind, let's start your journey toward financial security.

Figure 12.2: Build financial independence through disciplined decisions.

Reflection Questions

1. In your opinion, how significant are the factors beyond your control that impact your financial security?
2. Do you believe most people should feel content after achieving basic financial security?
3. How many of the ten steps in figure 12.2 have you already considered and implemented in your life?

CHAPTER 13

Understand Your Finances

You can't steer a ship if you don't know where you are on the map, even if you know where you're going. So before we talk about investing or building wealth, we need to locate your starting point and determine *exactly where you stand financially, right now*. That's why the first step in your LIVING360 financial plan is brutally simple: Track your income, spending, and net worth. Most people never do this, and they pay the price for it over a lifetime.

It was a late Thursday afternoon when Jordan, a thirty-six-year-old marketing executive, walked into my office. He was polished, confident, and dressed in a tailored suit. He drove a sleek European car, vacationed in Tuscany, and lived in a downtown high-rise with skyline views. By all appearances, Jordan had "made it." His father, a longtime friend, had urged him to come in. Jordan needed help with investments—or so he thought. But after exchanging pleasantries, he got straight to the point: "I make over $350,000 a year," he said. "But every month, I feel like I'm chasing my own tail. I have no idea where the money goes. By the

---

Please refer to Appendixes 7A and 7B for detailed disclosure information.

twenty-fifth, I'm broke. I'm putting everything on a credit card with a 19 percent interest rate. I'm scared—and frankly, a little ashamed."

We pulled up a whiteboard and started mapping his finances. Within forty-five minutes, the picture was clear: Jordan had negative cash flow. Despite his impressive income, lifestyle creep had taken over: private school tuition, mortgage, country club dues, dining out, and a dozen subscription services he barely used.

The second shock came when we calculated his net worth. Despite the car, wardrobe, and high-rise condo, Jordan was practically underwater. His debts nearly equaled his assets. His net worth was lower than a barista who lived frugally and saved consistently. Jordan didn't need a raise. He needed a reset.

Even if you're not already burdened by lifestyle creep the way Jordan was, we're going to take this opportunity now to take stock of your finances so you can make more intentional choices moving forward.

Jordan took this hard lesson to heart. Together we built a plan. He canceled unused subscriptions, downsized his condo, set up automatic investments, traded his fancy car for a more affordable one and within a year he was out of credit card debt and finally started growing his savings. He transformed embarrassment into empowerment. That reset begins here, with you. So, let's roll up our sleeves and start *your* reset.

Before building wealth, before investing, before real estate or retirement strategies comes a simple but profound step: Know where you stand. Track what comes in, what goes out, and what you truly own. You cannot improve what you do not understand. Financial independence isn't about income—it's about awareness and intentionality. It's not about appearing rich, but about actually being free.

Financial independence starts with living within your means. Regardless of your income level, spending less than you earn is foundational. Remember, wealth isn't built by spending. It's built by saving and investing wisely. Do you want to *look* rich or be rich?

ASSESSMENT: BUDGET AND CASH FLOW

Think of your finances as if they were a bathtub. Your income is the water coming in through the faucet. Your spending is the drain. If the faucet flows faster than the drain, the tub fills up—*that's your savings*. But if the drain is wider than the faucet, the water runs out faster than it fills. You'll never get ahead unless you control the outflow.

Take a moment to reflect:

- Do you know exactly how much money you spent last month?
- When was the last time you checked your net worth?
- Are you managing your money—or is your money managing you?

CONTROL YOUR CASH FLOW

Cash flow isn't about mere budgeting. It's about reclaiming control. You wouldn't launch a multimillion-dollar business initiative without understanding every dollar that goes in and out, yet many successful people run their personal finances with a "hope and pray" strategy. To break this cycle, the first step is to determine whether your net cash flow each month is positive or negative.

Let's get started:

- Make a quick budget → Know your cash flow
- Net cash flow = How much you make – How much you spend
- If you have a net cash flow surplus, meaning you are saving, it's a good start. If you have a deficit, meaning you are spending more than what you make, you have a challenge that needs immediate action.

Your Cash Flow = Net (After Tax) Monthly Income - Everything You Spend in a Month

Your Net Monthly Income = $________________
Your Total Monthly Expenses – $________________
Your Net Cash Flow = $________________

(Please find a detailed cash flow worksheet available in the Appendix 3.)

Even if your cash flow is temporarily negative due to specific circumstances (new business, property purchase, education costs), understanding your cash flow is crucial to your long-term financial security. Temporary negative cash flow due to an investment can be positive for future growth of income.

KNOW YOUR NET WORTH

What is your true financial situation? As a starting point, quickly create a net worth statement. A net worth statement gives a clear snapshot of your financial health.

To calculate your net worth, first add up the value of everything you own and then subtract all the money you owe. Your assets are your home, your savings in a bank or brokerage, cars you've paid off, and so on. Your liabilities include mortgage on your home, credit card balances, student loans, car loans, and so on. This is the true measure of your Financial Wealth, not cash flow or how much you are spending.

Net Worth = Assets (home, savings, investments, cars, etc.) - Liabilities (mortgages, credit card debt, student loans, etc.)

Your Current Net Worth = $ ________________________________

(Please find a detailed net worth worksheet available in the Appendix 4.)

If you are able to calculate your detailed net worth, you will know the true level of your wealth. Moreover, completing an honest financial evaluation places you among the top 20 percent of Americans in terms of financial awareness. A Discover® survey (2024) revealed that only 36 percent of Americans created a budget, while a Qualtrics study (2023) indicated 67 percent of Americans don't actively track their net worth, highlighting widespread financial illiteracy.[1]

From the net cash flow and net worth analysis, you now know how much you are spending, saving, investing, and the state of your financial net worth. Take stock of where you are today. Based on your life goals and vision for personal financial security, you can set up a target amount to save and determine where and how to invest.

Ultimately, knowing your net worth will help you strip away the noise of income, expenses, and asset values, boiling your financial life down to a single truth: the size and strength of your current financial foundation. Net worth is the number that tells you how many more options you have today than you did yesterday. By tracking it regularly, you will gain the clarity and motivation necessary to maintain your momentum, thus converting your abstract hopes of financial stability into measurable progress.

Reflection Questions

1. What is your current net monthly cash flow?
   (Money Earned – Money Spent)
2. What is your current net worth?
   (Total Assets – Total Liabilities)
3. Are you satisfied with your current net cash flow and net worth?

CHAPTER 14

Simple but Time-Tested Investment Principles

Albert Einstein is famously quoted as saying, "Compound interest is the eighth wonder of the world. He who understands it, earns it—he who does not, pays it." We've covered the mechanics of saving. Now let's talk about something just as crucial—your investing mindset. For most people, knowing how to invest and compound money does not mean becoming a stock market wizard. Instead, it means setting up a simple, powerful system where your money earns money automatically. Investing is an essential step in achieving the financial stability that underpins your life's endeavors. Investing is how you will harness the exponential force of compounding and allow yourself the freedom to pursue the life you want.

Of course, knowing *how* to invest matters: A Dalbar study showed that over a thirty-year period ending in 2021, the average equity fund

---

Please refer to Appendixes 7A and 7B for detailed general and investment-related disclosures.

investor earned 7.13 percent annually compared to the S&P 500's 10.65 percent.[1] That difference of 3.5 percent may not sound like much, but over a span of thirty years, it means retiring with $789,465 instead of $2,082,269 million ($100,000 invested for thirty years earning 7.13 percent versus 10.65 percent). That gap wasn't bad luck; it was bad behavior: chasing hot stocks, panicking during downturns, or trying to time the market. This discrepancy, due largely to emotional and impulsive decisions, costs investors significantly. Avoid being part of this statistic by developing a disciplined, informed investment approach.

Case Study: Two Sisters

Leila and Sofia went to the same college, had the same salary, and began at the same starting point. Leila dove into investing right away. She started small, kept it simple, bought index funds, and forgot about them. Sofia felt uncertain—she kept reading articles that highlighted risk in the economy, markets, and the world. She waited for the "right time," worried she might mess up and lose money

Ten years later, Leila had a $250,000 investment portfolio. Sofia was still on the sidelines with $45,000 in her checking accounts. The only difference? Leila mastered a few basic principles and stuck with them. That's what this chapter is about. Investing doesn't have to be hard. You just need to start and keep it simple.

Surprisingly, many people find saving easier than investing. While the US education system excels in teaching complex subjects such as calculus and chemistry, it often neglects practical financial education. Consequently, many adults lack essential financial skills despite regularly making critical decisions about budgeting, borrowing, insurance, and investments. Expecting everyone to magically grasp these concepts upon turning eighteen is unrealistic and absurd.

The Uncomplicated Path to Investment Success

For three decades, I've had the privilege of walking alongside thousands of investors, diving deep into portfolio philosophies, investment styles, and trading techniques. And what I've seen, time and time again, is a consistent pattern: The more complex and active an investment approach, the more likely it is to end in a "crash and burn."

But here's the good news: The clients who achieved good outcomes and solid financial security weren't doing anything crazy. Their success came down to a few surprisingly simple, yet profoundly powerful, principles.

KNOW YOUR INVESTING ABCS

As I mentioned, you don't need to be a Wall Street wizard, but successful investors do take the time to understand the basics. They know the core investment types: stocks, bonds, real estate, and good old cash. They're not intimidated by jargon; they learn the simple ideas they need to know to make smart choices.

Keep It Simple, Seriously

Who really benefits from overly complicated financial products? Usually, it's not you. Smart investors steer clear of these exotic offerings because they realize they're not experts in everything. Complexity can often hide high fees and unnecessary risks.

Don't Put All Your Eggs in One Basket

This isn't just an old saying. It's a golden rule of investing. I once had a client, an engineer, who put nearly all his savings into his own company's stock. When that company hit a downturn, his investments dropped 60 percent in a blink, all because his eggs were in one basket. If he'd spread his investments around, that one company's fall wouldn't have hurt so much. Lesson learned: No matter how much you believe in a single investment, it is very risky to bet your whole garden on one seed.

Successful investors embrace diversification. When they're young, they have a good mix of stocks. As they get older, they gradually add bonds to the mix. It's the oldest and still the best way to manage risk in your portfolio.

Minimize Costs

Every dollar you pay in fees or taxes is a dollar that isn't working for you. Successful investors are incredibly conscious of this. They prioritize low-cost investments and max out tax-advantaged accounts. Why? Because those "small" fees—anywhere from 0.50 percent to 3 percent annually—can eat away at your returns like termites.

Consider this: A $100,000 portfolio, over thirty years, earning 9 percent instead of 7 percent (thanks to lower costs), means an extra $565,000 in your pocket! High costs are a huge reason why many investors dramatically underperform the overall market. They simply crush the magic of compounding.

Focus on Tax Efficiency

In my experience, uninformed investors chase the highest gross returns, while smart investors focus on real after-tax performance.

Many investment options, such as actively managed mutual funds or high-turnover strategies, constantly trigger taxable events such as short-term capital gains or interest income, which are taxed at higher rates. These taxes erode your actual wealth.

Instead, savvy investors prioritize tax-efficient strategies such as low-turnover ETFs, index funds, and municipal bonds (for taxable accounts). They make the most of tax-advantaged accounts like IRAs and 401(k)s.

Let's look at an example to fully understand the negative impact of unnecessary taxes:

Imagine you invest $100,000 in corporate bonds earning 5 percent interest. If your combined federal and state tax bracket is 32 percent, your *net* (after-tax) return is a mere 3.4 percent. Here's the quick math:

After-Tax Return = (Your investment x Interest Rate) x (1 - Your Marginal Tax Rate)

After-Tax Return = ($100,000 x 5%) x (1 - 0.32)
Real After-Tax Return = $3,400

So, from that $5,000 in interest you *thought* you earned, you actually paid $1,600 in taxes, leaving you with only $3,400. The same principle applies to short-term gains or interest from CDs. And if you're *also* paying 1 percent in management fees? Your net return plummets to around 2.4 percent. You just lost over 50 percent of your earnings to taxes and fees!

Stay Calm and Carry On

Finally, and perhaps most importantly, successful investors are masters of their own emotions. They don't let "fear or greed" push them into bad decisions. They ignore the constant parade of "doom and gloom" headlines and resist the siren song of every "shiny new thing" promising quick riches. Emotional discipline is your superpower in investing. I know this is easier said than done. When the market dives and your account balance falls, it's *human* to feel fear; I've felt it too. No one really knows the future and uncertainty creates anxiety. I believe that sometimes I feel it more, because thousands of people have trusted me and my firm with their life savings and I feel responsible that my actions profoundly impact their life experience. But here's what I remind myself: those headlines screaming doom won't matter in ten years, but the choices I make today will.

History proves the virtue of patience. In the 2008–2009 crisis, those who stayed invested in the S&P 500 saw their portfolios nearly *double* in value over the next ten years, while those who sold at the bottom, locked in losses and often missed the rebound.[2] Every crash feels unique and scary in the moment, but the recoveries have been remarkably consistent for those who stay the course

A truly successful financial strategy isn't just smart on paper. It has to be something you can stick with through thick and thin. Investing isn't about beating the market or predicting the future; it's about consistent, disciplined, and prudent decisions made patiently over the long haul. Figure 14.1 highlights some of the lessons learned by my most successful clients.

Understand Investing: As Easy as Planting a Garden

Building wealth is like tending a garden. Each asset plays a different role—some provide shade, some offer steady nourishment, and others are there for resilience and variety. The key is patience, planning, and letting time do the heavy lifting.

- Stocks are like oak trees grown from acorns.
    - Tiny acorns. They start small, but with time and care, they become tall, wide, and strong—offering shade (financial security), strength, and long-term growth. Don't expect them to sprout overnight, but over time potential is unmatched.
    - Investing in stocks means buying a share of ownership in a company. As a shareholder, you become a partner in the

LESSONS FROM SUCCESSFUL INVESTORS

KNOW YOUR OPTIONS

Successful investors learned the basic types of investments–stocks, bonds, real estate, and cash. They were not intimidated by jargon.

KEEP IT SIMPLE

They avoided exotic financial products realizing that they are not experts. Complexity often masks high fees or unnecessary risks.

DIVERSIFY WISELY

They followed the age-old principle of "Don't keep all your eggs in one basket." When they were young, they maintained a diversified exposure to stocks.

MINIMIZE COSTS

They understood and controlled investment fees, which erode returns. Low-cost index funds and tax-smart accounts mattered.

ACHIEVE TAX EFFICIENCY

Smart investors sought real after-tax performance. They avoided over trading, prioritized long-term gains over short-term gains, and favored tax efficient investment vehicles such as stocks and ETFs.

STAY DISCIPLINED

Lastly, these successful investors managed their emotions. They did not allow fear or greed to make emotional decisions.

Figure 14.1: Timeless patterns of successful investing.

business, benefiting from profits and growth. As companies grow and increase their revenue and profits their stock price usually appreciates. Stocks are typically chosen for long-term appreciation and growth potential.

- Bonds are like vegetables.
    - They grow steadily and provide predictable nourishment. Steady growing carrots, cucumbers, and tomatoes that reliably feed you (provide income) season after season. They don't shoot up like trees, but they keep your portfolio healthy and balanced.
    - Buying bonds means lending money to corporations or governments. Bondholders receive interest payments, typically twice a year, and the initial loan amount is returned at maturity. Bonds are favored for their predictable income and stability. They are often selected based in part on the company or government's demonstrated ability to pay its debts (credit ratings).
- Real estate is like a fruit orchard.
    - It takes work—planting, pruning, and maintenance—but it can offer a reliable harvest year after year, plus strong roots that hold value over time. Once ripe, they are delicious and much in demand. Investing in properties such as single-family homes, condos, apartments, or commercial real estate can provide steady cash flow, long-term appreciation, and substantial tax benefits. A primary residence is usually the largest and most profitable investment people make. Real estate often utilizes leverage, meaning you use other people's money (OPM) by making a smaller down payment (10–30 percent) and borrowing the rest.

- Commodities are like wild herbs or sunflowers.
  - A few sprinkled in can add color, fragrance, or pest protection—but overdo it or they can take over the plot. Use sparingly and with intention.
  - Investing in physical goods like gold, silver, or other commodities can diversify your portfolio. Commodities usually make up a small portion of a well-balanced investment strategy.
- Alternative investments are like exotic plants.
  - Rare orchids. Bonsai trees. Cactus gardens. These are beautiful—but require expert care, special conditions, and lots of attention.
  - Hedge funds, private equity, and venture capital can offer outsized gains but come with high risk, high fees, and long lockups. Unless you're a professional or ultra-high-net-worth investor, these may not be suitable for your portfolio.
- Cash is your watering can and garden shed.
  - You need the right amount to cover regular upkeep and emergencies to survive dry spells. Without it, your garden can wither during tough times.

Holding cash in savings accounts or money market funds feels safe but typically earns returns lower than inflation. Use cash strategically for short-term needs or emergencies rather than long-term investment growth.

Your job as the gardener and investor? Choose your seeds wisely. Diversify your crops. Water consistently. And most importantly—be patient. Wealth doesn't sprout overnight. But with care, discipline, and time, your garden will thrive and your harvest will come and you will find financial security via LIVING360.

Know Your Risk Profile and Investment Horizon

The asset classes (stocks, bonds, real estate, alternatives, commodities, and cash) and investment choices we have discussed will suffice for a large majority of investors. When investing, you should have a clear vision of what you would like your investments to do for you. The answer to these questions comes from your investment time horizon (e.g., Will you need this money soon or can you let it grow for decades?), and how comfortable you are with risk (e.g., Can you sleep comfortably if the value of your savings goes up or down 10, 20, or even 40 percent?). When investing, most investors seek growth (capital appreciation) or income through dividends or interest. Your investment horizon can be an important factor in determining how to divide your assets and diversify. In the chart that follows, you can find ideas regarding how to mix and diversify your investments between two simple asset classes (stocks and bonds) based on when you will need to access your money (see figure 14.2).

Most people worry that they aren't experts and believe stocks, bonds, ETFs, and mutual funds are mysterious black boxes. But if you just master a few simple principles, you may very well outperform the majority of professionals.

Why? Because more than 85 percent of actively managed mutual funds underperform the market over long periods.[3] Not due to lack of intelligence—but because even the smartest minds can't predict a system as chaotic and interconnected as the financial markets. Attempting to predict precisely how thousands of interconnected variables will behave is practically impossible, even for seasoned professionals (see figure 14.3). Instead of trying to predict the unpredictable, embrace simple investment principles and disciplined practices to target financial independence.

INVESTMENT HORIZON

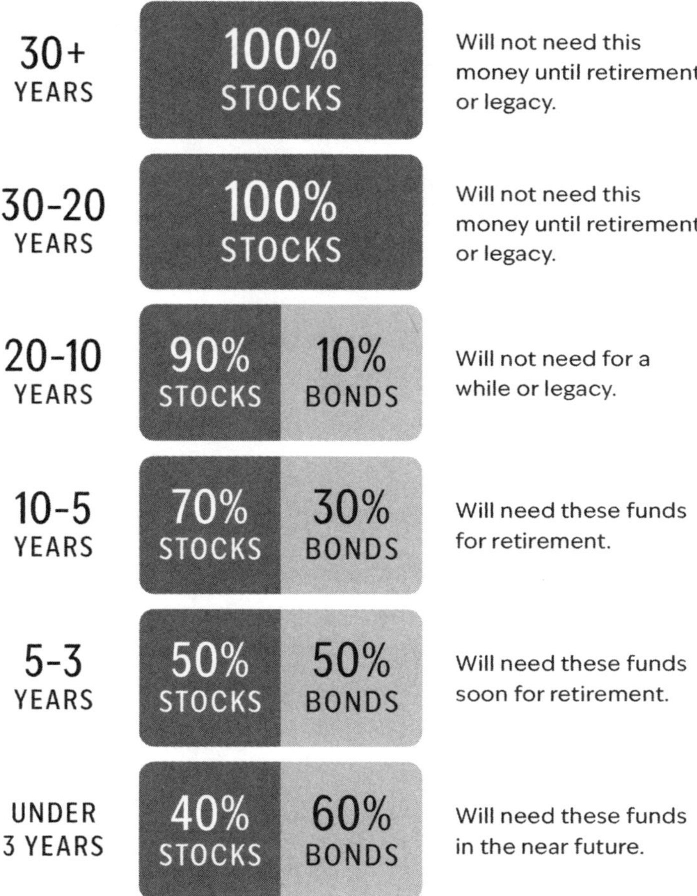

The more money you will not need for retirement, the higher your risk-taking capability.

Figure 14.2: Risk capacity is shaped by when you need the money and your comfort with volatility.

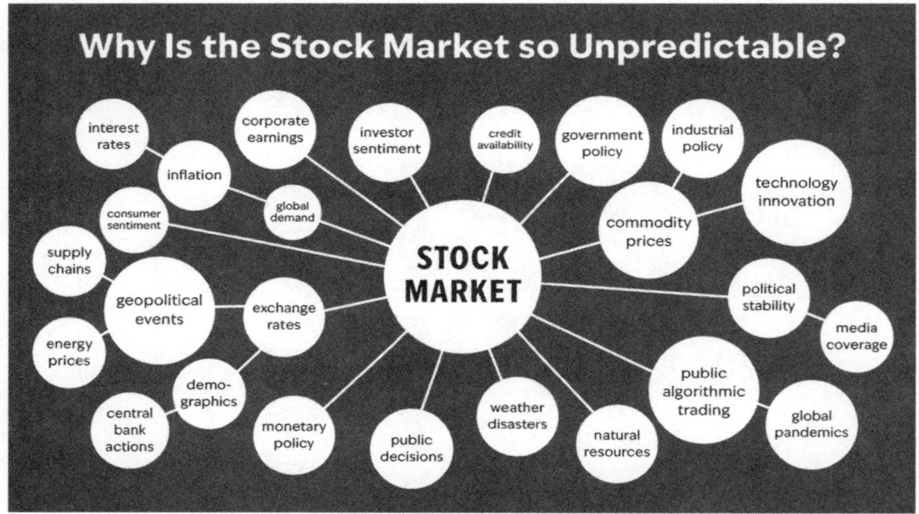

Figure 14.3: Market outcomes emerge from countless interacting forces.

If you internalize the ideas of LIVING360 and develop a disciplined and consistent approach to investing, I believe that you have a good chance of doing better than many investment professionals. You don't need a perfect strategy—you just need a good one, executed consistently. So take the pressure off yourself. No one knows what the market will do tomorrow. Your investments can perform well if you can follow a disciplined plan and allocate your savings to simple, low-cost, tax-efficient, and diversified investments and hold them for a long period of time. The next few sections provide a detailed explanation of how you may create investment strategies that align with your goal of financial security. Before we get there, let's first understand how your emotions and biases can impact your decisions.

Behavioral Finance

In the field of behavioral finance, Daniel Kahneman's and Amos Tversky's research found that losses feel roughly twice as painful as gains feel pleasurable.[4] If you've ever worried about the latest inflation reading or a war in a distant land, you've felt this instinct. It's normal, but it can harm your investments if you let fear drive your decisions. Your brain is wired to focus on avoiding loss and ensuring survival, not maximizing the long-term value of your retirement account.

Imagine you have a $500,000 investment account fully allocated to the S&P 500 (via the SPDR S&P 500 ETF Trust, which trades under the symbol "SPY"). If the market declines 15 percent—the average intra-year decline over the past forty-four years[5]—that's a $75,000 drop. Emotionally, research shows it would take a $150,000 gain for you to feel the same way you feel about that $75,000 loss. This lopsided fear leads many investors to sell during downturns, locking in losses and missing the recovery.

To succeed where others have failed, it is as simple as this: Expect declines, plan for them, and stay the course. Before making any investment decision, take a moment to reflect. Ask yourself, "How will I feel if my portfolio drops 15 percent or 30 percent? Will I be able to stay the course?"

Keep in mind also that when you are young, you can take more risks because time is on your side. As you progress in age and your time horizon is less or you will need to access the money for lifestyle needs, you will require an appropriate mix of investments. Even though an ETF like SPY or an equity mutual fund provides diversification through the large number of stocks they own, you will need to seriously consider allocating your investment across multiple asset classes and regions.

Planning for your emotional reactions is just as important as planning your investments. It will help you avoid decisions you later regret and allow you to continue your LIVING360 journey with confidence. Remember, the key is not to overthink your investments or spend your energy trying to outsmart the market. To achieve financial independence, just invest, start early, keep it simple, and stay the course.

AVOIDING FEAR OF MISSING OUT (FOMO)

Emotional discipline isn't only tested during downturns; it's tested when everyone else seems to be getting rich faster than you. We've all felt that twinge of envy or FOMO at some point. Picture this: You're at a family gathering, between bites of barbecue, your cousin Jane casually mentions how her Nvidia stock has doubled. Uncle Brown chimes in, grinning, "I told you all about it last Thanksgiving!" Then Mark—your golf buddy and armchair economist—leans over and whispers about the "next big thing" he's gotten into, a tech startup you've never heard of but is "going to be the next Amazon."

Suddenly, your rock-solid portfolio—diversified, disciplined, and carefully planned—feels . . . boring. That voice in your head begins to murmur: "What if I'm missing out?"

This, right here, is the most dangerous moment in investing. Not because markets are rising. Not because valuations are stretched. But because *everyone else* seems to be making easy money, and your fear of missing out (FOMO) takes the wheel.

Throughout modern history, markets have handed us these temptations in neatly packaged acronyms. They've come with stories of transformation, disruption, and guaranteed prosperity. And over and over, investors have taken the bait.

THE RISE AND FALL OF ACRONYM INVESTING

Throughout history, there's always a "next big thing" luring investors off a solid path. Don't believe it? Let's look at how *every decade has its fad* and its fallout.

Let's journey back to the late 1960s. The buzzword was Nifty Fifty—a glamorous group of blue-chip American companies such as Coca-Cola, McDonald's, and IBM. These weren't just stocks. They were seen as royalty. The mantra was "buy and never sell." Valuation didn't matter. These companies were the future. But when the bear market of the early '70s arrived, many Nifty Fifty names were cut in half. The lesson? Even great companies can be terrible investments if you pay too high a price.

Fast forward to the late 1990s. The air was electric with possibility. The internet was going to change everything—and it did. But first came the dot-com bubble. Pets.com, Webvan, eToys—companies with no earnings, no revenue, and no viable business models soared to sky-high valuations simply because they had "dot-com" in their name. Then, just as quickly, they vanished. Fortunes were lost. Dreams vaporized. Once again, reality struck back.

Next came BRIC—Brazil, Russia, India, and China. A new global order. These rising economies promised endless growth. Investors, eager not to miss this international train, jumped in with both feet. But geopolitical instability, corruption, and uneven development reminded everyone that growth without governance is a shaky proposition and does not automatically lead to stock market appreciation.

Then emerged TINA—"there is no alternative." After the 2008 crisis, interest rates were cut to zero, and bonds offered little reward. So, investors poured into stocks—not because they wanted to, but because they felt they had to. And for a while, it worked. But when rates began rising again, the cracks in this logic showed. TINA was never a strategy. It was a surrender.

Of course, no acronym is as famous in recent memory as FAANG—Facebook, Apple, Amazon, Netflix, and Google. These weren't just companies—they were verbs, habits, ecosystems. People built portfolios entirely around them. Some did very well. But others, who bought in at peak euphoria or failed to diversify, were exposed to major corrections.

Now, we live in the age of the Magnificent Seven: Apple, Microsoft, Nvidia, Meta, Amazon, Google, and Tesla. These giants are driving most of the market's returns, as well as the narrative. "AI," "hyperscalers," "cloud computing,""autonomous vehicles"—every buzzword is a promise of riches. But look closely and you'll see history rhyming again.

The modern Wild West of investing is, of course, cryptocurrency. What began with the mysterious rise of Bitcoin has exploded into a universe of over seven thousand digital coins, each promising innovation, disruption, or freedom from traditional finance. For many, the rise of crypto became the new gold rush. It represented a chance to get in early and strike it rich. Stories spread like wildfire—a teen who turned $1,000 into millions with Dogecoin; a friend-of-a-friend who bought Ethereum at $10. But beneath the hype lies a sobering truth: Most of these coins will likely vanish, just as many dot-com startups did in the early 2000s. The blockchain revolution may be real, but history reminds us that technological revolutions often begin with chaos, bubbles, and speculation before settling into sustainable value. Chasing every new token is not a strategy; it's a gamble. The winners in this space will be few, and they'll likely be the ones with real utility, regulation, and resilience. Not just the loudest Twitter following.

TIMELESS TRUTHS > TRENDY ACRONYMS

Here's what I've seen in my career: those who succeed in investing rarely do so by chasing shiny objects. Instead, they commit to a thoughtful process. Some allocate 90 percent of their portfolio in ETFs, index funds, or mutual funds and may invest 10 percent of their portfolio in handpicked stocks they understand deeply, often because they use the company's products, see the trend firsthand, and are willing to hold long-term. They know the risks. More importantly, they know they're not trying to get rich quick.

On the flip side, I've yet to meet anyone who achieved financial security by jumping into the latest "penny stock" or chasing a 50x return like a lottery ticket. Lottery thinking is entertainment—not investing.

Acronyms may come and go, but financial principles are timeless. When everyone's chasing the next big thing, ask yourself: "Am I making this decision because it aligns with my goals? Or because I'm afraid of being left behind?" Don't let FOMO derail you. History doesn't repeat itself, but it rhymes. The names and trends will change, but the strategy that wins remains the same—patience, diversification, and sticking to your plan.

The *Wisdom and Wealth Solution* isn't about the thrill of the moment. It's about peace of mind that lasts through all seasons.

AVOIDING THE LUCK TRAP

Buying and selling stocks online has never been easier. But identifying future market leaders such as Nvidia, Apple, Netflix, or Google is incredibly challenging. Even professional venture capital firms investing in innovative startups succeed spectacularly in only about 10–15 percent of their ventures, with the vast majority failing or performing modestly.[6]

Recently I met John, who had put half his savings into a single stock because he thought it was "the next Google." Two years later, the company went bankrupt. His pain wasn't just financial; it was emotional. The stress, regret, and lost time could have been avoided with a more balanced approach.

Instead of relying on luck to find the next big stock, adopt a more solid, strategic foundation for your financial goals. Investing like my successful clients does not require flawless market prediction. It's about disciplined strategies, simplicity, diversification, and understanding your choices clearly. Keep your investments aligned with your financial goals and emotional comfort. By mastering these basic principles, you empower yourself to build lasting financial security and independence. You don't need to outsmart Wall Street. You just need to out-discipline the average investor.

Reflection Questions

1. How important are taxes and cost for the long-term return of an investment portfolio?
2. Why do investors go in and out of the markets and how does it normally impact their investments?
3. Have you ever felt the need to chase an investment because other people are buying it (FOMO)?
4. Have you ever sold your investments because of fear of losing your nest egg?

CHAPTER 15

Your Long-Term Financial Vision and Strategy

Now you've moved beyond the basic mechanics of money. You know your net worth, have a firm grip on your cash flow, and have laid the groundwork for investing. You must engage the most powerful tools in your financial arsenal: vision and strategy. This chapter will help you stop measuring what *is* and start defining what *will be.*

As Paulo Coelho famously wrote in *The Alchemist*: "When you have a dream, the universe conspires to make it happen."[1] While the universe can certainly align circumstances for you, the conspiracy begins with your detailed and proactive plan. For the financially successful, a long-term vision isn't a vague hope; it's a blueprint for freedom and options. By intentionally projecting your desired financial stability five, ten, twenty, and thirty years into the future, you are doing more than simply setting goals. You are creating the space for meaning and purpose later in life.

Please refer to Appendixes 7A and 7B for detailed general and investment-related disclosures.

You are creating a powerful magnetic pull toward your desired future. This chapter will guide you from the hard facts of your current state to the precise, aspirational targets that will define your ultimate financial stability and personal freedom.

ASSESSMENT: YOUR TEN-, TWENTY-, AND THIRTY-YEAR HORIZON

Now comes the strategic element: envisioning your financial future. This isn't a passive exercise; it's an active projection of the life you want to lead, ten, twenty, and thirty years from now. Let's start the strategic planning by defining your targets.

- What is your current net worth?
- What is your current net cash flow (surplus or deficit)?
- Where do you want your net worth to be in ten years?
- Where do you want your net worth to be in twenty years?
- Where do you want your net worth to be in thirty years?

Envision Your Financial Future

A vague hope is not a plan. In business, no successful project begins without a comprehensive strategic plan. You wouldn't launch a product or scale an operation without first defining a clear vision of success—and your financial life deserves the same deliberate approach. A defined, long-term financial vision is the engine that converts today's diligent habits into tomorrow's financial freedom and flexibility.

Let's consider an example: You and your spouse are forty-five years old, and you have two children, ages eleven and fifteen. Your current net worth is $400,000. Together, you and your spouse earn $240,000 annually, with a net monthly income of approximately $17,000 after taxes. Your monthly expenses total around $16,000. You own a condo worth $700,000, with a mortgage balance of $450,000, and have $10,000 in credit card debt. Your combined 401(k) savings currently total $150,000.

Imagine you and your spouse sitting together over a drink, envisioning your financial future. Together, both of you decide that by age sixty-seven, you want your home fully paid off and to have retirement savings of $3 million. This is your personal financial security number!

Focus on Financial Discipline

The challenge of moving from $150,000 in savings today to $3 million may seem daunting, but it's achievable through disciplined saving in your 401(k). By contributing $2,000 monthly to your 401(k), you'll save roughly $500 in taxes, making your net additional contribution just $1,500 per month. With your current surplus of $1,000, finding an additional $500 to save each month—by slightly reducing expenses—is all you need to meet your goal.

The calculations in figure 15.1 help explain the power of compounding, driven by long-term, consistent, and disciplined investing. They are not a guarantee of returns and outcomes. Investments have risk of loss, including principal. (See Appendixes 7A and 7B for disclosures.)

BASIC INFO		PROJECTIONS	
Current age	45	Expected retirement age	67
Current annual salary	$240,000	Life expectancy	85
Current 401(k) balance	$150,000	Expected salary increase	3 % per year
Contribution (% of salary)	10 %	Expected annual return	9 % per year
Employer match	100 %	Expected inflation rate	3 % per year
Employer match limit	4 %		

Figure 15.1: Basic 401(k) info and projections.[2]

The information in figure 15.2 assumes your employer matches 4 percent of your salary, your salary increases 3 percent annually, and your investment returns average 9 percent per year. However, figure 15.3 illustrates what happens if your returns drop to just 3 percent.

RESULT

At the retirement age of 67, the 401(k) balance will be **$3,754,084**, which is equivalent to **$1,959,229** in purchasing power today.

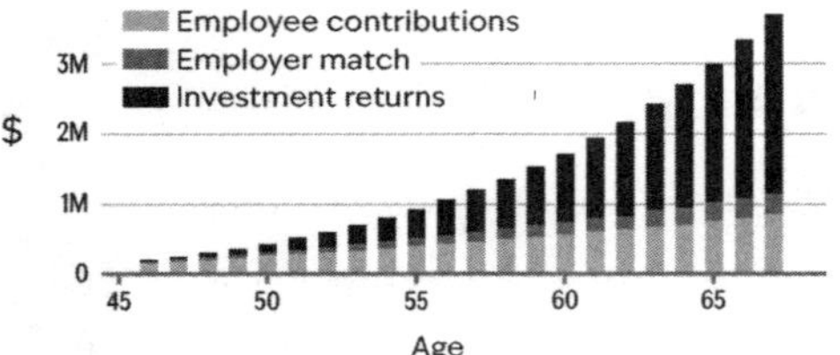

Balance at 67	$3,754,084
Total contributions:	$1,172,319
Employee contributions:	$880,228
Employer match:	$292,091
Investment returns:	$2,581,765

Figure 15.2: How to target $3.75 million with consistent saving and a 9 percent return.

RESULT

At the retirement age of 67, the 401(k) balance will be **$1,676,564**, which is equivalent to **$874,986** in purchasing power today.

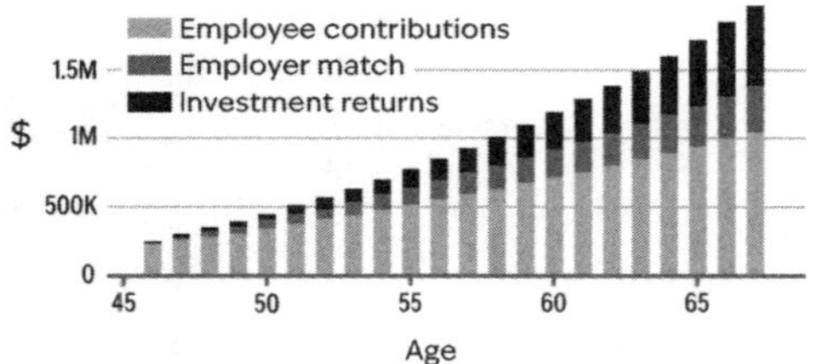

Balance at 67	$1,676,564
Total contributions:	$1,172,319
Employee contributions:	$880,228
Employer match:	$292,091
Investment returns:	$504,244

Figure 15.3: This figure illustrates the outcome with consistent saving but only earning a 3 percent return.

Under a hypothetical scenario, a lower annualized return could reduce the ending value of a retirement account by millions over several decades. Instead of 9 percent per annum you only earned 3 percent and your LIVING360 financial independence dream is not fulfilled. This is what happens to most people. They do not know what mutual fund to invest in, and they leave their money in cash or they get scared from all the negative headlines or social media feeds that are always calling for a recession, debt crisis, and a stock market crash.

If you can ignore all these headlines and manage your emotions to stay invested in a diversified portfolio, with an appropriate allocation to stocks based on your investment time horizon, you have a high probability of reaching your LIVING360 goals. We have just seen that getting to $3 million in retirement savings is an achievable goal, even when you start investing at forty-five and do not have a large nest egg. The key is to avoid falling into the 3 percent return trap. Avoiding this pitfall is critical to long-term success.

From 1950 through 2025, broad US equity markets—as represented by the S&P 500 Index—generated average annual returns of approximately 11.70 percent, while US bonds averaged around 5.2 percent (see Appendix 5).[3] These figures are presented solely to illustrate long-term historical behavior. They are not guarantees of future results, and actual markets can vary widely from one year to the next.

To understand why diversification matters so much, it helps to look at how markets have behaved over time. Between 1950 and 2025, the S&P 500 experienced a very wide range of annual outcomes. Its strongest calendar year delivered a return of +52 percent, while its worst year saw a decline of –37 percent. This demonstrates two important truths: The S&P 500 has historically offered substantial long-term growth, and that growth has come with periods of significant short-term volatility. (For detailed charts that visually compare the S&P 500, US bonds, and diversified portfolios, see Appendix 5).[4]

During this same seventy-five-year period, US bonds displayed a very different pattern. Their best year produced a gain of +33 percent, and their worst year declined –13 percent. Compared to the S&P 500, bond returns fluctuated in a narrower band and were typically more stable. Bonds often acted as a counterweight during periods when the S&P 500 experienced substantial stress.

Bringing these two asset classes together—using a portfolio of 60 percent S&P 500 and 40 percent US bonds—created a noticeably smoother experience. This blended portfolio still participated in much of the long-term growth associated with the S&P 500, but with smaller swings along the way. Its strongest year was +34 percent, and its worst was –20 percent, both significantly less extreme than the S&P 500 on its own.

But the most compelling evidence comes from looking at longer time horizons. When examining a seventy-five-year period (1950–2025), a 60/40 portfolio produced an average return of 9.4 percent per year. The combination of growth-oriented assets (represented by the S&P 500) and income-oriented, historically less volatile securities (US bonds) helped create a more consistent long-term experience (see Appendix 5).

Most notably, from 1950 through 2025, there has never been a negative ten-year or twenty-year rolling period for a portfolio of 60 percent S&P 500 and 40 percent US bonds. While past performance does not guarantee future results, this long-term record highlights how diversification has historically helped reduce the impact of short-term volatility and improved the likelihood of achieving positive long-term outcomes. (Please refer to Appendix 5 and Appendix 7B for detailed disclosure information.)

That's where the importance of long-term investing comes in. Our hypothetical forty-five-year-old couple has a twenty-two-year horizon until retirement. It makes sense for them to consider allocating their 401(k) into a low-cost S&P 500 index fund or a total stock market fund. This strategy provides simplicity, broad diversification, and a likelihood of achieving returns between 6 percent and 11 percent annually over a long period of time.

MAXIMIZE BENEFITS FROM RETIREMENT ACCOUNTS

If you work for a company that offers a 401(k) or 403(b), begin as a first step by logging into your account. Navigate through different pages, read about your investment choices. If you are self-employed, you have numerous options to open retirement accounts (IRA, SEP IRA, Solo 401(k), etc.) at a large brokerage firm and invest in tax-deferred accounts. If you are young or you will not need to access your retirement savings for ten years or longer, you can consider a larger allocation to S&P 500 or the US Total Stock Market index fund or ETF. You can also add international exposure though international ETFs, index funds, or mutual funds. Either of these options or their combination can give you immediate exposure to a broad and diversified portfolio comprising the largest companies in the United States and from around the world. Historically, this simple strategy has proven effective for long-term investors. For instance, if you had invested in the S&P 500 index in 1950 and remained invested continuously until 2025, your annualized return over the subsequent seventy-five years would have been approximately 11.70 percent (see Appendix 5).[5]

Investing entirely in an S&P 500 index fund ensures your returns closely mirror the performance of the broader US stock market (minus minimal fees, assuming you choose a low-cost fund and don't have to pay much, if anything, in commissions). Historically, investors who follow this approach can reasonably expect annual returns between 6 percent and 11 percent. As you age or if you desire more diversification to reduce volatility, you can introduce other asset classes such as international stocks or bonds. Of course, your portfolio may change as the market changes; however, the long-term trajectory has historically been positive, but individual results may vary.

Most employer-sponsored 401(k) plans offer a variety of mutual funds and low-cost index funds covering different asset classes. The index funds typically include the S&P 500, Total US Stock Market, International Stock Market Index, Emerging Markets Index, and Total Bond Market Index funds. In the following section, you'll find straightforward asset allocation ideas based on broad guidelines connected to age and personal risk tolerance. If the thought of significant market downturns—such as those experienced during bear markets—causes you anxiety and might prompt you to prematurely sell your investments, it's wise to choose a lower-risk, more diversified portfolio from the start. This approach helps you remain invested and disciplined during inevitable market fluctuations, greatly enhancing your chances of achieving long-term financial security and independence.

Address Portfolio Allocation Based on Age and Risk Tolerance

In this section, you will find practical asset-allocation ideas for both retirement accounts and taxable brokerage accounts. These simple frameworks are designed to help you assess your own risk appetite by considering two key questions: How long can you keep this money invested? And how do you emotionally respond to market volatility?

You may use these sample portfolios as a starting point to select an allocation that aligns with your goals, time horizon, and stage of life.

Adjust and fine-tune the strategy until it feels both financially feasible and emotionally viable.

As you review the portfolios, keep in mind that a higher risk number reflects a higher level of volatility—meaning your account value may experience larger ups and downs over time. Choosing the right balance is ultimately about finding a portfolio you can stick with through all market conditions.

The risk score is based on Morningstar's portfolio risk methodology. For complete details about how Morningstar calculated the risk score, please visit https://developer.morningstar.com/content/hidden-from-navigation/morningstar-portfolio-risk-score-methodology.pdf.

Here is a quick summary:

- Hybrid Approach: The system uses a combination of holdings-based analysis (from Morningstar's risk model) and returns-based analysis to capture risk across a broad range of assets, including mutual funds, ETFs, and individual securities.
- Risk Estimation: The system identifies the investments within a portfolio and uses the hybrid methodology to generate a risk estimate.
- Scoring: The estimated risk is then compared to the volatility of Morningstar's Target Allocation Indices to produce a score on a new 0–100 scale.
- Scale: A score of 0 represents the lowest risk (all cash), while 100 represents the highest risk end of the very aggressive range. A small percentage of levered portfolios may score above 100.
- Figure 15.4 illustrates the Morningstar Risk Profiler, while figures 15.5 to 15.9 depict sample investment portfolios ideas based on age.

Exhibit 1 Morningstar Risk Profiler and Portfolio Risk Scoring System–The Advice Flow

Risk Tolerance

Very Low | Low | **Avg** | High | Very High

Portfolio Risk Score

MODERATE | AGGRESSIVE | CONSERVATIVE | VERY AGGRESSIVE

45

0 | 100

Efficient Frontier

● Equity ● Fixed Income

0 / 100 | 22.5 / 77.5 | 40 / 60 | 60 / 40 | 77.5 / 22.5 | 92.5 / 7.5 | 110 / -10 | 140 / -40

45

0 | 25 | 50 | 75 | 100

Low Risk Highly Diversified | **High Risk** HighlyConcentrated

The Morningstar Risk Profiler provides a risk tolerance score that can be adjusted by additional "know your client" considerations for each goal.

The score from the Morningstar Risk Profile generates a range of Morningstar Portfolio Risk Scores (MPRS) that are a best fit for the portfolio goal.

MPRS represents the risk of a portfolio using the morningstar Risk Model and returns-based style analysis, in conjunction with risk ranges defined by the multi-asset Target Allocation Indexes

Source: Morningstar, as of February 27, 2025

Figure 15.4: Morningstar's risk profiler helps investors determine their risk tolerance.

SAMPLE INVESTMENT PORTFOLIO IDEAS BASED ON AGE OR INVESTMENT HORIZON (RISK APPETITE)

Age-Based Portfolio Allocations

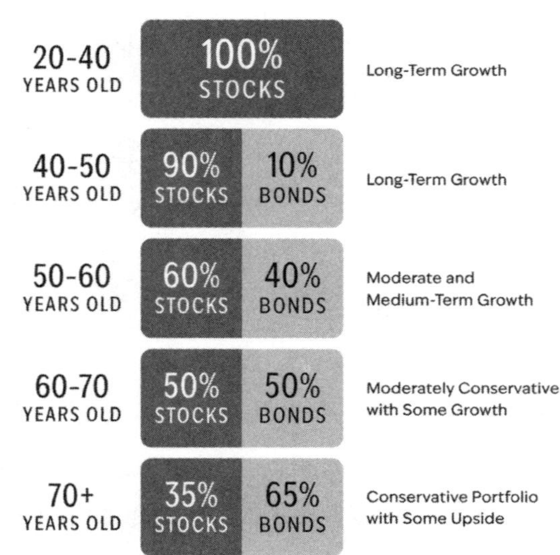

Figure 15.5: This figure provides sample investment portfolios based on age.

The asset allocation shown in figure 15.6 is considered aggressive because 100 percent of the money is invested in stocks. This portfolio may be appropriate for long-term investors who are looking for aggressive growth, are okay with their investment going up and down with the stock markets, and do not need to use money in the short term.

PORTFOLIO BASED ON AGE & RISK

Appropriate for Ages 20-40 & Aggressive/Long-Term Investors

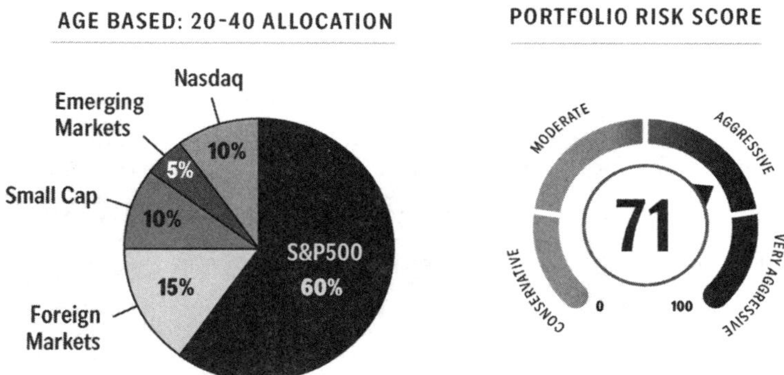

Figure 15.6: Illustrative portfolio for a long-term investor without near-term liquidity needs.

The asset allocation shown in figure 15.7 is still considered aggressive because 85 percent of the money is invested in stocks and only 15 percent of the allocation is in bonds. This portfolio may also be appropriate for long-term investors who are looking for growth, are comfortable with their investment going up and down with the stock markets, and do not need to use this money in the short term.

PORTFOLIO BASED ON AGE & RISK

Appropriate for Ages 40-50 &
Moderately Aggressive/Still Long-Term Investors (10 Years +)

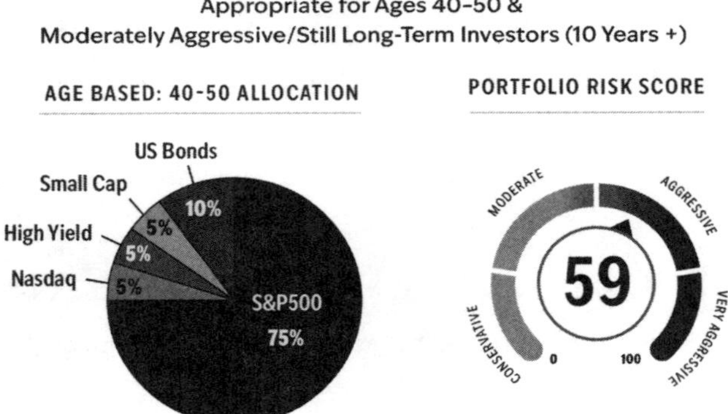

Figure 15.7: Illustrative portfolio for a long-term investor with moderate risk capacity and minimal liquidity needs.

The asset allocation shown in figure 15.8 is considered moderate because 60 percent of the money is invested in stocks and 40 percent of the allocation is in bonds. This portfolio may also be appropriate for investors who are seeking a balance between growth and stability. They may have a medium-term investment horizon and need to access this portfolio for their living or retirement expenses in seven to fifteen years.

PORTFOLIO BASED ON AGE & RISK

Appropriate for Ages 50-60 &
Moderate/Long-Term Investors (10 Years +)

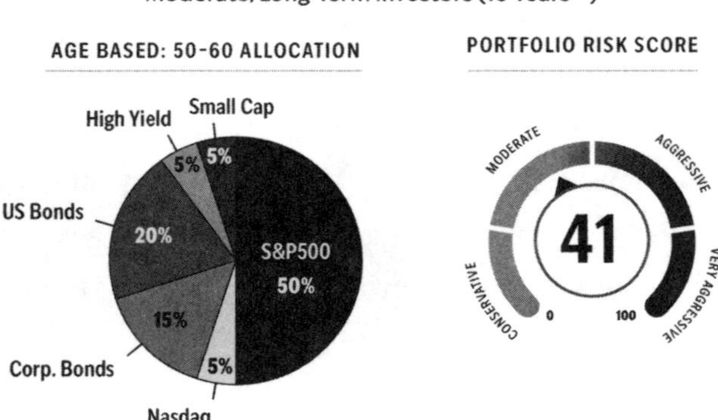

Figure 15.8: Illustrative portfolio for a long-term investor with reduced risk capacity and greater liquidity sensitivity.

The asset allocation shown in figure 15.9 is still considered moderate because 50 percent of the money is invested in stocks and 50 percent of the allocation is in bonds. This portfolio may also be appropriate for investors who are seeking a balance between growth and stability. They may have a medium-term investment horizon, and they need to access this portfolio for their living or retirement expenses in three to seven years.

PORTFOLIO BASED ON AGE & RISK

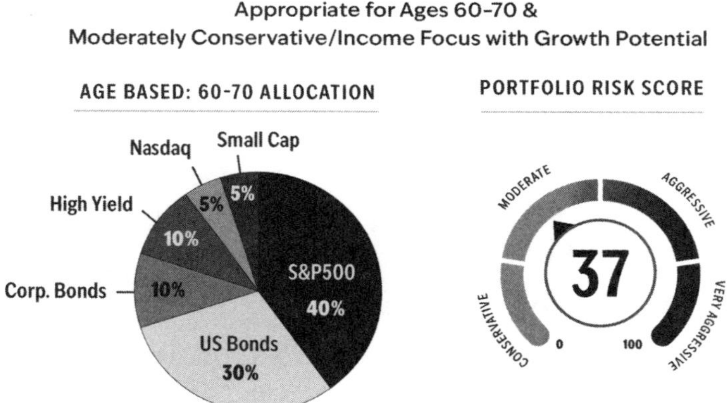

Figure 15.9: Illustrative portfolio reflecting lower tolerance for volatility and increased demand for income stability.

The asset allocation shown in figure 15.10 is moderately conservative because 35 percent of the money is invested in stocks and 65 percent of the allocation is in bonds. This portfolio may also be appropriate for investors who are seeking stability, income, and some growth. They may have a short-term investment horizon and need immediate access to a part of their portfolio for their living or retirement expenses.

PORTFOLIO BASED ON AGE & RISK

Appropriate for Ages 70+ &
Conservative/Income Focus with Some Growth Potential

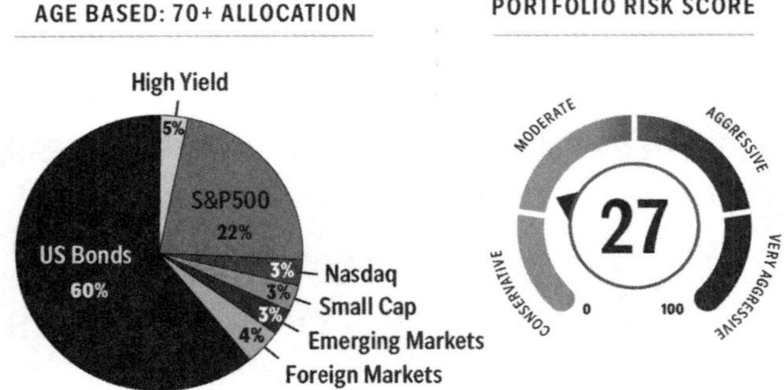

Figure 15.10: Illustrative portfolio reflecting heightened need for capital stability and sustained income reliability.

FURTHER RESOURCES FOR CALCULATING RETIREMENT ACCOUNTS

You can visit simple online calculators such as calculator.net to simulate the value of your retirement account: https://www.calculator.net/401k-calculator.html.

Your target allocation from the preceding pie charts and Morningstar's risk score can be a starting point to determine your own risk profile and asset allocation. Based on your liquidity needs and investment horizon, you can apply the same investing principles to your retirement and taxable accounts. While your company-sponsored, tax-deferred account may have limited choices, in your taxable brokerage account you can hold mutual funds, exchange-traded funds (ETFs), or individual securities such as stocks, bonds, REITs, or precious metals. For most investors, a reliable way to translate the pie chart into real dollars is to use a handful of low-cost, broad-market index funds, ETFs or mutual funds that mirror each slice of the allocation.

Mutual Funds Versus ETFs

It helps to know the difference between mutual funds and ETFs. Both are like a basket or container that holds different types of securities, such as individual stocks or bonds. By buying shares in the mutual fund or ETF, you end up having proportional exposure to the securities that mutual fund or ETF owns.

Mutual funds price once per day after markets close and many are actively managed, meaning a team of portfolio managers tries to beat the market. Over long stretches, most active funds (about 85 percent) fail to outperform their benchmarks after fees, which is why if you choose active funds, you should be selective and cost-conscious. To reduce the risk of underperformance, you can buy low-cost index funds or ETFs. This type of fund (ETF) trades all day like a stock and most of the large, familiar ones simply track an index.

For example, SPY seeks to match the performance of the S&P 500; when the S&P 500 rises 1 percent in a day, SPY will typically rise by roughly the same amount before fees. Be aware that index funds won't ever exactly match the index's returns. This is called "tracking error," and is due to things such as fees and costs, whether the fund is buying all the securities in the index or simply "sampling" a representative subset, and certain trading and rebalancing strategies. The smaller the tracking error, the more closely the fund or ETF matches the returns of its underlying index.

Today there are large, low-cost ETFs that track the Dow 30, Nasdaq100, S&P 500, mid- and small-cap US stocks, international stocks, and core bond markets. For the typical investor, a small set of these broad, tax-efficient funds is often enough to produce a good long-term outcome.

In your 401(k) or similar plan, you'll usually be dealing with mutual funds. Most 401(k) now also provide low-cost index funds as investment choice. When evaluating options, you can look at the expense ratios, consistency of the long-term record, and the stability of the portfolio management team.

Allocating your 401(k) to an appropriate portfolio is critically important for your financial security. You may consider the allocations presented earlier to invest your accounts, based upon your investment goals. The following list provides asset classes that you may find in your 401(k) account. For each asset class you may find passive choices (index funds) or active choices (mutual funds). Most retirement plan trustees are expected to undertake due diligence to find funds that are appropriate for the retirement plan. Your job is to make sure that you *invest* based on your goals. Either choose index funds or actively managed mutual funds but invest. If you leave your funds in money market accounts, achieving financial security will be an uphill climb. This is a brief introduction. In the Comprehensive Investment Guide, you can find more details and strategies for multiple investment solutions.

Tables 15.1 and 15.2 are educational and illustrative tools to help develop an understanding of how you can find funds belonging to different asset classes in your investment accounts. This is certainly not a recommendation or specific investment advice. Always remember that past performance is not indicative of future results. You may find similar funds in the same categories, so choose based on your investment goals and risk tolerance.

Retirement plans normally also provide target date funds. Target date funds are pre-packaged portfolios with diverse sets of asset classes that may match your risk profile based on your investment horizon. Target date funds can be an efficient option for investors looking for simplicity and ease of execution. When evaluating a target date fund, do consider the expense ratio of the fund and the other active and passive options available in the plans.

Because each 401(k) or retirement plan has different investment options, it is difficult to provide specific ticker symbols because those index fund (passive) or actively managed mutual funds may not be available in your retirement plan. Review the investment choices available in your retirement plan and develop an asset allocation using the asset class list in table 15.1. You can consult the sample asset allocation examples provided earlier in the chapter to determine how you may divide your money based on age and risk tolerance.

TABLE 15.1: COMMON TYPES OF MUTUAL FUNDS IN RETIREMENT PLANS

Category	What It Invests In	What It Means for You
US Stocks: Total Market	Thousands of large, mid, small, and micro-cap US companies across every sector	Broad diversification and steady exposure to the long-term growth of the US economy
US Stocks: Large-Cap (S&P 500)	Big, established companies like Apple, Microsoft, NVIDIA, Google, Coca-Cola	More stability, established businesses, foundation of most portfolios
US Stocks: Mid-Cap	Mid-sized companies valued between ~$2B and $10B	Balanced mix of growth potential and moderate volatility
US Stocks: Small-Cap	Smaller companies valued between ~$250M and $2B	Higher growth potential along with higher short-term volatility
International Stocks	Companies outside the US, across developed and emerging markets	Global diversification and participation in international growth
Developed Market Stocks	Foreign companies in mature economies (e.g., Japan, UK, Germany, Canada)	More stability and lower risk compared to emerging markets

continued

Category	What It Invests In	What It Means for You
Emerging Market Stocks	Rapidly growing economies (e.g., India, Brazil, Mexico, Indonesia)	Higher long-term growth with higher political and economic risk
US Total Bond Market	Government, corporate, agency, and mortgage-backed bonds across all maturities	Income, stability, and protection during market downturns
High-Yield Bonds	Lower-rated corporate bonds ("junk bonds") offering higher interest	Higher income but higher risk—behave more like stocks in stress periods
Commodity Funds	Energy, metals, agriculture, and other raw materials	Diversification and inflation protection; more volatility

(Please refer to Appendixes 7A and 7B for disclosures.)

For your taxable brokerage accounts, you may prefer ETFs due to their tax efficiency and lower cost. Today, over four thousand ETFs exist in the US market. Table 15.2 provides actual examples of the type of ETFs you can consider.

To keep your investment process manageable, the selected ETFs in the following table cover some of the biggest asset classes. As of the writing of this book, these ETFs were among the largest in their asset class. Each of these ETFs may differ in their methodology and tracking error. There are a number of other ETFs offered by other providers that may have a lower expense ratio and fit better with your risk profile, but you may use the following as a starting point.

TABLE 15.2: EXAMPLES OF EXCHANGE-TRADED FUNDS (ETFs)

Asset Class	ETF(s)
US Stocks (Diversified)	Vanguard Total Stock Market ETF (VTI) iShares Core S&P Total US Stock Market ETF (ITOT) Schwab US Broad Market ETF (SCHB)
US Stocks (S&P 500) Large-Cap	SPDR S&P 500 ETF Trust (SPY) Vanguard S&P 500 ETF (VOO) iShares Core S&P 500 ETF (IVV)
US Large-Cap Growth	Invesco Nasdaq-100 ETF (tracks NDX) (QQQ) Vanguard Growth ETF (VUG) iShares Russell 1000 Growth ETF (IWF) iShares S&P 500 Growth ETF (IVW)
Dow Jones Industrial Average or Similar	State Street SPDR Dow Jones Industrial Average (DIA) Invesco Dow Jones Industrial Average Dividend ETF (DJD)
US Stocks: Mid Cap	iShares Core S&P Mid-Cap (IJH) Vanguard Mid-Cap (VO) iShares Russell Mid-Cap (IWR)
US Stocks: Small Cap	iShares Core S&P Small-Cap (IJR) Vanguard SmallCap (VB) Schwab US SmallCap (SCHA)
International Stocks	Vanguard Total International Stock (VXUS) iShares Core MSCI Total International Stock (IXUS)
Developed Market Stocks	Vanguard FTSE Developed Markets (VEA) iShares Core MSCI EAFE (IEFA) iShares MSCI EAFE ETF (EFA)
Emerging Market Stocks	iShares Core MSCI Emerging Markets (IEMG) Vanguard FTSE Emerging Markets (VWO) iShares MSCI Emerging Markets (EEM)

continued

Asset Class	ETF(s)
US Total Bonds	iShares Core US Aggregate Bond (AGG) Vanguard Total Bond Market (BND) Schwab US Aggregate Bond (SCHZ)
High Yield Bond	SPDR Bloomberg High Yield Bond (JNK) iShares iBoxx $ High Yield Corporate Bond (HYG) iShares Broad USD High Yield Corporate Bond (USHY)
Commodity Funds	World Gold Trust Services - State Street Global Advisors (GLD) iShares Gold Trust (IAU) iShares Silver Trust (SLV) Sprott Asset Management Physical Silver Trust (PSLV) iShares GSCI Commodity Dynamic Roll Strategy (COMT)

(Please refer to Appendixes 7A and 7B for disclosures.)

Because a taxable brokerage account is outside the protective shield of a tax-deferred status, every sale of a security or trade is a potential taxable event. If you sell an investment that has gained value, you incur a tax liability. When you sell an investment you've held for one year or less to realize a gain, the government classifies that as a short-term capital gain, taxing it at your ordinary income rate for both federal and state income tax. Conversely, holding an investment for more than one year qualifies it for the favorable, much lower long-term capital gains tax rate.

This is why investment legend Warren Buffett has said his favorite holding period for a stock is "forever."[6] Financial research indicates that for individual investors, buying and selling frequently leads to underperformance.[7] Stick to a long-term plan and avoid over-trading.

The overall investment strategy for your LIVING360 portfolio is ultimately simple: Aim for efficiency and low costs. For your long-term savings in retirement accounts such as a 401(k), stick to low-cost index funds, which are simply affordable bundles of investments that aim to track the benchmark (underlying index). In your regular, nonretirement accounts, prioritize using simple and liquid ETFs for their flexibility and tax benefits. Beyond these choices, your success relies on discipline. You must contribute money regularly, choose the right mix of investments (known as asset allocation), and most importantly, avoid trading often. If you commit to this disciplined approach, you have the potential to unlock the powerful effect of compounding, allowing your money to start earning money itself and securing your financial future.

BUYING STOCKS

Students and sometimes clients ask if they should buy individual stocks. My answer to them is that based on my experience of decades, the stocks you pick will have a higher chance of underperforming the overall market over a reasonable period of time (you can always get lucky!).

ASSESSMENT: STOCKS

Ask yourself the following critical questions before jumping into individual stocks:

- Do I possess unique insights or skills to identify stocks that will outperform the overall market?
- Can I realistically outperform professional investors and market analysts, most of whom fail to consistently beat market indices?

Thousands of highly trained analysts and professional fund managers consistently struggle to outperform broad market indices like the S&P 500. Acknowledging this reality can help set realistic expectations and temper overconfidence.

While I have seen a few people get lucky with a few stocks, in my thirty years of experience in the wealth management profession it is rare that someone has consistently picked the next GOOG, NVDA, or AMZN. Very occasionally people get lucky. But it's like winning the lottery and buying lottery tickets certainly is not a reliable strategy for financial security!

In the Comprehensive Investment Guide section of the book, you can find detailed ideas and strategies for creating and managing an individual stock portfolio.

Real Estate, Automobile, and Risk Management for Financial Security

BUYING YOUR PRIMARY RESIDENCE

Buying a home is one of the most important financial decisions you will make in your lifetime. It is also one of the most powerful tools for building generational wealth. Home ownership provides a unique combination of leverage, tax advantages, and potential for long-term appreciation. A home represents more than shelter—it symbolizes security, prosperity, and a legacy that can uplift your family's financial trajectory for decades to come. (See Appendix 7D for all real estate–related disclosures.)

WHY HOMEOWNERSHIP BUILDS WEALTH

Historically, real estate has been one of the most reliable wealth-building assets. According to the Federal Reserve, homeowners have a median net worth that's nearly forty times greater than renters—approximately \$255,000 compared to \$6,300.[8] This stark difference highlights the incredible financial leverage homeownership offers.

Consider this: when you purchase a home, you typically put down between 10 percent and 30 percent, borrowing the rest via a mortgage. This leverage amplifies your returns significantly. If you buy a $500,000 home with a 20 percent down payment ($100,000) and the home appreciates by just 3 percent annually, in thirty years your home could be worth around $1,213,631—more than doubling your initial investment several times over.

Tax Advantages

Homeownership comes with substantial tax benefits. Mortgage interest payments and property taxes are generally deductible, reducing your taxable income. For example, if your annual mortgage interest and property taxes total $20,000, and you're in a 32 percent tax bracket, that's roughly $6,400 saved annually on taxes. Over thirty years, these tax savings alone can equate to nearly $200,000—funds you can reinvest, use toward retirement, or allocate to other financial goals.

Long-Term Appreciation and Inflation Protection

Real estate historically appreciates at a rate slightly above inflation, averaging around 4 percent annually nationwide.[9] In booming metropolitan or coastal areas, appreciation rates can be significantly higher. This growth not only builds your equity but also provides a hedge against inflation. While rent costs rise with inflation, your fixed mortgage payment remains stable, creating predictable financial stability.

Maria and Carlos Hernandez purchased their modest home in Southern California for $350,000 in 1995 with a 20 percent down payment of $70,000. Despite initial worries about mortgage payments, they knew homeownership was critical for their family's future. Over the next twenty-eight years, their neighborhood flourished, and their home's value appreciated significantly. By 2023, their home was worth over $1.2 million. This property provided Maria and Carlos with financial flexibility—they refinanced to help their children through college, funded their retirement comfortably, and knew their children and grandchildren would inherit substantial equity. Their home wasn't just a place to live; it became the foundation for generational prosperity.

GENERATIONAL WEALTH: THE GIFT THAT KEEPS GIVING

One of the most powerful yet often overlooked benefits of homeownership is generational wealth transfer. Upon inheritance, your heirs typically receive a "step-up" in the property's cost basis, which resets the home's value for tax purposes to its current market value. This effectively allows heirs to avoid paying substantial capital gains taxes on the accumulated appreciation—ensuring wealth stays in your family rather than going to the government.

OWNING VERSUS RENTING: A CLEAR WINNER

When renting, your monthly payments build your landlord's wealth. In contrast, homeownership ensures that your monthly payments contribute directly toward building your own equity. The longer you own your home, the more equity you accumulate, creating a secure financial base and enhancing your net worth.

PRACTICAL ADVICE: ACT SOONER, NOT LATER

Waiting to buy can be costly. Interest rates fluctuate, prices rise, and the longer you wait, the less time your property has to appreciate. If you're financially able to purchase and sustain the mortgage payments, the decision is straightforward—take action sooner rather than later.

Buying a primary residence is more than just acquiring property;

it's investing in your future and the future of generations to come (see figure 15.11). Take pride in knowing that your home is more than bricks and mortar—it's the bedrock of lasting financial security, prosperity, and your family's ongoing legacy, an important step for growing your Total Wealth.

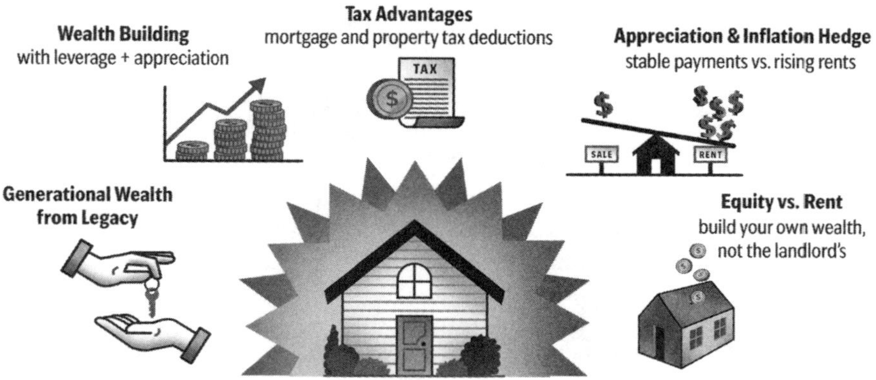

Figure 15.11: Your home's power: value far beyond four walls.

BUYING A CAR

Driving an expensive car might project an image of wealth, but in reality, it often delays true financial freedom. Until you reach a comfortable level of financial stability and security, spending heavily on a vehicle is more a reflection of impulse than wisdom. Remember, a car is a rapidly depreciating asset that not only loses value the moment you drive it off the lot but also demands ongoing costs for maintenance, insurance, registration, and fuel or electricity (see figure 15.12). The more you pay for a car, the more you will spend maintaining it.

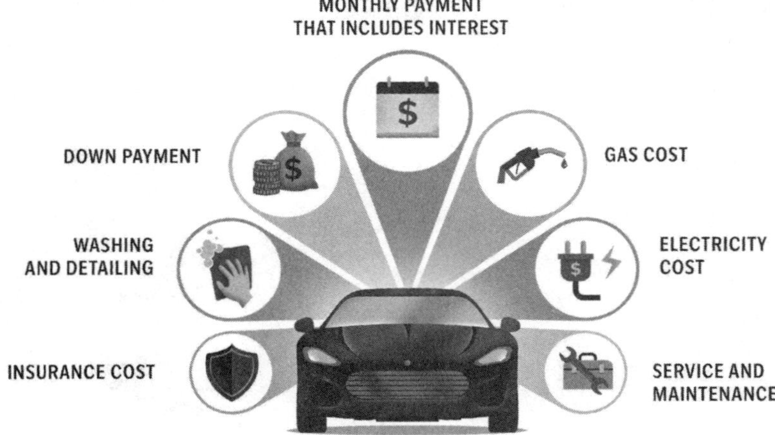

Figure 15.12: Total ownership costs can impede long-term compounding and wealth creation.

Your path to financial security is about creating a life of peace, independence, and intentional choices. Transportation should support your goals, not burden them. Your focus should be on finding a reliable, safe, and efficient vehicle—ideally a new or gently used car that meets your needs without draining your cash flow or forcing you into unnecessary debt. Driving a dependable car while investing the money you save will do far more for your long-term wealth and peace of mind than any luxury badge on your driveway.

RISK MANAGEMENT

A key pillar of financial security is understanding and managing risk wisely. Life is unpredictable, exposing us all to the potential of untimely death, illness, disability, or accidents that could derail our financial plans. Insurance exists to protect you from these potentially catastrophic events, but it is essential to approach it with strategy and awareness, not fear.

Transferring risk to an insurance company comes at a cost, which is why you must discern which risks are worth insuring against and which can be managed or self-insured. The financial consequences of an unexpected death can devastate a family's stability, making life insurance an essential safeguard, especially during your working years. Health insurance, auto insurance, and homeowners insurance similarly protect against severe financial losses from medical emergencies, car accidents, or property damage.

The Risk Management Strategy Matrix

Every risk you face falls along two axes (see figure 15.13):

- Frequency—How likely is the event?
- Severity—How damaging would it be if it happened?

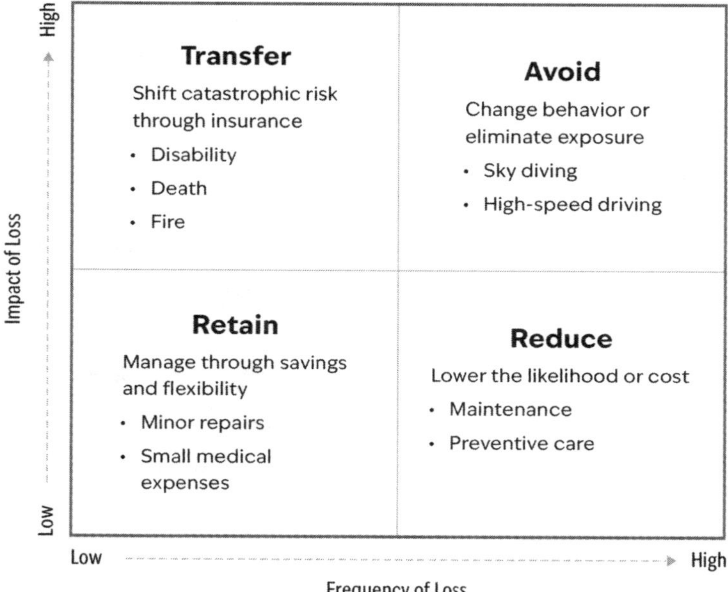

Figure 15.13: Risk management depends on capacity, frequency, and impact.

Based on this, you can choose from four strategies:

1. Avoid the risk: Don't do the activity (e.g., don't drive on icy roads).
2. Reduce the risk: Take precautions (e.g., wear a helmet, use smoke detectors).
3. Transfer the risk: Buy insurance to shift financial burden to an insurer (e.g., home insurance, automobile insurance, life insurance).
4. Retain the risk: Accept the risk and self-insure (e.g., minor electronics).

The essence of risk management in your LIVING360 journey is to regularly ask: What can go wrong? What would the financial impact be? Can I handle this risk on my own, or should I transfer it to an insurer? By thoughtfully protecting against significant, low-probability events while managing smaller risks directly, you create a financial safety net that supports your independence and peace of mind without unnecessary costs.

Annuities Simplified*

Consider Arthur, a civil engineer only three years away from retirement. Arthur has built a comfortable nest egg but worries deeply about the potential for an imminent recession and a deep bear market, which could erode his investments at the worst possible moment. At the same time, he understands the importance of investing in stocks to grow his wealth, achieve his retirement goals, and leave a meaningful legacy. For Arthur, annuities may offer an attractive compromise: the ability to stay invested in the market, but with guarantees like minimum returns,

* Please see Appendix 7C for annuities-related disclosures.

lifetime income, or protection of his capital—even though this security comes at a much higher cost.

TYPES OF ANNUITIES

Annuities come in several varieties, each with different risks, costs, and rewards:

- Fixed Annuities: Think of these as the insurance company's version of a bank CD. You provide the company with your money, and they promise a fixed return over a set period. They typically pay more than your local bank, but your safety net relies on the insurer's stability and ability to pay its claims—not FDIC backing available to banks.
- Variable Annuities: These are similar to mutual funds wrapped in insurance policies, allowing you to invest your money in the market. They offer potential tax deferral, growth, and sometimes lifelong guaranteed payments. But nothing's free: the fees can be high, and exiting early can be costly.
- Fixed Index Annuities: These annuities blend safety with potential growth. It's like standing safely on land while dipping your toe into the market. You partially participate in market gains while having some protection against losses.
- Immediate Annuities: With this option, you exchange a lump sum of your savings today for a guaranteed paycheck for life. It provides simple peace of mind—but once invested, your capital is no longer available to you. While Immediate Annuities may provide peace of mind and security, you limit any potential capital growth. In most cases you also trade life-time income (payments) for legacy money that could go to your heirs.

Annuities can be beneficial for those seeking certainty—especially retirees looking for steady income or individuals who want market participation but fear significant downturns.

There is no doubt that annuities can be very complex and your money is invested in them for the long-term. If you need all your money back, there can be a surrender charge of up to 10 percent. When you see a disclosure that annuities are complex, it is most certainly accurate. You have to spend time, effort, and energy to fully understand the costs and benefits.

> The principles and different investment products you've just explored are clear, actionable, and proven. They are not based on hype or overnight riches but on timeless truths: Spend less than you earn, invest wisely, protect against risks, and let time and discipline do the heavy lifting through the power of compounding.

The Power of Compounding and Starting Early

Starting your investment journey right now is the most impactful decision you can make for your financial future. The key is that time works as a powerful engine, creating a cycle where the returns you earn begin to generate returns of their own. By simply pairing this early start with a consistent strategy and sound financial understanding, you can watch modest savings bloom into the significant wealth required to purchase true financial freedom and options later in life.

How does it work? Suppose you start investing in your 401(k) at age twenty-five, earning a $75,000 salary growing at 3 percent (see figure 15.14). You contribute 10 percent annually ($7,500), your employer matches 4 percent, and your investments grow at 8 percent annually. By the time you retire at sixty-seven, based on these assumptions, your account would be worth approximately $4,778,352 (see figure 15.15).

BASIC INFO		PROJECTIONS		
Current age	25	Expected retirement age	67	
Current annual salary	$75,000	Life expectancy	90	
Current 401(k) balance	$1	Expected salary increase	3 %	per year
Contribution (% of salary)	10 %	Expected annual return	8 %	per year
Employer match	100 %	Expected inflation rate	2 %	per year
Employer match limit	4 %			

Figure 15.14: This figure illustrates the power of consistent savings and compounding at 8 percent.

At the retirement age of 67, the 401(k) balance will be **$4,778,352**, which is equivalent to **$2,080,036** in purchasing power today.

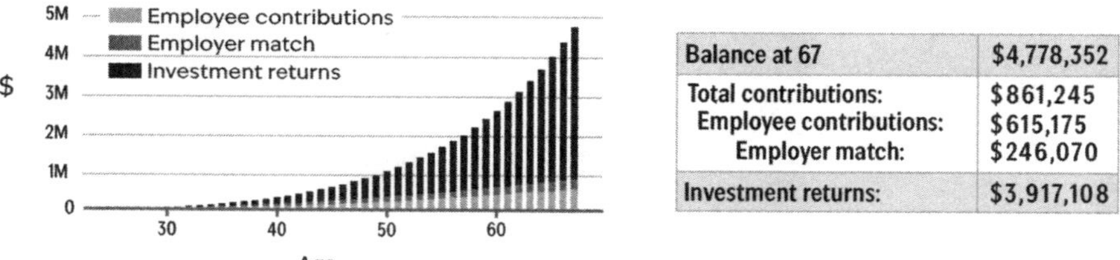

Balance at 67	$4,778,352
Total contributions:	$861,245
Employee contributions:	$615,175
Employer match:	$246,070
Investment returns:	$3,917,108

Figure 15.15: This figure illustrates the results of consistent 401(k) investment at age sixty-seven.

Now imagine a different path. You still save the same amount, but instead of investing in stocks, you keep your money in cash or low-yield bonds earning 3 percent (see figure 15.16). Your account would grow to just $1,503,945 (see figure 15.17).

BASIC INFO		PROJECTIONS		
Current age	25	Expected retirement age	67	
Current annual salary	$75,000	Life expectancy	90	
Current 401(k) balance	$1	Expected salary increase	3 %	per year
Contribution (% of salary)	10 %	Expected annual return	3 %	per year
Employer match	100 %	Expected inflation rate	2 %	per year
Employer match limit	4 %			

Figure 15.16: Here is the outcome of the projected investment at just 3 percent.

At the retirement age of 67, the 401(k) balance will be **$1,503,945**, which is equivalent to **$654,673** in purchasing power today.

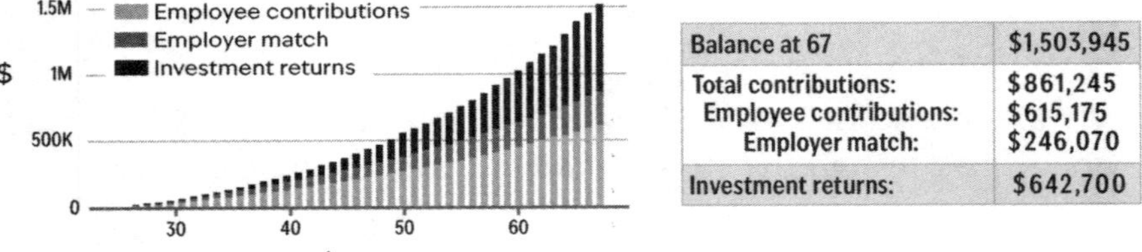

Balance at 67	$1,503,945
Total contributions:	$861,245
Employee contributions:	$615,175
Employer match:	$246,070
Investment returns:	$642,700

Figure 15.17: The change in investment return from 8 percent to 3 percent is significant.

What made the $3.2 million difference? Not luck. Not income. Just knowledge, consistent investing, and the power of compounding. It also requires understanding that while stocks are more volatile (their prices go up and down, sometimes dramatically) than cash, they are also the investment most likely to help you keep up with and even exceed the rate of inflation. Cash, in contrast, is worth less every year when you factor in inflation.

Charting the Path to Independence

Before any meaningful progress can be made, you must know where you're headed. Clarity of vision is the cornerstone of financial independence. If your mind's eye can truly picture where you want to go—how much you want to have, what kind of life you want to live—then your mind, habits, and decisions will begin to align in that direction. The journey begins with a thoughtful, personal inventory.

The exercise that follows isn't just about numbers. It's about purpose. It's about aligning your financial trajectory with your life goals, security, freedom, dignity, and impact. Take a few quiet minutes to complete the following assessment. Be honest. Be aspirational. And above all, be intentional.

ASSESSMENT: YOUR PATH TO FINANCIAL SECURITY

Where are you now? Where do you want to go?

- What is your current net worth? $________
- Target net worth five years from now: $________
- Target net worth ten years from now: $________
- Target net worth thirty years from now: $________
- Target net worth at age seventy: $________
- Target net worth at age eighty: $________
- Target net worth at age ninety: $________

Savings and Investment Discipline

- How much do you currently save each month in 401(k), IRAs, or other investment accounts? $________
- If this number is zero or low, ask yourself: *What am I spending money on today that I might regret not saving for tomorrow?*

continued

Home Ownership and Real Estate Vision

- Do you currently own a home? Yes / No
- If yes, what is its current market value? $________
- What do you believe the value of your home will be twenty years from now? $________
- If you do not yet own a home:
    - Do you plan to buy a home?
    - In what time frame?
    - What kind of home and location aligns with your life goals?

Your financial freedom = Your life freedom.

- Do you have adequate life insurance?
- Do you have health insurance?
- Have you thought about disability insurance, long-term care insurance, and umbrella insurance?
- What does financial independence mean to you?
- What will you do with your time and energy when you no longer have to work for money?
- Who will benefit from your financial security—just you, or will you use it to lift others?

You now have a LIVING360 Financial Wealth road map. If you follow it patiently and consistently you will transform your financial trajectory. For those who are striving not thriving or feel that they are in a state of stifled enlightenment, having a long-term vision for financial security itself can be empowering and liberating.

This chapter covered the essentials of financial planning and investing. You know what needs to be done. Most people learn profound ideas that can transform their life but never act on them. You will be different; you will act and implement!

(When you are ready to go deeper—to master the why behind each strategy, understand financial planning and risk management deeply, and learn the nuances of building a portfolio that can support you for decades—please review the Comprehensive Investment Guide.)

Simply taking the time to envision your future is the most powerful first step. It puts your subconscious to work, aligns your priorities, and prepares you for disciplined action. You wouldn't start building a house without a blueprint. Don't try to build your financial life without one either. Let this be your blueprint. Keep it close. Update it annually. And remember: Every great journey begins with a vision, followed by consistent, intentional steps. This is the start of your financial freedom.

Reflection Questions

1. Have you clearly defined what financial security means to you?
2. Are you saving the maximum amount possible in your retirement accounts or can you save more?
3. Is your investment strategy keeping up with the market, and is it simple, low cost, and tax efficient?
4. Are you covered in case of a negative event? Do you have appropriate insurance?
5. Can you invest more in real estate?

CONCLUSION

Live Your 360

Every great story comes to an end, yet in that ending we often find the seed of a new beginning. As you reach the end of this book, pause—to notice what has shifted. The change may be subtle, but it is real. You are thinking differently. You are asking better questions. You are more aware of how you see the world—and how that view was formed. As you move forward, your decisions feel different, urgency softens, and comparison loses its grip.

For most of your life, your concrete box blended into the background. It felt like "just the way things are"—the beliefs, habits, and stories inherited from family, culture, faith, politics, and money. It told you what success should look like, how much you should earn, what you should own, what you should fear, and what you should never question.

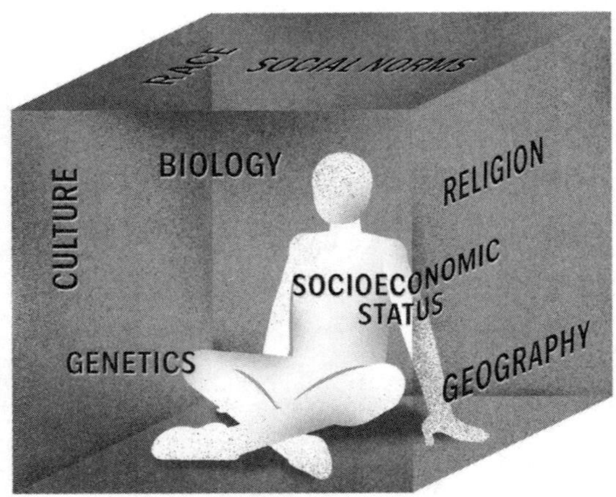

Figure 0.1: Awareness of the inherited concrete box and your choice to step outside.

In these pages, you did something rare. You stopped long enough to look at that box. You traced its edges: the unspoken rules, the scripts you replayed, the comparisons that stole your peace. You noticed how it shaped your career decisions, your spending, your giving, even your relationships. What you once called "normal" was often inherited ideas, not your own considered choices.

The box did protect you. For a time, it offered the comfort of structure, the safety of identity, and the warmth of belonging. But as you looked closer, you saw the cost—the dreams you never voiced, the conversations you avoided, the risks you never took, the joy you postponed. The box started to feel darker, the walls slowly narrowing around you.

The work you've done here was not about escaping the box entirely. We all live within some structure and a belief system we create. The deeper task is to make that structure fully conscious and personally authentic—to ensure it reflects who you truly are, not just what you were handed.

Today, you hold the key to your concrete box.

You can open the door and step outside when opinions and decisions demand distance and clarity. And just as importantly, new windows have appeared. These windows are glass. They let in fresh light—new ideas, perspectives, and experiences that expand how you see yourself and the world. Through Wisdom Wealth, awareness grows without requiring you to abandon your identity. You are no longer confined; you are informed.

From that awareness, your perspective widened. You came to understand your life within the context of history, technology, economics, and culture—recognizing that many of the pressures you feel are not personal shortcomings, but reflections of a complex and fast-changing world. With that understanding came resilience to navigate the risks and opportunities.

You then confronted the heart of fulfillment: meaning, purpose, relationships, and gratitude. You saw that a good life is not something postponed until success arrives, but something practiced daily—through presence, connection, and intention. And you grounded all of this in financial security—not as an end in itself, but as a foundation for freedom, dignity, and peace of mind.

This is Total Wealth: the alignment of Wisdom Wealth and Financial Wealth. Not more for the sake of more, but enough—your definition of enough—to support a life that reflects your deepest values. In a world that worships more, choosing "what is enough for me" is an act that reflects self-respect and freedom.

The discipline that sustains this alignment is simple, yet demanding: the 3As—Awareness, Action, and Acceptance.

Awareness sharpens how you seek and process knowledge. It helps you notice, in real time, when comparison poisons your joy or fear is driving your decisions.

Action turns insight into vision and lived reality. It's small steps that compound over time, fully funding your 401(k), postponing a purchase, investing in relationships, taking care of your health, and making time for experiences that matter.

Acceptance—often the hardest. It is humility to know that you will not control outcomes, markets, other people, or time. Sometimes you will do everything "right" and still face loss, illness, volatility, or disappointment. Acceptance is not surrendering your agency; it is releasing the illusion of total control. You meet success with humility. You meet failure with empathy—for yourself and others. And you let experience, even difficult experience, become wisdom through greater Awareness.

The journey does not end here. New boxes will form. Old assumptions will return. Life will push you back inside the concrete box—locking the door, drawing the curtains over the windows. But now, you recognize the walls as they rise. You know how to open the door.

You carry the key now. Live your 360.

Your Final Call to Action

- **Measure Your Progress:** Before you close this book, complete the LIVING360 Grid and Compass one final time. (You can find them both in Appendix 1.) This exercise will reveal the progress you have made across the four critical dimensions: Know Yourself, Know the World, Know Your Purpose, and Build Financial Security.
- **Define Your Next Step:** Identify the dimensions on your LIVING360 Compass that need the most immediate attention, and commit to one deliberate, joyful movement in those areas every week. You can access www.wisdomandwealthsolution.com to explore additional tools and valuable resources to continue your Total Wealth journey.
- **Revisit Your Blueprint:** The book is now your operational manual. Use it, update it annually, and remember that the true aim has always been progress, not perfection.
- **Master Financial Planning and Investment Strategy:** Continue on to the Comprehensive Investment Guide in the next section.

If these pages have helped you live with greater clarity, balance, and financial security, then the work has already begun. You now have the LIVING360 framework and the tools—what matters most is how you choose to live them.

Comprehensive Investment Guide

In Part IV of this book, we explored the "why" and "how" of financial security—not just strategies to grow your money, but how to align it with your values, purpose, and peace of mind. We discussed the guiding principles and easy-to-understand solutions that form the foundation of Financial Wealth: awareness of the value of financial security, disciplined actions of saving and investing, and acceptance of outcomes with patience for long-term success.

Now, in this Comprehensive Investment Guide, we go deeper. Think of this section as your *field manual*—a place where the ideas of Wisdom Wealth meet the mechanics of Financial Wealth. In this guide, you'll find clarity on how different investments work, what roles they can play in your portfolio, and how you can navigate the ever-changing financial landscape with confidence and calm.

This guide isn't meant to predict markets or prescribe products. It's meant to empower you. To replace confusion with understanding, fear with perspective, and complexity with simplicity.

Please refer to Appendix 7 for detailed disclosures.

My goal is to help you see investing not as a game of chance or speculation, but as a lifelong partnership between your money, your goals, and your values. The chapters ahead offer a practical overview of the major investment building blocks available to you:

- The Stock Market: Understanding the overall market structure
- Exchange-Traded Funds (ETFs): The modern tools of diversification and efficiency
- Mutual Funds: Professional management, and how to understand what's beneath the surface
- Asset Classes and Diversification: Building strength through variety and balance
- Investing in Individual Stocks: Risks, opportunities, and investment methodologies
- Fixed Income, Bonds, and Bond Ladders: Creating stability and income through structure and patience
- Alternative Investments: Opportunities beyond the traditional, with measured awareness
- Real Estate: Understanding the financial and emotional value of the homes we live in and invest in
- Buying a Car: Making smart choices about one of the most common financial decisions
- Annuities: Knowing options and understanding complexity and opportunity
- Risk Management and Insurance Solutions: Protecting your family, your dreams, and your legacy
- My Ten Investment Principles

Each topic is designed to bring you one step closer to financial clarity, to help you ask better questions, make wiser decisions, and understand the moving parts of your financial life.

This comprehensive guide provides detailed information for you to confidently navigate the world of finance, so that your saving and investment strategy, like your life, reflects the balance of wisdom and wealth: LIVING360 with financial security. Remember that wealth is not built with a single decision. It's built through a thousand thoughtful choices and over a long period of time.

1. Demystifying the Stock Market*

When you think of investing or buying stocks, one question may come to mind: where is all this trading taking place? Historically, stocks traded on exchanges, and when you wanted to buy a stock, you called your "broker" and they placed the order that ended up on the floor of the exchange. Those days are gone. All stock trades are done electronically. All the buyers and sellers are matched through automated trading. On your evening news or CNBC, when you see the floor of the New York Stock Exchange, know that people standing there are not really engaged in trading. They are simply looking at fancy monitors. They or their trading gurus are choosing from a set of programs (algorithms) that are constantly quoting prices.

Simply put, the stock market is a platform where company shares are bought and sold. You often hear about major market indices. Every news bulletin ends with a report on the performance of major stock market indices. This normally includes the following:

- The Dow Jones Industrial Average (DJIA) tracks thirty large, established US companies like Coca-Cola, Apple, and McDonald's, giving a quick snapshot of market sentiment.

---

* Please see Appendixes 7A and 7B for all investment-related disclosures.

- The S&P 500 Index represents five hundred of America's largest corporations across various sectors, offering an excellent gauge of the overall US market performance. When you hear "the market is up 1 percent," it usually refers to this index.
- The NASDAQ Composite encompasses over three thousand companies, heavily weighted toward tech giants like Apple, Microsoft, Amazon, Google (Alphabet), Meta (Facebook), and Tesla. It's often used as a barometer for the technology sector.

Next time someone mentions "the Dow rose 2 percent," it means the average stock price of its thirty companies increased by 2 percent. A "1 percent drop in the S&P 500" signals an average decline across those five hundred companies.

2. Investing in ETFs: Your Simple Path to Financial Freedom

Exchange-traded funds (ETFs) have revolutionized investing in the last thirty years. They provide a simple, cost-effective way for everyone to build wealth without having to invest much thought into it. Imagine buying a diverse basket of investments—stocks or bonds—with just one transaction. That's the magic of ETFs: they offer instant diversification, accessibility, and ease, making investing straightforward and stress-free.

An ETF is like purchasing a ready-made investment portfolio. When you buy a single ETF, you're investing in multiple stocks or bonds simultaneously. For instance, an ETF tracking the S&P 500 Index allows you to invest in five hundred of the largest US companies with just one transaction.

ETFs do the same for your investments as a good tour design does for travel to a new country. They simplify the journey, save time, reduce costs, and give you broad and diversified exposure without constant second-guessing. They could constitute your entire portfolio, or you can use them as a base for some percentage.

REMARKABLE GROWTH OF ETFs

The first ETF (SPY) was introduced in 1993, tracking the S&P 500. Today, SPY remains the world's largest ETF, managing over $600 billion. Since then, the ETF industry has exploded:

- By 2000, fewer than one hundred ETFs existed globally.
- The 2008–2009 financial crisis boosted interest in transparent, low-cost investing, fueling further ETF growth.
- Today, there are over ten thousand ETFs worldwide, with the US alone hosting over four thousand ETFs and managing more than $8.5 trillion in assets.

This explosive growth reflects one thing: more investors are choosing simplicity, transparency, and control—values that align perfectly with *The Wisdom and Wealth Solution*.

ETFs IN ACTION: SIMPLE EXAMPLES

To see how this works in real life, here's how investors use ETFs to mirror the market without the stress of picking individual stocks:

- **SPY ETF**: If you buy the SPY ETF, you're essentially investing in all five hundred companies in the S&P 500 Index. If the index rises 1.3 percent in a day, SPY rises about the same. If it drops by 0.75 percent, SPY mirrors this decrease. Over long periods, such as ten years, SPY's performance closely matches the overall market return (minus very small management fees).

- **DIA ETF**: This ETF tracks the Dow Jones Industrial Average (Dow30), representing thirty of America's most iconic companies like JP Morgan, Apple, Coca-Cola, Walmart, and Microsoft. If the Dow30 rises 1 percent, DIA typically follows suit. This offers a simple way to invest in the strength and stability of America's leading businesses.

DIVERSE ETF CHOICES FOR SMART INVESTORS

In addition to SPY and DIA, table CG.1 (as seen in Chapter 15) lists some popular, low-cost ETFs to consider as you build your portfolio:

TABLE CG.1: EXAMPLES OF EXCHANGE-TRADED FUNDS (ETFs)

Asset Class	ETF(s)
US Stocks (Diversified)	Vanguard Total Stock Market (VTI) iShares Core S&P Total US Stock Market (ITOT) Schwab US Broad Market (SCHB)
US Stocks (S&P 500) Large-Cap	SPDR S&P 500 ETF Trust (SPY) Vanguard S&P 500 (VOO) iShares Core S&P 500 (IVV)
US Large Cap Growth	Invesco Nasdaq-100 (tracks NDX) (QQQ) Vanguard Growth (VUG) iShares Russell 1000 Growth (IWF) iShares S&P 500 Growth (IVW)
Dow Jones Industrial Average or Similar	State Street SPDR Dow Jones Industrial Average (DIA) Invesco Dow Jones Industrial Average Dividend (DJD)

Asset Class	ETF(s)
US Stocks - Mid-Cap	iShares Core S&P Mid-Cap (IJH) Vanguard Mid-Cap (VO) iShares Russell Mid-Cap (IWR)
US Stocks - Small-Cap	iShares Core S&P Small-Cap (IJR) Vanguard SmallCap (VB) Schwab US SmallCap (SCHA)
International Stocks	Vanguard Total World Stock (VT) Vanguard Total International Stock (VXUS) iShares Core MSCI Total International Stock (IXUS)
Developed Market Stocks	Vanguard FTSE Developed Markets (VEA) iShares Core MSCI EAFE (IEFA) iShares MSCI EAFE ETF (EFA)
Emerging Market Stocks	iShares Core MSCI Emerging Markets (IEMG) Vanguard FTSE Emerging Markets (VWO) iShares MSCI Emerging Markets (EEM)
US Total Bonds	iShares Core US Aggregate Bond (AGG) Vanguard Total Bond Market (BND) Schwab US Aggregate Bond (SCHZ)
High Yield Bond	SPDR Bloomberg High Yield Bond (JNK) iShares iBoxx $ High Yield Corporate Bond (HYG) iShares Broad USD High Yield Corporate Bond (USHY)
Commodity Funds	World Gold Trust Services - State Street Global Advisors (GLD) iShares Gold Trust (IAU) iShares Silver Trust (SLV) Sprott Asset Management Physical Silver Trust (PSLV) iShares GSCI Commodity Dynamic Roll Strategy (COMT)

(Please refer to Appendixes 7A and 7B for disclosures.)

POWERFUL ADVANTAGES OF ETFs

- **Instant Diversification**: A single ETF holds numerous stocks or bonds, spreading your risk effectively. For instance, one share of SPY gives you exposure to five hundred major companies.
- **Low Cost**: ETFs are usually cheaper than mutual funds due to passive management, offering expense ratios as low as 0.03 percent for popular funds.
- **Liquidity and Flexibility**: ETFs trade like stocks on exchanges, letting you buy and sell throughout the trading day at market prices, unlike mutual funds that only trade once daily.
- **Transparency**: ETFs typically disclose holdings daily, ensuring you always know precisely what you own.
- **Tax Efficiency**: ETFs often incur fewer taxes due to their unique "in-kind" trading mechanism, minimizing capital gains distributions.
- **Accessibility**: ETFs have no minimum investment requirements, making investing affordable for everyone.
- **Automated Rebalancing**: ETFs automatically adjust holdings to match their indices, eliminating frequent manual adjustments.
- **Ideal for Dollar-Cost Averaging**: ETFs facilitate regular investing, smoothing market volatility, and removing the guesswork of timing the market.

NAVIGATING ETF RISKS AND CHALLENGES

With growth comes more choice but also greater complexity and higher cost. Be cautious about specialized ETFs. Consider the following:

- **Higher Fees**: Specialized ETFs (leveraged or thematic funds) often carry higher expense ratios.
- **Leveraged ETFs**: Aim to amplify daily returns by multiples (e.g., 2x or 3x). Due to daily compounding, their long-term returns can significantly differ from expectations and their underlying index.
- **Niche ETFs**: These focus narrowly on specific sectors (cannabis, robotics, genomics), increasing risk due to less diversification and potential market hype.
- **Shiny Object Syndrome**: Beware of ETFs promising to capitalize on trendy sectors or themes. Chasing these can lead to subpar performance.

Don't let these complexities scare you off. You can easily avoid these niche ETFs. Just focus on broad, diversified, and low-cost ETFs, and you may avoid most of these pitfalls.

KEEP IT SIMPLE—THE KISS PRINCIPLE

The key to success with ETFs is simplicity:

- Stick to broad, diversified ETFs tracking major indices.
- Avoid complex or overly specialized ETFs unless thoroughly researched.
- Consistently invest and maintain a disciplined, long-term approach.

Simplicity is your superpower. With ETFs, you don't need to beat the market—you just need to join it consistently.

YOUR ETF INVESTMENT JOURNEY

By embracing ETFs, you may simplify investing, reduce risk, and build toward financial independence. By choosing simplicity, you are choosing confidence. Let your money compound and benefit from the excellent historical performance of stock markets while you focus on living a richer, more purposeful life.

Welcome to your ETF-powered path to financial success, another essential step on your LIVING360 journey! Some ETFs mentioned in this section—SPY, DIA, QQQ, IVV, EFA, IWM, VTI, VXUS, AGG, LQD, and BNDX, etc.—are shown for educational illustration purposes only and do not represent investment recommendations. Their inclusion is intended to demonstrate asset-class diversification, portfolio construction, and the role of index-based investing. Similar ETFs are available from other providers, which may offer lower fees, greater liquidity, or more efficient index tracking. Past performance is not indicative of future results, and all investing involves risk, including possible loss of principal.

3. Mutual Funds: Your Gateway to Easy, Effective Investing

I once worked with a client, Ali, who let his 401(k) sit in cash for years because he was afraid of making a mistake. When he finally started investing with a simple mutual fund strategy, he told me, "I wish I had started earlier. This feels like freedom." If you look across 401(k) accounts of American workers, you will find a large percentage of participants who think like Ali!

Imagine you want to start investing but feel overwhelmed picking individual stocks or bonds. What if you could pool your money with thousands of other investors and let professionals do the heavy lifting, giving you instant diversification and a clear path to building wealth? That's the power of mutual funds.

The modern mutual fund industry in the US began in 1924 with the launch of the Massachusetts Investors Trust (MITTX)—the nation's first open-end mutual fund available to the public. Today, investors have access to approximately seven thousand mutual funds in the United States alone, providing countless opportunities to build wealth efficiently.

A mutual fund is simply a pooled investment vehicle managed by financial experts, designed to invest in a diverse set of stocks, bonds, or other securities. Instead of selecting individual investments, you own a fraction of a professionally managed portfolio, instantly spreading your investment risk across multiple assets.

Most people have access to mutual funds through retirement plans such as 401(k) and 403(b). Most companies provide about fifteen to thirty mutual funds that employees (plan participants) can invest in. It is truly tragic that a lot of employees do not have any idea on how to allocate the money they are saving through the retirement plan and they leave it in a cash or a money market account. A significant barrier to proper allocation of the retirement account is due to a lack of understanding (not knowing which mutual fund to pick). On other occasions, the retirement plan participants are scared that the stock market will decline, and they will lose their hard-earned money.

MUTUAL FUNDS: TAILORED TO YOUR GOALS

One of the best aspects of mutual funds is their flexibility. No matter your age, goals, or comfort with risk, there's likely a mutual fund that fits your needs. An abbreviated list of different types of mutual funds follows. Each type of fund carries its own risk and reward potential:

- Stock funds primarily invest in equities, offering potential long-term growth.
    - The all cap, go-anywhere funds may be domestic, that is, focused on US stocks, or global, meaning they can also invest in international stocks.
    - You can find funds that invest in micro-cap companies, small-cap companies, mid-cap companies, or large-cap companies.
    - There are funds that invest in developed markets and emerging markets stocks.
    - If you favor a particular investment theme such as "value" stocks or "growth" stocks, you can also find plenty of those as well.
- Bond funds focus on fixed-income securities, providing regular income and greater stability. Within this category, there are funds that invest in all types of bonds: some that focus on government bonds, while others target investment-grade, high-yield, or international and emerging market bonds.
- Balanced or hybrid funds blend stocks and bonds, balancing growth potential and income stability.
- Money market funds invest in short-term, low-risk instruments, ideal for safely parking cash.
- Index funds replicate specific market indices (e.g., the S&P 500), often at a lower cost.
- Sector or thematic funds target specific industries like technology, healthcare, or renewable energy.

CHOOSING THE RIGHT MUTUAL FUND

With thousands of mutual funds to choose from, it's easy to feel overwhelmed. But you don't need to analyze every fund—just focus on a few key factors that will guide you to smart, confident choices. You don't need to find the perfect fund to succeed. Your evaluation can begin by reviewing fees and expenses on websites like morningstar.com. High fees can significantly diminish returns. Always compare management fees and commissions with similar funds.

Many fund managers fail to outperform their benchmarks consistently. Review historical performance over five-year period, ten-year period, and since inception. While past returns do not predict future performance, funds with long-term outperformance are often better managed.

Later in this section, we'll guide you on developing a diversified portfolio of mutual funds or ETFs based on your financial goals and risk appetite.

Most 401(k) plans only offer mutual funds. Some of the mutual funds are actively managed and some are passive index funds. Selecting index funds is normally a simpler choice. If you choose a broad, low-cost index fund that tracks an index like the S&P 500 or the average of all international markets, you know what the outcome will most likely be. With actively managed mutual funds, there is always an additional level of risk that your mutual fund manager may perform much worse than the index. Whether you use an active mutual fund or a passive index fund for the growth of your retirement savings, the key is to invest and not leave your savings to lose value in cash. It is hard to come up with simple rules for investing, but the risk profile based on age and time to retirement liquidity needs, along with the concept of diversification, have stood the test of time as sound investment principles.

Adapting Your Strategy as Your Financial Situation Evolves

If you are under the age of forty and saving for retirement in your 401(k) or individual retirement account (IRA), you could allocate your savings to just a few equity (stock) ETFs or index mutual funds. For example, if you started with $10,000 in January 1993 and saved $500 per month until January 2025 and earned the actual SPY return of 10.43 percent, your account balance will be about $1,816,223—this figure does not include any employer contribution, etc.[1] This is the power of long-term compounding, driven by the discipline to invest every month and stay the course.

In the preceding scenario, if you had a 4 percent match from your employer (which is normally the minimum) during your thirty-three years of employment and your starting salary was only $40,000, your 401(k) would have over $2.4 million.

If you are saving for the long-term (at least ten years), don't think too hard or too long—you can invest in the stock market using a simple ETF or index fund and let it grow. There is a high probability that you will earn an attractive return.

If you are about to retire and you will need to use your savings to fund your lifestyle, then your investment portfolio should be more conservative with a lower proportion of stock and a larger allocation to bonds. The actual mix will be a function of your financial situation. You may consult a financial advisor to help you access your financial needs and risk profile to develop an appropriate asset allocation.

In Chapter 15, I have provided age and risk-based sample portfolios. These portfolios can be implemented with ETFs, index mutual funds, or actively managed mutual funds.

Age is an important factor because it determines your investment horizon, meaning that if you are young and don't need your money in the short term and the market declines, you don't have to sell and realize your losses. But age is not the only factor; imagine you have money in your retirement account, but you have already paid off your home, and your expenses are fully covered by a Social Security income and a pension. In this situation, you will not need to use your savings for lifestyle expenses and in twenty or thirty years, your savings will be passed on to your kids as a legacy. Here, you have the financial capability to take more risks and keep your money in the stock markets versus allocating a large percentage to bonds. Remember, your emotional comfort with market ups and downs matters as much as your financial capability to take on risk. Emotions and irrational fear of losses, driven by market noise, are two factors that often derail financial freedom and LIVING360.

The discussion of mutual funds in this chapter is provided for educational purposes to illustrate concepts such as diversification, professional management, and long-term investing. It is not intended as a recommendation or solicitation to buy, sell, or hold any mutual fund or security. Mutual funds involve market and management risk, and the value of shares will fluctuate with market conditions. Returns vary based on investment strategy, holdings, and expenses. Past performance is not indicative of future results. Before investing, readers should review each fund's prospectus, objectives, risks, and fees, and consult a qualified financial professional to determine suitability.

4. Diversification: Don't Put All Your Eggs in One Basket

Think of building a portfolio the way a coach builds a championship team. No team relies on just one star player. A basketball team needs point guard, shooting guard, small forward, power forward, and a center. A soccer team needs strikers, midfielders, defenders, and a goalkeeper. If you only field one type of player, you might dominate in one situation but lose badly in another.

Your portfolio works the same way. By diversifying across different asset classes, you ensure you're not betting everything on one "player." Some assets will shine when the economy is strong, while others step up when conditions turn tough. Together, they create a resilient team that can compete in any environment.

WHY DIVERSIFICATION MATTERS

Diversification is not just about balance—it's about stability and protection. Asset classes move in cycles, and what thrives in one year may underperform the next. It is incredibly difficult—if not impossible—to predict which asset class will be the top performer in any given year. Even seasoned investors and analysts get it wrong more often than they get it right.

Over the years, I've witnessed trends rise and fade unpredictably. Real estate might top the charts one year and drop to the bottom the next. Investors may flock to emerging markets one moment, then abandon them just as quickly. Small-cap stocks might dominate for a stretch, only to be overshadowed by large-cap growth. Commodities might be hot when inflation spikes, then languish when the economy slows.

In my experience, trying to predict and rotate through sectors or styles is a strategy riddled with risk. Some investors get lucky and make a well-timed call—but luck is not a strategy. Worse, when it works once, people tend to believe they've discovered a repeatable formula. They anchor that belief, even as the market moves on.

I have yet to see a sector rotation strategy that consistently outperforms a broadly diversified portfolio over time.

UNDERSTANDING THE KEY ASSET CLASSES

Here are the major asset classes most investors can access:

1. US Stocks

   These represent ownership in American companies. Investors gain when companies grow and share profits through dividends or stock price appreciation.

   - Large-Cap Stocks: Shares in big, established companies like Apple, Microsoft, or Coca-Cola. Generally more stable, with slower growth.
   - Mid-Cap Stocks: Medium-sized firms with growth potential, offering a balance between risk and return.
   - Small-Cap Stocks: Smaller companies with higher growth prospects—but also more volatility.

2. International Stocks

   Ownership in companies based outside the United States.

   - Developed Markets: Includes stable economies like Japan, France, Spain, Germany, or the UK. Offers diversification away from US markets.
   - Emerging Markets: Countries with developing economies such as India, Brazil, or Vietnam. Offers higher growth potential, but also greater economic, political, and currency risk.

3. Bonds

   Loans to governments or companies in exchange for regular interest payments and eventual return of principal. Bonds tend to be less volatile than stocks and are often used to reduce portfolio risk.

4. Real Estate Investment Trusts (REITs)

   REITs allow investors to access property income—such as from malls, apartments, or office buildings—without owning physical property. REITs can be publicly traded and offer income and diversification benefits.

5. Commodities

   Physical goods like gold, oil, or agricultural products. Commodities may do well during inflationary periods but can be highly volatile and influenced by unpredictable factors like weather, war, or policy shifts.

6. Cash and Cash Equivalents

   Includes money market funds, savings accounts, Treasury bills, or short-term certificates of deposit. These assets are low-risk and highly liquid but offer the lowest long-term return potential. Useful for capital preservation and emergency needs.

The Unpredictable Rotation of Performance

Every year, different asset classes lead the performance tables—and the order changes constantly. Charts that show annual returns of each asset class resemble a colorful patchwork quilt, with no clear or consistent pattern. It's tempting to try to chase last year's winners, but history shows that those who do often end up disappointed.

That's why I caution against style chasing, regional bets, or sector-specific fads. While some areas may shine temporarily, making concentrated bets can increase your risk of long-term underperformance. The goal isn't to pick a few winners—it's to ensure your overall portfolio remains resilient no matter which asset class is in favor.

Diversification doesn't guarantee profits or eliminate all losses—but it provides balance, stability, and a much greater chance of long-term success. It protects you from being overly exposed to any single risk and gives each part of your portfolio time and space to grow.

Just as you wouldn't fuel your body with only one food group, don't bet your financial future on a single investment type. A well-diversified portfolio—built with discipline and patience—is a powerful tool for enhancing your Financial Wealth and LIVING360.

How to Diversify Your Investments

Creating a diversified portfolio with the two largest asset classes often involves balancing stocks and bonds. A very simple and common approach for someone who has under ten years of needing money is the 60/40 model—60 percent stocks for growth, 40 percent bonds for stability (see figure CG.1). Such a portfolio can be easily established using just a few ETFs or mutual funds.

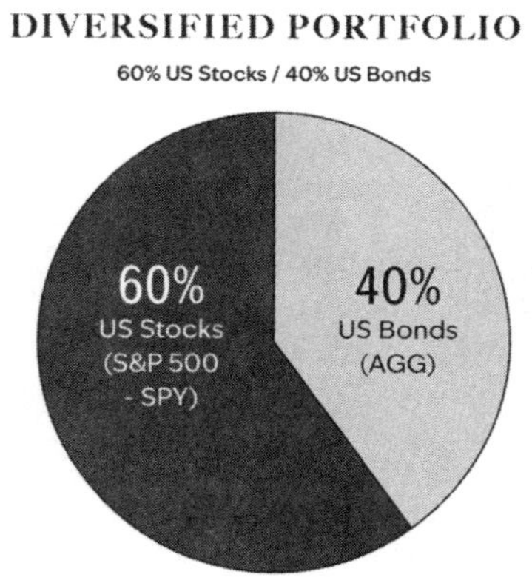

Figure CG.1: This chart depicts a diversified portfolio using the 60/40 model. (See Appendixes 7A and 7B for disclosures.)

Building a Globally Diversified Portfolio

To further strengthen your moderate risk investment portfolio and increase diversification, consider adding international stocks and small allocations (around 5 percent each) of commodities, real estate, and cash. A globally diversified and balanced portfolio might include:

- US Stocks: 35 percent
- Developed Markets International Stocks: 15 percent
- Emerging Market Stocks: 5 percent
- US Total Bonds: 25 percent
- Global High Yield Bonds: 5 percent
- Real Estate Investment Trusts (REITs): 5 percent
- Commodities (Gold/Silver): 5 percent
- Cash/Money Market: 5 percent

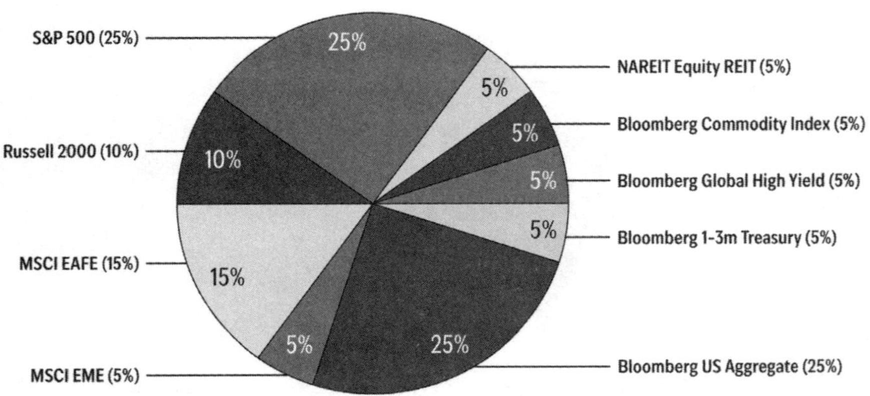

Figure CG.2: This pie chart illustrates a more globally diversified investment strategy. (Please refer to Appendixes 7A and 7B for disclosures.)

The investment strategy depicted in figure CG.2 is a globally diversified investment strategy with all major asset classes represented. If you are younger or would like to target a higher rate of return, you can have more allocation to stocks and less in bonds.

To simplify implementation and create a diversified portfolio that aligns with your risk profile, I have previously listed low cost and liquid ETFs that are available for investment in all brokerage accounts. This strategy may also be replicated in most retirement accounts through index funds or mutual funds that invest in each of the represented asset classes.

ASSESSMENT: INVESTMENT CHOICES

Ask yourself:

- How diversified is your current investment portfolio?
- Are your index or mutual fund choices aligned with your financial goals and comfort with risk?
- What steps can you take to improve your portfolio diversification?

If you are a long-term investor, you may be able to create an efficient and effective portfolio with two to six ETFs or mutual funds. As your investment horizon gets shorter, you may need more asset classes. The real value will come from starting early, maintaining a disciplined approach, and not overthinking every decision.

5. Investing in Individual Stocks: Taking Charge of Your Investment Destiny

You can skip this section if you are not interested in buying individual stocks. It is not necessary for you to invest in individual stocks and bonds to get financial independence. The goal of this chapter is not to make you a financial analyst, but to provide a realistic strategy that you can pursue with a reasonable amount of effort. If you want to spend time and energy, investing in individual stocks can be one of the most exciting and rewarding, yet challenging, methods to grow your wealth.

Imagine sipping your morning coffee while scanning financial headlines, and a bold statement catches your eye: "Nvidia Shares Skyrocket on Explosive AI Demand." You vividly recall your first encounter with Nvidia years ago when the potential of AI, gaming, and advanced graphics cards piqued your interest. Trusting your instincts and personal experience, you invested early. Now, as the stock surges, you feel the thrill of seeing your insight pay off spectacularly. This exhilarating rush of "winning" as your stock climbs is the unique excitement of individual stock investing.

But investing in stocks isn't about thrill; the goal is financial security, which demands knowledge, patience, discipline, and emotional resilience. You just don't need to have one big winner; your entire stock portfolio should deliver better return than the index for this exercise to bring financial value to you. Unlike mutual funds and ETFs, which provide instant diversification and professional oversight, investing directly in stocks places control—and the accompanying responsibilities—firmly in your hands.

Over the years, I've met many thoughtful clients who say something like this: "I'm comfortable having 80–90 percent of my portfolio in professionally managed funds or ETFs, but I want to invest 10 percent in stocks I personally believe in." This is reasonable and it can be incredibly rewarding. Treating a portion of your portfolio as an intellectual sandbox allows you to stay actively engaged with the markets, global trends, and the stories behind the companies shaping our world. When approached with discipline and curiosity, this personal investing journey doesn't just grow your wealth—it expands your awareness, sharpens your thinking, and deepens your connection to the evolving economy.

Done right, it becomes more than a financial strategy—it becomes part of your LIVING360 experience.

UNDERSTANDING STOCKS

When you buy stocks, you're acquiring partial ownership in a business. Picture yourself as an Apple shareholder, smiling as enthusiastic customers line up overnight for the newest iPhone. Each sale contributes directly to your investment success, rewarding you through:

- Capital Appreciation: Your investment grows as the company succeeds
- Dividends: Regular profit-sharing payments that put cash directly into your pocket

Critical Reflections Before Investing

Before diving into individual stocks, honestly consider the following questions:

- Do you possess unique insights or personal experience that could help you identify stocks with potential?
- Can you realistically outperform seasoned professionals who routinely struggle to beat the market?

In my career, successful investors have typically leveraged personal experience and early insights into products poised for explosive growth. They fully accepted the risks involved and were ready to hold their investments for the long term. On the other hand, I have never met anyone who achieved financial independence by chasing speculative "penny stocks" hoping for quick 10x or 50x returns—much like playing the lottery. Financial security comes from informed, patient investing, not gambling.

STRATEGIC APPROACHES TO INDIVIDUAL STOCK INVESTING

If individual stocks still excite you, adopt structured strategies to balance risk and reward. The following are a few ideas for you to evaluate:

- Top Fifty S&P 500 Approach: Consider allocating 1–5 percent to each of the top forty to fifty companies in the S&P 500, capturing much of the index's performance.
- Dow Jones Industrial Average (DOW30) or NASDAQ: Distribute investments across DOW30 or top one hundred NASDAQ companies. You can develop a portfolio of forty to sixty stocks. The percentage of investment in each stock can be a function of your conviction.
- Conviction Picks: Reserve 5–10 percent of your portfolio dedicated to individual stocks for a few high-conviction stocks. These could be rooted in your personal experiences and confidence in their long-term success, such as recognizing early-stage potential in innovative products or services.

STARTING YOUR JOURNEY: PRACTICAL STEPS

1. Establish Clear Goals: Define your objectives—short-term gains, long-term growth, dividend income, or a balanced approach. Clear goals shape successful stock selection.
2. Deep-Dive Research: Examine key aspects of potential investments:
    - Company Fundamentals: Evaluate revenue, profits, debt levels, and cash flows.
    - Market Position: Understand competitive advantages and market leadership.
    - Management Quality: Assess the leadership team's competence, integrity, and history.

3. Understand Basic Valuation: Become comfortable with important valuation metrics:
   - Price-to-Earnings (P/E) Ratio: How much you pay per dollar of earnings
   - Price-to-Book (P/B) Ratio: Helps identify undervalued or overpriced stocks
   - Dividend Yield: Crucial for those seeking steady income

Choosing Your Path: Three Stock-Investing Styles

Every investor, whether seasoned or just starting out, eventually finds themselves drawn to a particular approach to stock investing. It's not just about numbers—it's about personality, goals, and even life stages. Over the years, I've seen three classic investing styles rise above the rest: growth, value, and income. Let me introduce you to each one—not through technical jargon, but through the eyes of relatable characters you can imagine actually living these strategies.

1. Growth Investing: Focusing on the Future

Meet Maya, a twenty-nine-year-old software engineer from San Jose. She's always been fascinated by innovation. Back in 2016, she noticed how everyone in her office was suddenly using Zoom. Even though Zoom had low revenue and was burning cash, Maya began researching the company to determine if it could be a good investment for the future. She didn't expect overnight riches—but she believed in the long-term growth potential.

Growth investors like Maya seek companies with explosive potential. These are firms that reinvest their profits to fuel expansion—think DocuSign, Tesla, Shopify, and Nvidia in their early days. There's often little to no earnings or dividends because the money is going back into innovation. The ride can be bumpy, with stock prices swinging wildly on earnings reports or economic forecasts. But for growth investors, the thrill lies in being part of the next big thing.

2. Value Investing: Geared Toward a Comeback

Then there's James, a retired Air Force pilot in his sixties. He isn't chasing trends—he's hunting for bargains. After reading Benjamin Graham's *The Intelligent Investor*,[2] James adopted the value investing mindset. He looks for solid companies whose stock prices are temporarily beaten down—perhaps due to bad news, poor sentiment, or being overlooked by the market.

One of his moves was investing in Ford back in 2009 during the financial crisis, when the company was trading below book value but had strong leadership and a credible turnaround plan. James waited, and waited some more—and eventually, his patience paid off.

Value investors like James are like disciplined treasure hunters who search for undervalued stocks. They believe that the market often misprices companies, and that with enough research and a cool head, they can find diamonds in the rough. They don't mind waiting years for the market to catch up to their analysis.

3. Income Investing: The Dividend Dream

Finally, meet Margaret. A seventy-two-year-old former school principal, Margaret isn't trying to beat the market—she's looking for peace of mind. She loves receiving dividend checks every quarter from companies she's trusted for decades: Coca-Cola, Procter & Gamble, and Johnson & Johnson. She calls them her "financial friends."

Income investing is about stability. These investors prefer mature companies with a proven track record of paying consistent dividends. It's a strategy especially appealing to retirees or those who want a passive income stream. The goal isn't just appreciation—it's reliability.

UNDERSTANDING RISKS AND LESSONS FROM HISTORY

Consider companies like Kodak, Blockbuster, Bear Stearns, or Lehman Brothers—once deemed invincible but destroyed by lack of innovation, poor decisions, or economic turmoil. The 2008 financial crisis exposed the devastating impact of a nondiversified portfolio overly concentrated in financial or real estate stocks. Entire portfolios were wiped out overnight, emphasizing the critical importance of diversification.

Diversification Is Essential

Even when investing in individual stocks, diversifying across sectors (e.g., technology, healthcare, finance) and regions helps protect against volatility and unforeseen company failures.

Practical Advice from Legendary Investors

- Warren Buffett advises investing only in companies you thoroughly understand and holding them patiently.
- Peter Lynch promotes investing based on your everyday experience—"Invest in what you know."

Individual stock investing offers participation in the success of businesses you understand and believe in. With realistic expectations, disciplined execution, and thoughtful diversification, you have the potential to successfully manage risks and rewards.

6. The Power of Bonds and Fixed Income: Stability with Purpose

Imagine you're on a long journey across rugged financial terrain. Your equity investments—those exciting, high-growth stocks—are the engine propelling you forward. But no seasoned traveler would set off without seatbelts, brakes, and a solid suspension system. That's where bonds come in. Bonds are the stabilizers of your financial vehicle: they keep your ride smoother during turbulence, help you slow down safely in a downturn, and ensure that you don't fly off the road during moments of market mania.

Let me tell you about Ray. In his younger years, Ray was all about speed—investing heavily in tech stocks, chasing high returns, riding the waves of booms and busts. His mantra was, "I am a long-term investor, and I am OK with my portfolio having wild swings, but I want a 10 percent annualized return." But when he hit fifty, something shifted. "I don't mind going fast," he told me over coffee, "but now I want to make sure I have brakes that work." That's when we began to embrace bonds. He started with a simple 10 percent allocation to diversified bond ETFs. Every year, he increased his bond allocation by 2 percent and when he reached age sixty, he had a 70 percent stock and 30 percent bond portfolio. At age sixty-seven, when he decided to retire and needed a source of reliable income, we arrived at a split of 60 percent stocks and 40 percent bonds. At this point, we built a ladder of individual bonds that would mature year after year, providing predictable income well into retirement, similar to the allocations illustrated in figure CG.3.

That's the essence of fixed income. It's not about beating the market—it's about balancing it. Bonds offer yield, consistency, and peace of mind. They don't sparkle like stocks, but they show up every day—reliable, measured, and often quietly powerful.

The following are several smart, accessible ways to invest in bonds:

- Bond ETFs: Low-cost, diversified, and easy to trade
- Bond Mutual Funds: Professionally managed diversified portfolio of bonds for those seeking simplicity
- Bond Ladders: A structured, elegant way to create steady cash flow and reduce interest rate risk

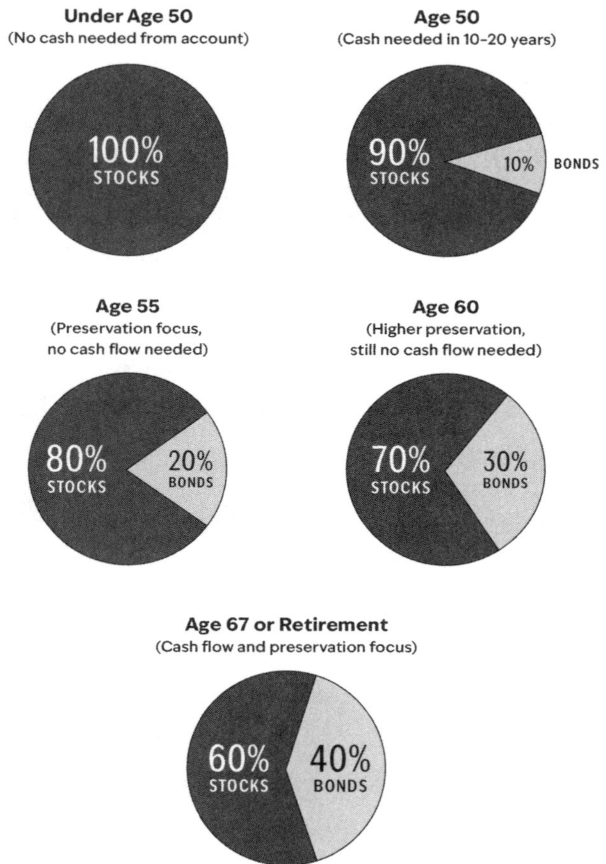

Figure CG.3: These pie charts illustrate age- and risk-based bond allocation. (See Appendixes 7A and 7B for disclosures.)

Historically, from 1950 to 2025, a diversified bond portfolio delivered a 5.2 percent annualized return (see Appendix 5).[3] While bonds don't supercharge your savings, they have historically beaten inflation and added peace of mind for investors. When you decide you need bonds, determine the allocation percentage, which will be based on your need for preservation of capital and cash flow. Once you know how much of your portfolio will go to bonds, you can weigh the risk, benefits, and suitability of bond ETFs, bond mutual funds, or a bond ladder composed of diverse bond types across multiple maturities.

A SURPRISING TRUTH ABOUT PROFESSIONAL BOND MANAGERS

Now here's something that surprises many: Just as most professional stock pickers struggle to beat the index, active bond fund managers often underperform too—despite all their models, teams, and resources.[4]

- Over the past ten years, 98 percent of active managers in Treasury fixed income failed to outperform their benchmark.
- In public investment-grade credit, the failure rate was 82 percent.
- Even in high-yield bonds—where you'd expect more opportunity—79 percent underperformed.

The data paints a clear picture: simple, low-cost fixed income strategies can outperform complex, high-fee ones.

When you are investing in bonds, you must consider default risk (credit risk), time to maturity, and the interest rate you will receive (interest rate risk).

There are various credit rating agencies that evaluate the creditworthiness of bonds. Moody's and Standard & Poor's are the two biggest. A brief primer on ratings follows.

The Standard & Poor's bond ratings range from AAA to D. A bond rated AAA is considered very secure and has a negligible chance of default. A company with a rating of C– has a high probability of default. A rating of D means the company has defaulted on payment of interest or principal. As you go down the credit rating from AAA to AA to A and then to BBB, the risk increases. Anything below BBB is considered high yield (junk bonds) and have a higher chance of defaulting. The higher the credit rating of a bond, the lower the interest it will have to pay. This is logical because higher-rated bonds have lower risk.

In addition to credit risk, individual bonds, bond ETFs, and bond mutual funds also carry interest rate risk. Imagine that you hold a bond with five years to maturity, and it pays 6 percent interest. If the interest rates increase in the economy by 1 percent, and five-year bonds start paying 7 percent interest, then the bond you are holding will be less valuable and it will trade below the par value of $1,000. The case is reversed if the interest in the economy declines and five-year bonds only pays 5 percent—then, your bond will become more valuable and will trade at a premium. We can generalize this as: When interest rates go up, bond prices go down, and when interest rates go down, bond prices go up (see figure CG.4). Interest rates and bond prices are negatively correlated.

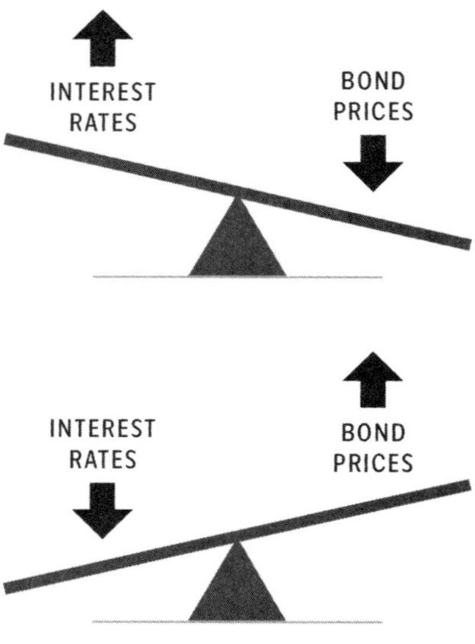

Figure CG.4: When interest rates go up, bond prices go down, and vice versa.

When you are buying bonds or investing in bond ETFs or bond mutual funds, learn about the type of bonds they invest in. What is their credit quality, what is the chance of default, and what is the maturity profile of the bonds. This will help you estimate the potential impact on the price of the ETF or the mutual fund if interest rates in the economy move up or down.

WHAT IS YIELD TO MATURITY (YTM)?

Imagine you buy a $1,000 bond that promises to pay you $50 every year for the next five years and then return your $1,000 when it matures. If you bought that bond for exactly $1,000, your return would be simple: 5 percent per year. But what if you bought the same bond for $950? Now you're not only getting $50 per year—you're also gaining $50 more when the bond matures. Your real return is higher than 5 percent. That higher, more accurate number is called the yield to maturity, or YTM.

The yield to maturity is a bond's true annual return if you hold it until it matures—including both the interest you receive, and any gain or loss based on the price you paid. In simple terms: YTM is the total return you'll earn if you buy a bond today and hold it until the end.
It accounts for:

- The bond's annual interest payments
- The price you paid (which may be more or less than the bond's face value)
- The time left until the bond matures

As an investor in bonds, the YTM is the most important term for you. YTM is your return if you hold the bond until maturity.

BOND LADDERS: PREDICTABLE INCOME AND REDUCED RISK

A bond ladder is a series of individual bonds with staggered maturity dates—think of it as rungs on a ladder. Instead of putting all your money into one bond that matures in ten years, you divide your investment across bonds that mature in one, two, three, four, and five years (or longer). As each bond matures, you reinvest the proceeds into a new bond at the end of the ladder. This approach has the following advantages:

- Steady Income: You receive regular interest payments (called *coupon payments*) from each bond, creating a predictable income stream.
- Reduced Interest Rate Risk: By staggering maturities, you don't lock in all your money at one interest rate. If rates rise, you'll soon be able to reinvest at higher yields.
- Liquidity and Flexibility: A portion of your portfolio matures each year, giving you access to cash without having to sell anything prematurely.

How Have Bonds Performed Historically?

While bonds may not deliver the higher returns of stocks, they've historically provided solid, dependable results—especially when stocks stumble. Over the past seventy-five years bonds have delivered a 5.2 percent return (see Appendix 5).

High-yield (junk) bonds can offer higher returns but come with increased credit risk. Junk bonds or (high yield bonds) are issued by companies that have a higher chance of defaulting. In terms of credit rating, these bonds are rated BB+ or lower by Standard & Poor's. Since these bonds carry a lot more risk, they may not be suitable for most conservative investors.

During periods of stock market turmoil—like the dot-com bust

(2000–2002) or the 2008 financial crisis—bonds often acted as a buffer, preserving capital while equities dropped.

How to Build a Bond Ladder

Creating a bond ladder is easier than you think. Here's a simple five-step process:

1. Decide on the Time Horizon

   Start with your goal. Is this income for the next five years or a twenty-year retirement plan? The longer your ladder, the more stable your income stream.

2. Choose the Rungs (Maturity Years)

   For example, a five-year ladder might include bonds that mature in one, two, three, four, and five years. A ten-year ladder includes maturities from one to ten years.

3. Diversify Across Bond Types

   Depending on your risk appetite and tax bracket, you can consider:

   - Treasuries (safe, government-backed)
   - Municipal bonds (tax-free for many investors)
   - Investment-grade corporate bonds (higher yield, slightly more risk)

4. Invest Equal Amounts (or Adjust for Yield)

   Put equal amounts into each maturity rung. For example, if you have $100,000, you'd invest $20,000 into each year's bond for a five-year ladder.

5. Reinvest Maturing Bonds

   As bonds mature, roll them into new long-term bonds to maintain the ladder and lock in current interest rates.

To explain how a bond ladder can be created I have developed a sample for you. You can go into your brokerage account and easily purchase bonds that align with your goals and risk profile. Alternatively, you can ask your financial representative to create an appropriate bond ladder for you.

The six-year bond ladder shown in table CG.1 uses a balanced mix: 50 percent US Treasuries for safety and 50 percent high-quality corporate bonds (ranging from AAA to BBB) for higher yield.

TABLE CG.1: SIX-YEAR BOND LADDER

Year	Type	Issuer	Coupon	Rating	Amt ($)	Annual Int. ($)
Year 1	Treasury	US Treasury Note	5.00%	AAA	10,000	500
	Corporate	ABC Company Bond	5.70%	BBB	10,000	570
Year 2	Treasury	US Treasury Note	4.80%	AAA	10,000	480
	Corporate	XYZ Company Bond	5.50%	BBB+	10,000	550
Year 3	Treasury	US Treasury Note	4.60%	AAA	10,000	460
	Corporate	ZZ Company	4.70%	AA	10,000	470
Year 4	Treasury	US Treasury Note	4.50%	AAA	10,000	450
	Corporate	XX Company	5.60%	BBB	10,000	560
Year 5	Treasury	US Treasury Note	4.40%	AAA	10,000	440
	Corporate	YY Company	5.25%	BBB+	10,000	525
Year 6	Treasury	US Treasury Note	4.30%	AAA	10,000	430
	Corporate	YXY Company	6.00%	A-	10,000	600

Portfolio Snapshot

- Total investment: $120,000
- Treasuries (AAA): $60,000 | Avg Coupon: ~4.6 percent
- Corporate bonds (A to BBB): $60,000 | Avg Coupon: ~5.6 percent
- Total annual income: ~$6,035
- Average credit rating (corporate): Mix of AA to BBB

A PACKAGED SOLUTION FOR A BOND LADDER

Let's say you're nearing retirement, or just looking for steady, predictable income without the stress of picking individual bonds. You want simplicity, safety, and a way to plan your cash flow year by year. That's where set maturity date self-liquidating bond ETFs come in.

These set maturity bond ETFs are built to act just like a traditional bond ladder, but with the convenience of ETFs. Think of it as a pre-packaged bundle of bonds—hundreds of them—carefully selected to all mature in the same year. For example, when you buy a set maturity bond ETF maturing in 2027, you're essentially buying a slice of a well-diversified portfolio of bonds that all mature by December 2027. Until then, you receive regular interest payments; when the ETF reaches its final maturity, you get your money back, just like a bond (subject to market and credit risk).

Imagine you're building a personal orchard. Instead of planting and caring for each individual tree (bond), someone hands you a crate of saplings that will all bear fruit in exactly one year, another crate for the next year, and so on. Every year, a new group ripens, gives you fruit (interest), and then clears out to make room for fresh planting. That's what a ladder of set maturity bond ETFs feels like—a harvest of income year after year, with very little effort.

Why Set Maturity Bond ETFs Make Bond Laddering Easier

- Simple: Each Bond ETF matures in a fixed year—2026, 2027, 2028, etc.
- Diversified: Each ETF holds dozens or even hundreds of bonds, reducing individual bond credit risk.
- Liquid: Unlike individual bonds, set maturity bond ETFs can be bought or sold on the stock market anytime.
- Predictable: You receive regular income, and the fund matures on a known date.

You can easily build a six-year bond ladder by buying set maturity bond ETFs maturing in 2026, 2027, 2028, 2029, 2030, and 2031. This way, one part of your investment matures each year, returning principal to reinvest or use as income.

Bond ladders are especially useful in retirement or conservative portfolios where *preserving capital and generating income* is more important than chasing high returns. They let you sleep well at night while your money works quietly in the background.

Think of it as an insurance policy for stability—a way to smooth out market ups and downs and avoid surprises, providing peace of mind for LIVING360.

The discussion of bonds, bond ETFs, mutual funds, and fixed-income strategies in this chapter is provided for educational purposes only and does not represent a recommendation or solicitation to buy, sell, or hold any security. All bond investments involve risk, including interest-rate risk, credit risk, reinvestment risk, and inflation risk.

References to products such as set-maturity bond ETFs are intended solely to illustrate the concept of maturity-based, diversified bond investing. These examples do not represent endorsements or recommendations of any specific issuer or product.

7. Alternative Investments: Exploring Opportunities Beyond Traditional Stocks and Bonds

As investors seek to diversify their portfolios and enhance returns, alternative investments have gained traction. These assets fall outside the conventional categories of stocks, bonds, and cash. Common types include private equity, hedge funds, real estate, venture capital, private credit, commodities, art, collectibles, and even newer vehicles like cryptocurrencies. While these alternatives offer potential for enhanced returns and diversification, they also carry distinct risks—and are not suitable for every investor.

Historically, many alternative investments have delivered attractive long-term returns. For example, private equity has outperformed public equities over the last two decades, with annualized returns between 10 and 15 percent, compared to 7–9 percent for the global stock market return.[5] Similarly, private credit has offered stable income streams in the 7–10 percent range, often with less volatility than equities.[6] Hedge funds, while varied in strategy, can offer downside protection and uncorrelated returns—but results can be highly inconsistent. Real estate, particularly in the form of income-generating property or REITs, has been another favored alternative, offering both yield and inflation protection. However, these strategies often come with complex structures, long lock-up periods, and reduced liquidity, which must be carefully considered.

It's important to understand that many alternative investments are restricted to qualified purchasers (QPs)—typically individuals with $5 million or more in investable assets. This high bar exists for a reason: alternatives often require higher risk tolerance, greater sophistication, and the ability to tie up capital for five to ten years or longer. For investors without sufficient liquidity who may need to access their money soon, these strategies can be ill-suited and even harmful if misunderstood.

NEW INVESTMENT PRODUCTS: THE RISE OF INTERVAL FUNDS AND PROTECTIVE ETFs

Financial innovation continues to make previously exclusive investment opportunities more accessible. One such development is the emergence of interval funds, especially in private equity. Historically, investing in private equity required long-term commitments to institutional funds. Now, large private equity managers offer interval funds that allow individual investors to gain exposure to private equity with quarterly liquidity—a game-changer for accessibility. This shift is especially relevant as the number of public companies dropped from eight thousand in 1995 to under four thousand eight hundred by 2021, while private businesses have proliferated.[7]

In parallel, structured ETFs with built-in downside protection—sometimes called "buffer ETFs" or "defined outcome ETFs"—have emerged as tools for risk-averse investors. These ETFs offer limited upside potential in exchange for protection against a percentage of market losses over a specified period (usually twelve months). While they won't outperform in bull markets, they may provide peace of mind during volatile periods, particularly for retirees or conservative investors.

In short, alternative investments offer unique ways to grow and protect wealth, but they demand careful due diligence, an understanding of risk, and sufficient net worth and liquidity. They are not shortcuts—but for the right investor, they can be important tools in building a resilient and diversified portfolio.

8. Real Estate Investing*

Real estate is often considered a pillar of wealth creation because it's a powerful vehicle for both compounding and leverage. If you want to move beyond the linear growth of traditional investments, this combination

* Please refer to Appendix 7D for disclosure.

may offer an accelerated path. Compounding in real estate is the steady growth in your property's value (and rental income, if applicable) building upon itself over time. Leverage is the strategic genius of using borrowed money—like a mortgage—to control a large, valuable asset by only using a small fraction of your own cash. When these two forces are channeled effectively, they create a highly efficient engine that can multiply your net worth and deliver the financial options required for long-term freedom.

To develop an understanding of rental real estate and the power of leverage and rental income, imagine that you buy a condo for $500,000, make a 20 percent down payment, borrow 80 percent at 6 percent interest for thirty years, and rent it for $2,975 per month. If you include HOA fees, taxes and other fees, insurance, maintenance, and vacancy and assume a 3 percent price appreciation, here is your return profile:

- Your total profit at sale after thirty years would be $1.7 million.
- This translates to a cash-on-cash return of 1,646 percent, and
- An internal rate of return (IRR) of 12 percent per year.

Actual real-estate returns vary widely and depend on market conditions. Let's review additional details in figure CG.5, which illustrates some more of the assumptions and risks. Figure CG.6 demonstrates the profit gained after thirty years.

In addition to working hard in our profession, it is imperative that we understand the basics of investing, the power of compounding, and the value of the right level of leverage. We need to invest with discipline in a diversified set of asset classes and not let our biases and emotions control our decisions. To evaluate different scenarios and assumptions, you can use online tools to model your current savings, investment outcomes, and real estate returns. One good online source is www.calculators.net. If you implement these simple, yet powerful ideas, your vision may well become a reality.

PURCHASE

Purchase Price	$500,000
Use Loan?	(•) Yes ( ) No
Down Payment	20 %
Interest Rate	6 %
Loan Term	30 years
Closing Cost	$4,000
Need Repairs?	( ) Yes (•) No

INCOME

		Annual Increase
Monthly Rent	$2,975	4 %
Other Monthly Income	$0	3 %
Vacancy Rate	5 %	
Management Fee	0 %	

RECURRING OPERATING EXPENSES

	Annual	Annual Increase
Property Tax	$5,000	3 %
Total Insurance	$1,000	3 %
HOA Fee	$100	3 %
Maintenance	$1,500	3 %
Other Costs	$300	3 %

SELL

Do you know the sell price?	( ) Yes (•) No	
Value Appreciation	3 %	per year
Holding Length	3	years
Cost to Sell	5 %	

Figure CG.5: This figure provides additional details regarding the purchase and income for a real estate investment.

RESULTS

For the 30 Years Invested

Return (IRR):	**12.00% per year**
Total Profit When Sold:	**$1,711,871.80**
Cash on Cash Returns:	**1,646.03%**
Capitalization Rate:	**5.20%**
Total Rent Income:	$1,902,120.66
Total Mortgage Payments:	$863,352.76
Total Expenses:	$375,845.78
Total Net Operating Income:	$1,526,274.88

First Year Income and Expense

	Monthly	Annual
Income:	$2,975.00	$35,700.00
Mortgage Pay:	$2,398.20	$28,778.43
Vacancy (5%):	$148.75	$1,785.00
Property Tax:	$416.67	$5,000.00
Total Insurance:	$83.33	$1,000.00
HOA Fee:	$8.33	$100.00
Maintenance Cost:	$125.00	$1,500.00
Other Cost:	$25.00	$300.00
Cash Flow:	**$-230.29**	**$-2,763.43**
Net Operating Income (NOI):	$2,167.92	$26,015.00

First Year Expense Breakdown

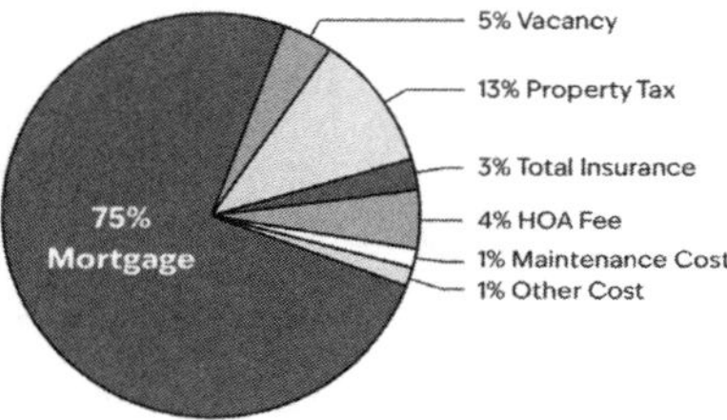

Figure CG.6: After thirty years of investment, the total profit would equal more than $1.7 million.

Real estate can be a powerful tool for wealth creation, but it involves a range of financial, operational, and market risks, and should be approached with careful analysis and professional guidance.[8]

9. Buying a Car: A Practical Approach to Financial Health

Unlike purchasing a home, buying a car is not an investment—it's an expense. A car loses value rapidly, depreciating significantly the moment you drive it off the dealership lot. According to automotive data experts at Edmunds, a new car can lose as much as 20 percent of its value in the first year and roughly 60 percent over the first five years of ownership.[9] This rapid depreciation emphasizes why cars should be viewed primarily as practical tools rather than symbols of wealth or success.

UNDERSTANDING THE TRUE COST OF CAR OWNERSHIP

Beyond the initial purchase price, owning a car entails several ongoing expenses that can substantially impact your finances. These include insurance, fuel, regular maintenance, repairs, and registration fees. AAA reports that in 2023, the average annual cost to own and operate a new car is approximately $10,728, or nearly $900 per month.[10] This cost can increase significantly with luxury vehicles or cars requiring specialized maintenance.

Case Study: Jake's New Car

Jake, a young professional, received a significant promotion at work and celebrated by purchasing a luxury sports car. While the new vehicle temporarily boosted his self-image and initially provided a sense of accomplishment, he quickly realized the financial strain it created. Monthly payments, premium insurance rates, high fuel costs, and expensive maintenance bills began to impact Jake's ability to save and invest. After three years, he traded the car in at a substantial loss. The experience taught Jake a valuable financial lesson: prioritizing practicality over prestige is crucial in car ownership decisions.

PRACTICAL CAR-BUYING STRATEGIES

1. **Buy Used Instead of New:** Buying a reliable used car that's two to three years old can save thousands of dollars and reduce depreciation significantly.
2. **Prioritize Reliability and Fuel Efficiency:** Choosing a vehicle known for reliability and efficiency reduces long-term maintenance and operating costs.
3. **Avoid Extended Loans:** Car dealerships often encourage longer-term loans, but opting for shorter terms (three to four years) reduces overall interest paid and helps you avoid owing more than the car is worth (negative equity).

The Hidden Cost of Luxury Vehicles

Luxury cars come with elevated costs at every turn. Beyond the initial sticker price, maintenance, repairs, tires, and even basic oil changes can be far more expensive. Luxury cars also require premium fuel, further adding to operating expenses. Edmunds estimates the five-year ownership costs of a luxury vehicle can exceed those of an average mid-size sedan by more than $25,000.[11]

Maria's Smart Move

Maria faced a choice between purchasing a new luxury SUV or a practical, lightly used sedan. After considering her long-term financial goals and calculating the costs, Maria opted for the sedan. She saved money each month on her car payments, insurance, and fuel, allowing her to increase her monthly retirement contributions and fund a future home purchase. Maria's decision wasn't flashy, but it was wise—and it significantly improved her financial security and peace of mind.

Make a Wise Choice

Enjoying a nice vehicle isn't inherently wrong if your core financial objectives—such as homeownership, retirement savings, and emergency funds—are already secure. However, if you're still building your financial foundation, prioritize practicality and affordability. Treat your car as a functional tool rather than a status symbol, and you'll be rewarded with greater financial stability and freedom.

10. Investing in Annuities: Good or Bad? It Depends!*

If there's one financial product that sparks heated debates among financial planners and investors, it's the annuity. Walk into a room full of seasoned investors, mention annuities, and you're likely to hear a chorus of conflicting opinions. Some passionately label them as expensive, overly complicated, and inflexible. Others see them as reliable safeguards, offering stable income and peace of mind in an uncertain world. The truth, as with most financial tools, lies somewhere in between.

Think about Michelle, a careful and conservative investor who had built a nest egg over decades of diligent saving. As retirement approached, she faced a common worry: "What if I outlive my savings?" Her family was known for longevity—her mother had just celebrated her ninety-sixth birthday. For someone like Michelle, who prioritized guaranteed income and financial security, annuities offered real value.

Annuities come in different flavors. Each type and product has its

* Please refer to Appendix 7C for a detailed disclosure.

own features and benefits. For example, a fixed annuity is completely different from a variable annuity in terms of cost, growth potential, and complexity. Also, annuities offered by different insurance companies may have different features. It is critical to fully understand an annuity before you commit any funds, because in most cases access to your funds is limited until maturity (during the surrender period).

UNDERSTANDING ANNUITIES: TYPES, BENEFITS, AND FEATURES

1. Fixed Annuities: Stability and Simplicity

These are the simplest of the annuity family—like a dependable old friend who never surprises you. You lend a lump sum of money to an insurance company, and in return, you receive a guaranteed, fixed interest rate for a defined period.

Example: If you invest $100,000 into a three-year fixed annuity at 5 percent interest, you'll earn a predictable $5,000 per year. At the end of the three years, you get your principal back plus earned interest. It's straightforward and reassuring, especially for cautious investors like Michelle who value predictability over growth.

2. Fixed Index Annuities: Controlled Growth with Protection

Think of a fixed index annuity as an escalator that can only go up, never down—but sometimes it moves slower than you'd like. Your returns are linked to a market index like the S&P 500, and you benefit from market growth. However, if the market plunges, your principal remains protected. The catch? Your gains are capped—meaning if the market soars by 20 percent, you might only get a 4–7 percent gain.

This structure could be perfect for Mike. Having lost heavily in the 2008 financial crisis, Mike liked knowing that his principal was safe—even if he had to trade upside potential. But be aware—fixed index annuities are complex products that require careful evaluation of participation rates, caps, and floor rates.

3. Immediate Annuities: A Personal Pension

Immediate annuities function much like a traditional pension. Imagine trading a lump sum of cash today for guaranteed monthly checks for the rest of your life. For example, an investor could choose an immediate annuity, investing $500,000. In return, she could receive around $40,000 annually, guaranteed for life. She could sleep better knowing she had a steady, dependable stream of income no matter what happened in the markets.

Immediate annuities can also be structured for couples through joint-life annuities. While joint-life payments are lower than single-life, they continue for the surviving spouse, providing peace of mind for partners who worry about financial security if they lose their loved one. Once you purchase an immediate annuity, you no longer have your principal. You give your money away for lifetime income. In most cases you can't get your money back.

4. Variable Annuities: Balancing Growth Potential with Guarantees

Variable annuities stand apart from other annuities because they offer investors the chance to actively participate in the financial markets. Some also offer a layer of protection against significant losses. Think of a variable annuity as a hybrid—part investment account, part insurance policy—designed to provide growth potential, tax deferral, and optional guarantees. Variable annuities are most complex among annuity options. Each type of variable annuity offers idiosyncratic investment choices (sub-accounts), varying lifetime income benefits, different downside protection, and very specific early surrender charges.

The key to investing in variable annuities is to fully understand the true and total cost of the potential benefits of the specific product and carefully evaluate whether those costs and benefits fit with your financial security goal.

COMPLEXITY, COST, AND BENEFITS

Imagine you're approaching retirement and have built a substantial nest egg, but every stock market drop leaves you anxious and sleepless. Some variable annuities offer a unique solution: they let you invest actively in market-based options (like mutual-fund-style investments) while providing safeguards that help you sleep soundly at night. One appealing feature is the guaranteed lifetime withdrawal benefit (GLWB), which guarantees a steady stream of income for life, regardless of market performance. Picture this: Even if markets decline significantly, your annuity guarantees you'll still receive a predictable monthly paycheck, protecting you from the fear of outliving your money.

Additionally, some variable annuities include principal protection or death-benefit riders, reassuring you that your loved ones will inherit at least part of your original investment, regardless of what happens in the market. In short, variable annuities provide the flexibility to invest aggressively—potentially increasing your returns—while ensuring you have a financial safety net in place.

Case Study: Linda and Robert's Retirement Dilemma

Imagine Linda and Robert, both nearing retirement at age sixty-two, nervous about the big decision. They had diligently saved, but the 2008 financial crisis, the 2020 COVID-19 deep decline, and the 2022 bear market had left them deeply fearful of stock market volatility. Robert said, "We've worked our whole lives. The last thing we want is to see our retirement funds plummet right when we need them most."

They considered several options, including bonds and fixed annuities. But Linda also wanted growth, concerned about inflation eroding their purchasing power. A variable annuity with a GLWB offered them an ideal compromise. They chose a variable annuity, selecting more aggressive investment options—mostly stocks, partly bonds—along with a lifetime income rider.

Even if the market crashed again, Linda and Robert knew their annuity guaranteed a minimum annual income stream for life, regardless of how their investments performed. Knowing their income was secure, they felt comfortable investing more aggressively, balancing growth and safety. This strategy helped them overcome their fear and participate in market opportunities they might otherwise have missed.

For investors nervous about market volatility, a variable annuity with some type of downside protection can act as a psychological safety net. By securing a guaranteed minimum lifetime income, investors often become more comfortable investing in equities. Without this guarantee, many investors—particularly retirees or those approaching retirement—might remain too cautious, keeping large amounts in low-yield savings accounts or bonds, sacrificing potential growth and risking insufficient retirement income.

THE HIDDEN COSTS: KNOW WHAT YOU PAY

However, these appealing features come at a significant cost. Behind the scenes, variable annuities carry multiple layers of expenses that can quietly eat into your returns year after year. There's the mortality and expense (M&E) charge, usually around 1.25 percent annually, covering the insurance component. Add administrative fees of roughly 0.15–0.50 percent, and investment management fees between 0.50–1.50 percent, depending on your chosen investment options. On top of that, optional riders—like lifetime income guarantees or death-benefit protections—can tack on another 0.75–1.50 percent. Altogether, these fees often amount to 2–4 percent per year, sometimes even more. While that may seem small, over the years, the compounded effect of these fees can significantly reduce your investment growth. Before choosing a variable annuity, always pause, review the fine print carefully, and weigh whether the guarantees justify these expenses (sometimes hidden) in your specific situation.

ANNUITIES: KNOW WHAT YOU'RE GETTING INTO

Annuities aren't inherently good or bad—they're simply a tool. Just like a power saw is perfect for carpentry but dangerous in the wrong hands, annuities can be valuable or damaging depending on your circumstances. Here are the key factors to consider carefully:

1. Fees and Expenses

   Annuities often come with administrative fees, investment management fees, and hefty sales commissions. These costs can significantly impact your returns, so always seek transparency before committing.

2. Liquidity Constraints

   Many annuities have surrender periods, ranging from five to ten years, during which accessing your money early can trigger substantial penalties.

3. Complexity

   Annuities, especially variable and indexed ones, often come with intricate fine print. Be sure to understand exactly what you're buying. Ask plenty of questions, seek independent advice, and never feel pressured into a quick decision.

THE BOTTOM LINE: WHEN DO ANNUITIES MAKE SENSE?

While there is always debate whether annuities are good or bad, in 2024, a record-breaking $434.1 billion was invested in annuities in the US, representing a 13 percent increase from 2023.[12] This marks the third consecutive year of record-high annuity sales. In my experience, annuities can be effective under the right conditions. They can solve the anxiety of potentially outliving your money or offer a guaranteed baseline income to complement other investments. If your priority is guaranteed income and principal protection, an annuity can make sense, provided you've fully understood the terms, fees, and limitations.

But if you're looking primarily for growth, liquidity, and low-cost investing, other strategies might serve you better. As always, your personal financial plan should reflect your unique goals and values, with annuities playing a thoughtful, carefully chosen role if they align with your priorities.

11. Risk Management: Protecting What Truly Matters

Long before formal insurance policies existed, humans found ways to share and reduce risk. Chinese merchants would divide their cargo across multiple ships to prevent total loss from a single shipwreck. In ancient Babylon, the Code of Hammurabi (circa 1750 BCE) outlined agreements that protected merchants from losing their entire investment if their shipment was stolen or lost.

Fast forward to 1347, in Genoa, Italy—the first known formal insurance contract was signed. It was a marine insurance policy, drafted in Latin, guaranteeing compensation for a ship's cargo if lost at sea. That contract laid the foundation for the modern insurance industry—a system built on the timeless idea of sharing risk to reduce individual catastrophe.

LIVING360 requires us to understand what can go wrong in life and have a plan to manage these risks in a manner that will provide financial security at a cost we can afford. Good financial planning involves a mix of these strategies, based on your lifestyle, values, and resources. In the following section, we will review the types of risks you are exposed to and how certain types of insurances can help mitigate it.

LIFE INSURANCE: LOVE IN FINANCIAL FORM

Life insurance is the ultimate act of financial love. If you have children, a spouse, aging parents, or anyone who relies on your income, life insurance is essential. According to the Life Insurance Marketing and Research Association (LIMRA), almost one-in-three families would experience financial hardship within a month of losing their primary breadwinner.[13]

A healthy forty-year-old non-smoker can secure a twenty-year, $1 million term life policy for just $600–900 per year. Wait a decade, and that cost nearly triples.

David and Emily's Gift of Certainty

David, a vibrant thirty-eight-year-old father of two, dismissed life insurance as something "old people talk about." But when his childhood best friend died unexpectedly, leaving behind a wife and baby with nothing but debt, David had a wake-up call. He bought a term policy that would pay off the mortgage, fund college, and cover living expenses if anything ever happened to him. His wife, Emily, described it best: "That policy is our Plan B—for a future we pray we never need, but sleep better knowing we have."

DISABILITY INSURANCE: PROTECTING YOUR INCOME ENGINE

Your income is your greatest financial asset. What happens if illness or injury takes it away? The Social Security Administration reports that one in four workers will face a disabling event lasting more than ninety days before age sixty-seven.[14] Yet most people overlook this risk entirely. Disability insurance can replace 50–70 percent of your income if you're unable to work—enough to cover the essentials and protect your financial progress.

Sarah's Redefinition of Strength

Sarah, a high-powered attorney and triathlete, fractured her spine in a cycling accident. Recovery would take a year. Her firm's disability coverage was minimal. With bills piling up, she burned through savings and began borrowing from retirement accounts. After returning to work, she purchased an individual disability policy. "Strength isn't just surviving the fall," she said. "It's learning how to soften the landing."

LONG-TERM CARE INSURANCE: DIGNITY IN AGING

By age sixty-five, you have a 70 percent chance of needing long-term care.[15] Long-term care insurance is a policy designed to help cover the cost of extended care when you can no longer perform everyday activities on your own, such as bathing, dressing, or eating. It helps pay for services provided in your home, an assisted-living facility, or a nursing home. These policies are meant to protect your savings and provide financial support if illness, injury, or aging leads to the need for ongoing personal or medical care.

Depending on the level of care needed, long-term care can be very expensive. According to Genworth's 2024 cost data for different long-term options:[16]

- Assisted living can cost about $4,500/month
- Nursing home expenses range from $9,000–11,000/month

Medicare does not cover long-term custodial care. Without insurance, families often exhaust savings or burden adult children.

Robert and Linda's Second Chance

Robert and Linda watched helplessly as Robert's mother, once fiercely independent but now suffering from advanced Alzheimer's disease, drained her savings and then her children's to afford quality care. They swore not to let history repeat. At sixty-two, they bought a hybrid life and long-term care policy. "It's not about fearing the future," Linda said. "It's about honoring the life we've worked so hard to build."

HOMEOWNERS INSURANCE: FORTRESS PROTECTION

Your home is your fortress—and one of your biggest investments. Homeowners insurance protects the structure, belongings, and your liability if someone is injured on your property. Common risks include fire, theft, hail, and water damage. Yet many homeowners are underinsured. Rising construction costs means your policy may no longer reflect what it would actually cost to rebuild.

The Patel Family's Night of the Storm

A sudden tornado ripped through the Patels' Kansas neighborhood. Their home's roof was torn off; water damaged everything. Thanks to full replacement cost coverage, they rebuilt. Their neighbor, who'd opted for a cheaper policy years ago, was forced to relocate. "It's not about betting against disaster," Mr. Patel said. "It's about making sure your worst day isn't your last financially secure one."

AUTO INSURANCE: STEERING CLEAR OF FINANCIAL WRECKAGE

The average American driver files an insurance claim every 17.9 years. Auto insurance isn't just required—it's essential for protecting your vehicle and your liability. Automobile insurance protects you financially if your vehicle is damaged, stolen, or involved in an accident.

Auto insurance policies generally include:

- Liability: Covers injury or damage to others

- Collision: Covers damage to your car from an accident
- Comprehensive: Covers theft, fire, floods, or vandalism
- Uninsured motorist: Protects you when others have no insurance coverage

Jamal's College Crash Course

Jamal, a college student on a very tight budget, had an accident that totaled his car. His comprehensive coverage covered a rental and reimbursed the car's full value, allowing him to keep his part-time job and graduate on time. "I didn't just insure my car," he said. "I unknowingly insured my degree."

HEALTH INSURANCE: YOUR SHIELD AGAINST MEDICAL BANKRUPTCY

Medical expenses are the leading cause of bankruptcy in the US. Even a short ER visit or surgery can cost tens of thousands. Health insurance protects your finances while ensuring access to lifesaving care. Health insurance helps pay for medical expenses such as doctor visits, hospital care, prescriptions, and preventive services.

Health insurance plans vary in:

- Deductibles: How much you pay before coverage kicks in
- Out-of-pocket maximums: The most you'll pay in a year as a single person or a family
- Networks: Reimbursement for out-of-network care

Elena's Lifesaving Policy

Elena, a self-employed designer, almost skipped coverage one year. But her annual checkup revealed early-stage cancer. Her ACA marketplace plan covered nearly $45,000 in treatment costs. Today, she's in remission. "That monthly premium saved my life—literally and financially."

UMBRELLA INSURANCE: THE FINAL LAYER OF PEACE OF MIND

Umbrella insurance provides extra liability protection beyond the limits of your home, auto, or other insurance policies. It helps cover large claims or lawsuits, protecting your income and assets from unexpected financial loss. Umbrella insurance adds $1 million or more of extra liability coverage on top of your auto and home insurance. It kicks in when your primary policy limits are exceeded. It's affordable—often $250–400/year—and protects your assets from lawsuits, medical claims, or legal judgments.

The Jones Family's Backyard Surprise

At their son's birthday party, a guest tripped on a garden hose and suffered a spinal injury. The lawsuit quickly surpassed their homeowners' coverage. Their $1 million umbrella policy absorbed the excess. "We nearly lost everything due to an unfortunate accident over a hose," Mrs. Jones later said. "That umbrella policy saved our financial future."

> Risk is a fact of life. Insurance isn't just about avoiding loss—it's about protecting what matters most: your family, your freedom, your future. It's not the cost of fear; it's the price of responsibility.

12. My Ten Investment Principles

1. **If Starting Young, Go All-In (on Stocks)**

   If you're young and don't need the money for at least a decade, consider investing 100 percent in stocks. Stocks historically offer the highest long-term returns. You can add bonds later as you age and your need for stability increases.

2. **Don't Try to Time the Market**

   Trying to jump in and out of the market sounds smart, but the odds are against you. From July 1,1995 to June 30, 2025, the S&P 500 returned 8.4 percent annually (price return). If you missed just the ten best days? Your return drops to 5.26 percent. Miss the thirty best days? A dismal 2.11 percent, which is less than the inflation during the same period.[17]

3. **Let Compounding Work Its Magic**

   The earlier you start, the more time your money has to grow. Regular contributions and compounding over decades create exponential wealth.

4. **Max Out Retirement Accounts**

   Maximize contributions to tax-deferred accounts like 401(k)s and IRAs. By contributing to the retirement accounts, you reduce your taxable income today and let your money grow tax-free until retirement. Your future self will thank you.

5. **Control What You Can: Costs and Taxes**

   You can't control the market, but you can control costs. Consider using low-cost investment options and avoiding frequent trading. A long-term investment strategy not only reduces costs but minimizes capital gains taxes.

6. **Rebalance Intelligently**

   Rebalancing means realigning your portfolio back to your original asset allocation. You can do this annually—by buying more of what has lagged. It's a disciplined way to buy low and sell high.

7. **Invest in What You Understand**

   Avoid complexity. Prioritize index funds, ETFs, or mutual funds unless you deeply understand a business or sector. Remember Buffett's wisdom: "Never invest in a business you cannot understand."

8. **Diversify Across Asset Classes**

   Don't put all your eggs in one basket. Spread your investments across stocks, bonds, international markets, real estate, and even a small allocation to commodities or cash.

9. **Know Your Cash Flow and Always Have a Safety Net**

   Know how much money comes in and where it goes. Maintain an emergency fund. If you have a stable income, two to three months' expenses in cash may suffice, especially if you have access to a HELOC or credit. Certificates of deposit (CDs) can also serve this purpose in a pinch.

10. **Master Your Emotions**

    The biggest threat to your financial success? You. Fear, greed, envy, and pride can derail even the best strategy. Market chaos is normal. Recessions, booms, bubbles, and breakthroughs are part of the journey. Stay calm, stay humble, stay focused, stay invested.

APPENDIX 1

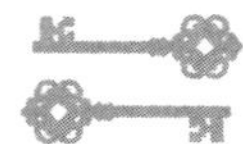

My LIVING360 Compass and Grid

The following is a self-reflection survey to see how balanced and fulfilled your life really is. Answer to what extent you agree with the following statements.

PART 1: KNOW YOURSELF

1. I have reflected on religion and faith (or lack of it) and can respect both my own beliefs and those of others.

   Answer: Yes / Somewhat / No

2. I understand where my political views come from and why others might think differently.

   Answer: Yes / Somewhat / No

3. I have thought about free will and how much control we really have over our choices.

   Answer: Yes / Somewhat / No

4. I understand how genetics and biology influence health, personality, and opportunity.

   Answer: Yes / Somewhat / No

5. I know that my thinking (like everyone's) is shaped by biases and blind spots.

   Answer: Yes / Somewhat / No

PART 2: KNOW THE WORLD

1. I see how history, politics, science, and culture have shaped the world I live in today.

   Answer: Yes / Somewhat / No

2. I believe life for most humans has improved in the last fifty years (less war, poverty, and hunger).

   Answer: Yes / Somewhat / No

3. I recognize the risks we face (climate change, pandemics, nuclear conflict) but also human creativity in solving problems.

   Answer: Yes / Somewhat / No

4. I pay attention to new technologies like AI and think about how they may affect my work and life.

   Answer: Yes / Somewhat / No

5. I stay aware of major political and economic changes that could impact my home, work, and community.

   Answer: Yes / Somewhat / No

PART 3: KNOW YOUR PURPOSE

1. I have at least one person in my life I can trust fully and share anything with.

   Answer: Yes / Somewhat / No

2. I have at least three close people in my life who I connect with often and who would be there if I needed them.

   Answer: Yes / Somewhat / No

3. I make time for people I care about, listen deeply, and offer real support.

   Answer: Yes / Somewhat / No

4. I regularly reflect on what's good in my life and practice gratitude.

   Answer: Yes / Somewhat / No

5. I take care of myself—healthy weight, good sleep, regular exercise, and some spiritual or community activity.

   Answer: Yes / Somewhat / No

PART 4: BUILD FINANCIAL SECURITY

1. I know my income, expenses, net worth, and credit score, and I feel I'm on track financially.

   Answer: Yes / Somewhat / No

2. I save regularly, maximize retirement accounts, and invest with discipline based on my goals.

   Answer: Yes / Somewhat / No

3. I own my home (or have a clear plan to).

   Answer: Yes / Somewhat / No

4. I believe I'll have enough savings to fund the lifestyle I want in retirement.

   Answer: Yes / Somewhat / No

5. I have thought carefully about risks (illness, disability, long-term care, lawsuits) and use insurance or planning to protect myself.

   Answer: Yes / Somewhat / No

SCORING

- Each **Yes = 2 points, Somewhat = 1 point, No = 0 points.**
- Maximum **10 points per part, 40 points total**.
- Plot your scores on the **LIVING360 Compass** (see figure 0.6) to see how balanced your life is. Transparent bars are left open for you to write your score directly on the chart—a visual snapshot of where you shine and where growth is calling.

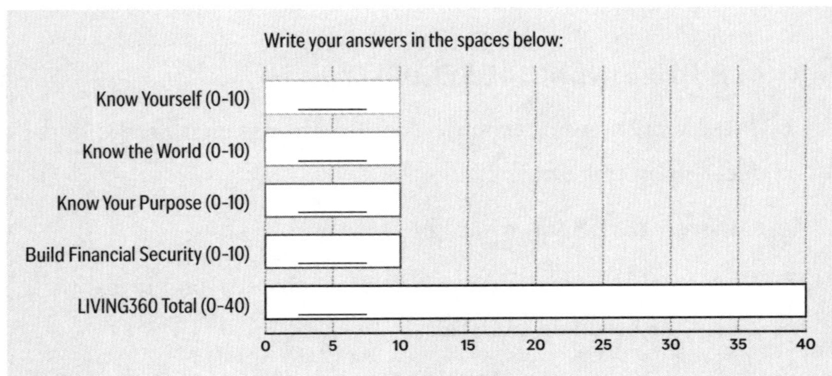

Figure 0.6: The LIVING360 Compass scorecard helps you determine where you are on your journey to LIVING360.

The Compass you just completed isn't about judgment—it's about awareness. Every "Yes," "Somewhat," and "No" is a clue to where you can focus your energy and attention.

Go back to the introduction of the book and copy your old Compass score from figure 0.6. Write your new score from the earlier page. Compare your scores in table A1.1 for each of the four points on your LIVING360 Compass. The difference between the old and new is you opening doors and creating windows in your concrete box. High scores represent more light and greater understanding and financial security.

TABLE A1.1: THE LIVING360 COMPASS SCORES

Compass Dimension	Old Score	New Score
Know Yourself		
Know the World		
Know Your Purpose		
Build Financial Security		
LIVING360 Total (0-40)		

THE LIVING360 GRID

We are now starting the LIVING360 Grid. On the next page, walk through each quadrant slowly, marking the descriptions on figure 0.4 that truly reflect your life today—be honest. The quadrant with the most checks is your current home on the grid.

And then, pause. Feel the weight of where you are now . . . and the pull of where you want to be.

THE LIVING360 GRID

Quadrant II

- ☐ I have significant assets and investments.
- ☐ I earn strong income from my career or business.
- ☐ I focus heavily on luxury, status, recognition, and success.
- ☐ I see my professional success as my identity.
- ☐ I approach relationships with limited emotions and maintain distance.
- ☐ I spend minimal time in self-reflection.
- ☐ I sometimes feel an inner void despite my success.
- ☐ I have low interest in global issues or learning new ideas.
- ☐ I maintain a work-dominated schedule.
- ☐ I seek fulfillment through consumption or achievement.

Count and Enter Total Checked Boxes in Quadrant II = ______

Quadrant I

- ☐ I have a strong retirement and investment plan.
- ☐ I consistently save and maintain surplus income.
- ☐ I have a clear life purpose and align my actions with it.
- ☐ I practice gratitude and emotional balance.
- ☐ I have deep, supportive relationships with family and friends.
- ☐ I stay curious and informed about the world.
- ☐ I actively give back to society.
- ☐ I balance work, leisure, and rest.
- ☐ I prioritize lifelong learning and growth.
- ☐ I make thoughtful decisions and try my best to maintain objectivity.

Count and Enter Total Checked Boxes in Quadrant I = ______

Quadrant III

- ☐ I live paycheck to paycheck.
- ☐ I carry persistent debt without a repayment plan.
- ☐ I lack emergency savings.
- ☐ I have no long-term financial plan.
- ☐ I lack a reliable support network.
- ☐ I feel unclear about my life purpose.
- ☐ I experience high stress and frustration.
- ☐ I react impulsively to life challenges.
- ☐ I have low awareness of new opportunities.
- ☐ I often feel stuck or left behind.

Count and Enter Total Checked Boxes in Quadrant III = ______

Quadrant IV

- ☐ I experience income instability or low earnings.
- ☐ I have limited savings or investments.
- ☐ I feel concern about retirement.
- ☐ I value purpose over possessions.
- ☐ I nurture deep, meaningful relationships.
- ☐ I am active in my community.
- ☐ I practice gratitude and mindfulness.
- ☐ I value learning, reflection, and self-awareness.
- ☐ I live a simple lifestyle, but money is a concern.
- ☐ I live in a rental apartment and worry about making rent.

Count and Enter Total Checked Boxes in Quadrant IV = ______

Figure 0.4: The LIVING360 Grid reveals where you are today and where you would like to be in the future.

Place yourself in the area with the most check boxes in the following grid. You may find that there are two or three areas with a similar number of checks, which indicates the balance or tension in your life today. While the dominant quadrant is important to understand your assessment of your thinking and life circumstances, the scores in other quadrants also reveal important insights. The following chart reveals what each area means and where you are on the LIVING360 Grid.

THE LIVING360 GRID

High Wealth / Medium / Low Wealth (vertical axis); Low Wisdom / Medium / High Wisdom (horizontal axis)

Quadrant II

Prosperity Without Peace

On the outside, you look successful. The bank account is full, the resume polished, the lifestyle enviable. But inside, something is missing. Relationships feel shallow, purpose feels thin, and the question lingers: *Is this all there is?* Consider the executive or a successful business owner who "has it all" but lies awake at night, haunted by loneliness and unspoken regret.

From the Previous Page, Count and Enter Total Checked Boxes in Quadrant II = ______

Quadrant I

Total Wealth: LIVING360

This is the destination, the goal, of LIVING360. Here, financial security is not a burden but a foundation. Relationships are rich, purpose is clear, and life feels whole. Think of the person who has enough, loves deeply, and wakes up each day with both security and meaning.

From the Previous Page, Count and Enter Total Checked Boxes in Quadrant I = ______

Quadrant III

Surviving, Not Thriving

Life feels like a constant uphill struggle. Bills press in, worries pile up, and deeper meaning feels out of reach. Survival takes center stage, leaving little space for reflection. Think of the young couple working two jobs just to keep the lights on—exhausted and anxious but still dreaming of a freer tomorrow.

From the Previous Page, Count and Enter Total Checked Boxes in Quadrant III = ______

Quadrant IV

Stifled Enlightenment

You've built a rich inner life. You read, reflect, perhaps even meditate. You know who you are, but you lack the financial security to fully live your vision. Consider the passionate artist whose work touches hearts but whose empty bank account limits the life they want to create.

From the Previous Page, Count and Enter Total Checked Boxes in Quadrant IV = ______

You can compare the new grid placement and quadrant scores to the location and scores at the start of this journey. *The Wisdom and Wealth Solution* is your blueprint to LIVING360. You can also visit www.wisdomandwealthsolution.com to complete the LIVING360 Compass and Grid exercises and access all the additional resources to enhance your life experience.

APPENDIX 2

Four-Month Gratitude Tracker

The next four pages have been left blank for you to document the implementation of your plan to enhance your life experience. Every week, update your progress. You may write whatever is important. You might include two to four good things for which you are grateful. These can be small events; they certainly do not have to be very significant. You can also list how you appreciated others, celebrated, shared, or noticed what was good.

MONTH ONE

Week 1

- Grateful for: ______
- Grateful for: ______
- Celebrated: ______
- Noticed: ______
- Appreciated: ______

Week 2

- Grateful for: ______
- Grateful for: ______
- Celebrated: ______
- Noticed: ______
- Appreciated: ______

Week 3

- Grateful for: ______
- Grateful for: ______
- Celebrated: ______
- Noticed: ______
- Appreciated: ______

Week 4

- Grateful for: ______
- Grateful for: ______
- Celebrated: ______
- Noticed: ______
- Appreciated: ______

MONTH TWO

Week 1

- Grateful for: ______________________
- Grateful for: ______________________
- Celebrated: ______________________
- Noticed: ______________________
- Appreciated: ______________________

Week 2

- Grateful for: ______________________
- Grateful for: ______________________
- Celebrated: ______________________
- Noticed: ______________________
- Appreciated: ______________________

Week 3

- Grateful for: ______________________
- Grateful for: ______________________
- Celebrated: ______________________
- Noticed: ______________________
- Appreciated: ______________________

Week 4

- Grateful for: ______________________
- Grateful for: ______________________
- Celebrated: ______________________
- Noticed: ______________________
- Appreciated: ______________________

MONTH THREE

Week 1

- Grateful for: ____________________
- Grateful for: ____________________
- Celebrated: ____________________
- Noticed: ____________________
- Appreciated: ____________________

Week 2

- Grateful for: ____________________
- Grateful for: ____________________
- Celebrated: ____________________
- Noticed: ____________________
- Appreciated: ____________________

Week 3

- Grateful for: ____________________
- Grateful for: ____________________
- Celebrated: ____________________
- Noticed: ____________________
- Appreciated: ____________________

Week 4

- Grateful for: ____________________
- Grateful for: ____________________
- Celebrated: ____________________
- Noticed: ____________________
- Appreciated: ____________________

MONTH FOUR

Week 1

- Grateful for: ____________________
- Grateful for: ____________________
- Celebrated: ____________________
- Noticed: ____________________
- Appreciated: ____________________

Week 2

- Grateful for: ____________________
- Grateful for: ____________________
- Celebrated: ____________________
- Noticed: ____________________
- Appreciated: ____________________

Week 3

- Grateful for: ____________________
- Grateful for: ____________________
- Celebrated: ____________________
- Noticed: ____________________
- Appreciated: ____________________

Week 4

- Grateful for: ____________________
- Grateful for: ____________________
- Celebrated: ____________________
- Noticed: ____________________
- Appreciated: ____________________

Sustained gratitude alters not the conditions of your life, but the way you experience it. After four months of reflecting on what is good and worthy of thanks, happiness becomes less an object of pursuit and more an act of recognition. This shift is the beginning of a happier life—and the essence of LIVING360.

APPENDIX 3

Personal Cash Flow Statement

Income | Amount ($)

Salary/Wages (net): $ _______

Business Income: $ _______

Rental Income: $ _______

Investment Income: $ _______

Other Income: $ _______

Total Income: $ _______

Expenses | Amount ($)

Housing: $ _______

Food & Groceries: $ _______

Transportation: $ _______

Health Care & Insurance: $ _____

Personal & Household: $ _______

Debt Payments: $ _______

Entertainment: $ _______

Education: $ _______

Charitable Donations: $ _______

Miscellaneous: $ _______

Total Expenses: $ _______

Net Cash Flow:

Total Income ($________) - Total Expenses ($________) = $________

Positive Cash Flow: surplus for savings/investing
Negative Cash Flow: reduce expenses/increase income

Example:
Income: $8,000 | Expenses: $6,500 | **Net Cash Flow: $1,500**
(surplus available)

This simplified statement helps you to clearly see financial inflows and outflows, facilitating better budgeting, savings, and long-term financial planning.

APPENDIX 4

Personal Net Worth Statement (as of ________)

Assets (What You Own)

Cash & Checking Accounts: $ _______

Savings Accounts: $ _______

Certificates of Deposit (CDs): $ _______

Retirement Accounts [401(k), IRA]: $ _______

Taxable Investment Accounts
(Stocks, Mutual Funds, ETFs, Bonds) _______

Primary Residence (Market Value): $ _______

Other Real Estate: $ _______

Vehicles: $ _______

Jewelry, Art & Collectibles: $ _______

Home Furnishings: $ _______

Business Interests: $ _______

Life Insurance (Cash Value): $ _______

Miscellaneous Assets: $ _______

Total Assets: $ _______

Liabilities (What You Owe)

Mortgage(s): $ _______

Home Equity Loans: $ _______

Credit Card Debt: $ _______

Personal Loans: $ _______

Auto Loans: $ _______

Student Loans: $ _______

Outstanding Taxes: $ _______

Medical Bills: $ _______

Other Debts: $ _______

Total Liabilities: $_______

Net Worth:

Total Assets ($_______) - Total Liabilities ($_______) = $_______

Positive Net Worth: financially healthy

Negative Net Worth: immediate attention needed

APPENDIX 5

Historical Returns

Time, diversification and the volatility of returns GTM | U.S. | 57

Range of stock, bond and blended total returns

Annual total returns, 1950 - 2025

	Annual avg. total return	Growth of $100,000 over 20 years
Stocks	11.7%	$908,783
Bonds	5.2%	$277,814
60/40 portfolio	9.4%	$606,792

Source: Bloomberg, FactSet, Federal Reserve, Standard & Poor's, Strategas/Ibbotson, J.P. Morgan Asset Management.
Returns shown are based on calendar year returns from 1950 to 2025. Stocks: S&P 500; Bonds: Strategas/Ibbotson for periods prior to 1976 and the Bloomberg U.S. Aggregate thereafter. Growth of $100,000 is based on annual average total returns from 1950 to 2025.
Guide to the Markets – U.S. Data are as of December 31, 2025.

J.P.Morgan
ASSET MANAGEMENT

Figure A5.1: Time, Diversification, and Volatility of Returns[1]

APPENDIX 6

Choosing a Financial Advisor

Investing is not as mysterious as it may seem. With a few hours of study, anyone can learn the basics of ETFs, mutual funds, and portfolio diversification. Most investors can easily set up and manage their own accounts in an employer retirement plan or brokerage platform.

However, wealth management goes beyond picking investments; it's about integrating your money, goals, and life decisions. A qualified financial advisor can bring professional insight and structure to that process, helping you navigate the complexities of LIVING360, the harmony between wisdom and wealth.

The Value of Professional Advice

A good financial advisor can help you develop a clear financial roadmap, provide accountability, and allow you to focus your time and energy on the things you value most. While some investors enjoy managing their own portfolio, others find it stressful or time-consuming.

Having a trustworthy advisor can reduce the emotional burden of decision making and help you maintain discipline through market ups and downs.

Vanguard Research, in its widely cited paper "Putting a Value on Your Value: Quantifying Vanguard Adviser's Alpha," estimates that a skilled financial advisor can potentially add about 3 percent in net returns over time, depending on the client's situation, goals, and implementation.[1] This "adviser's alpha" isn't a guaranteed or annual number; rather, it reflects the cumulative benefit of sound financial behavior, planning discipline, and tax-efficient implementation.

According to Vanguard's analysis, the primary drivers of this potential value include:

- Behavioral coaching: Helping clients stay the course during volatility rather than making emotional decisions
- Cost-effective implementation: Managing costs and emphasizing tax efficiency
- Asset location: Placing investments in the most tax-advantageous accounts
- Rebalancing discipline: Periodically realigning portfolios to maintain the intended risk profile

Finding the right financial professional can feel daunting, but you can make it easier by doing due diligence and accessing the right resources. In the following section, I have listed a few ideas to help you evaluate and choose an advisor.

- Check Credentials and Background

  Every investment adviser representative and registered representative must pass regulatory exams and disclose past disciplinary or financial issues. You can verify any advisor's record through

FINRA's BrokerCheck (for broker-dealers) or the SEC's Investment Adviser Public Disclosure (IAPD) database for investment advisors. Many investment professionals are associated with both types of investment firms, and either site will point you to the other one as needed. These websites are free and publicly accessible. Some of this information may be found on form CRS and/or form ADV part 3.

- Understand How They're Compensated

  Broker-dealers typically earn commissions per transaction, while investment advisers usually charge an asset-based or flat fee. The best structure depends on your involvement, frequency of trades, and service needs. Investment advisers often manage assets on a *discretionary* basis (they can trade without prior approval within agreed parameters), whereas brokers must obtain consent before executing trades. High investment costs and fees can be a drag on your portfolio and lower your net returns. Always ask if you can get a discount on fees.

- Look for Professional Designations

  The Certified Financial Planner® (CFP®) credential signifies comprehensive training, exam completion, and adherence to fiduciary and ethical standards set by the CFP Board of Standards. CFP professionals are accountable to their firm, regulators, and the CFP Board itself.

- Use Official Resources

  The US Securities and Exchange Commission (SEC) provides an excellent overview titled "Investor Bulletin: How to Select an Investment Professional" on its official website: https://www.investor.gov/introduction-investing/general-resources/news-alerts/alerts-bulletins/investor-bulletins/investor-0.

Why Consider a Financial Advisor?

A qualified advisor does much more than manage investments. They can help you:

- Plan for Retirement: Create a sustainable income strategy for your later years
- Manage Taxes: Coordinate investment and withdrawal strategies to minimize tax drag
- Control Risk: Evaluate insurance, debt, and portfolio exposure to unexpected events
- Find Peace of Mind: Build confidence in your financial plan and avoid reactive decisions

Ultimately, whether you choose to manage your investments independently or work with a professional, the key is to stay intentional and ensure that you follow a disciplined approach, investing your savings based on your goals and risk profile. Financial security comes from understanding your money, investing consistently, and aligning your resources with your values.

APPENDIX 7

Disclosures

Appendix 7A: Important Regulatory and Compliance Disclosure

This book, *The Wisdom and Wealth Solution*, is written for educational, philosophical, and informational purposes only. It explores concepts at the intersection of financial literacy, philosophy, behavioral psychology, and personal well-being. Nothing contained in this book constitutes investment, legal, tax, or accounting advice, nor should it be construed as a solicitation or offer to buy or sell any security or to engage in any investment strategy or transaction.

The views expressed are solely those of the author, in his individual capacity, and do not necessarily represent the views or positions of his investment adviser firm, broker-dealer, or any affiliated organization.

Throughout this book, various anecdotes, case studies, and "client stories" are used to illustrate principles of personal finance and human behavior. Many of these are composite narratives—drawn from years of professional experience and synthesized from multiple real-world situations. Names, professions, and circumstances have been changed to preserve confidentiality and emphasize lessons rather than individual outcomes. Any resemblance to specific persons or events is coincidental. Numerical examples (returns, account balances, growth rates, etc.), as well as statements of satisfaction or outcome, are for illustrative purposes only and are not representative of actual results.

ON MENTION OF SPECIFIC SECURITIES, FUNDS, OR INDICES

Mentions of investment vehicles such as exchange-traded funds (ETFs), mutual funds, market indices (e.g., S&P 500, Nasdaq 100), or specific securities are provided solely as examples to demonstrate concepts such as diversification, asset allocation, compounding, market behavior, cost efficiency, or risk management. These mentions are not recommendations to buy, sell, or hold any security. Actual investment decisions should be made in consultation with a qualified professional who understands the reader's individual circumstances, objectives, and risk tolerance. Historical performance figures (e.g., for the S&P 500 index, bonds, or real estate) are based on publicly available data but are provided for illustration only. Economic conditions, geopolitics, market volatility, inflation, interest rates, and policy changes can all affect investment outcomes.

Certain products discussed in this text also involve insurance and annuity contracts. Insurance policies and especially annuities are complex financial products, with long lock-up periods, surrender charges, and high fees. Please consult with an appropriately licensed insurance agent and/or tax and investment professional for more information.

The author, publisher, and affiliated firms receive no direct compensation from mentioning any of these products or companies. All examples are used solely to demonstrate structure, characteristics, fees, diversification concepts, or historical context and do not constitute investment advice.

NO PERFORMANCE GUARANTEES OR RECOMMENDATIONS

Illustrations and calculations are for educational purposes only. You and your financial professionals should independently review any information prior to making investment decisions. Past performance is not indicative of future results, and no representation or warranty is made regarding future market behavior, rates of return, or outcomes. All investments involve risk, including the potential loss of principal. Any historical data, including illustrations of index returns as proxies for theoretical investment portfolios, or long-term averages are presented solely for educational illustration.

No statement in this book should be interpreted as a guarantee, projection, or promise of any specific financial outcome. Readers should not assume that any strategy, method, or investment mentioned will be profitable or suitable for them. Any investment in real estate carries its own set of risks due to leverage, illiquidity, taxes, local laws, tax treatment, etc. Always consult a real estate professional and your financial advisor before any real estate transaction. Any discussion about real estate in the book is to demonstrate the long-term value of real estate investment and purchase of a primary residence. It is not a recommendation.

REGULATORY STANDING AND COMPLIANCE

The author is a principal and investment adviser representative of an SEC-registered investment adviser. He is also principal and a registered representative of a FINRA-member broker-dealer. Nothing in this publication is written for advertising or a solicitation for clients of any investment advisory firm or broker-dealer. The views herein are solely of the author.

NO CLIENT TESTIMONIALS OR ENDORSEMENTS

The book does not contain, and should not be construed as containing, testimonials or endorsements from current or former clients. All depictions of client situations are generalized composites meant to illustrate concepts, not to promote advisory or broker-dealer services.

READER RESPONSIBILITY

Readers are encouraged to conduct independent research and to consult their own financial, legal, and tax professionals before implementing any strategy discussed herein. Examples and stories are intended to promote reflection and awareness—not to prescribe specific investment actions.

TAX AND FEE CONSIDERATIONS

Investment results are reduced by management fees, transaction costs, and taxes. Mutual funds, ETFs, and managed portfolios charge annual expenses that reduce returns. Investors may also incur brokerage commissions and bid–ask spreads.

Because tax treatment varies by account type (taxable accounts, IRAs, 401(k)s, etc.), jurisdiction, and individual circumstances, readers should consult qualified tax professionals for personalized guidance. Tax laws are subject to change, and future legislation may materially alter investment outcomes.

Use of Indices and Benchmarks: Benchmarks such as the S&P 500®, Nasdaq 100®, Dow Jones Industrial Average®, MSCI EAFE®, and Bloomberg US Aggregate Bond Index® are referenced solely for general comparison and educational discussion. Indices are unmanaged, cannot be directly invested in, and do not include transaction costs, management fees, or expenses. Mentioning these indices does not imply that any investment or strategy will achieve similar or comparable results.

TRADEMARK AND OWNERSHIP NOTICE

All company names, fund names, trademarks, and ticker symbols appearing in this book are the exclusive property of their respective issuers and owners (including but not limited to Morningstar, Vanguard, BlackRock iShares, Schwab, and State Street SPDR).

Certified Financial Planner Board of Standards Center for Financial Planning, Inc. owns and licenses the certification marks CFP®, CERTIFIED FINANCIAL PLANNER®, and CFP® (with plaque design) in the United States to Certified Financial Planner Board of Standards, Inc., which authorizes individuals who successfully complete the organization's initial and ongoing certification requirements to use the certification marks. Their inclusion is for identification and educational purposes only and does not imply sponsorship, endorsement, or affiliation with the author, publisher, or affiliated entities.

Appendix 7B: Investment Disclosure

The discussions, examples, charts, and tables in this book that reference mutual funds, exchange-traded funds (ETFs), index funds, individual stocks, bonds, commodities, alternative investments, real estate, or other investment products are presented solely for educational and illustrative purposes.

They are intended to explain broad financial principles such as diversification, asset allocation, compounding, market behavior, and cost efficiency—not to recommend, endorse, or solicit investment in any particular fund, security, company, or strategy.

NO OFFER, SOLICITATION, OR RECOMMENDATION

The inclusion of any specific security, company, issuer, product name, or ticker symbol (for example, SPDR S&P 500 ETF Trust [SPY], Vanguard S&P 500 ETF [VOO], etc.), is not a recommendation to buy, sell, or hold that investment.

The author, publisher, and affiliated firms receive no compensation or economic benefit from mentioning any of these products or companies.

All examples are used solely to demonstrate structure, characteristics, fees, diversification concepts, or historical context and do not constitute investment advice.

No portion of this book constitutes an offer to sell securities, a solicitation of an offer to buy securities, or a solicitation of clients for investment-advisory, brokerage, or insurance services.

PAST PERFORMANCE AND HYPOTHETICAL ILLUSTRATIONS

Any reference to past performance, long-term averages, or comparative returns of securities, indices, or asset classes is strictly historical.

Past performance does not guarantee future results, and all investments involve the risk of loss, including the potential loss of principal.

Charts, tables, growth illustrations, and compounding examples may include hypothetical, backtested, or simulated performance data created solely to demonstrate financial principles. Such illustrations are inherently limited, do not reflect actual trading or market conditions, and should not be interpreted as indicative of future or achievable results.

INVESTMENT AND MARKET RISKS

All forms of investing carry risk. Among them:

- Stocks and Equity ETFs: Subject to market volatility, business risk, and valuation risk. Prices can fluctuate widely due to company performance, interest rates, or investor sentiment.
- Bonds and Fixed Income: Exposed to interest-rate risk, credit risk, call risk, and inflation risk. Bond values typically fall when interest rates rise.
- International and Emerging Markets: Carry additional risks including currency fluctuations, political instability, liquidity issues, and differences in accounting standards.

- Alternative Investments (Private Equity, Hedge Funds, Private Credit, Real Estate, Commodities, Venture Capital): often speculative, illiquid, and may employ leverage or complex strategies that amplify gains and losses. Such investments are generally suitable only for qualified or accredited investors.
- Commodities and Precious Metals: Highly volatile and influenced by global supply-demand dynamics, geopolitical events, and macroeconomic trends.
- Real Estate Investments: Subject to property-value fluctuations, leverage risk, tenant and liquidity risk, and local market conditions.

Diversification and asset allocation do not ensure profit or protect against loss in declining markets. In some periods, a diversified portfolio may underperform more concentrated or narrowly focused investments, especially during strong market rallies or sector-specific advances. Asset allocation is a framework for managing risk, not a guarantee of superior performance or capital preservation.

TAX AND FEE CONSIDERATIONS

Investment results are reduced by management fees, transaction costs, and taxes.

Mutual funds, ETFs, and managed portfolios charge annual expenses that reduce returns. Investors may also incur brokerage commissions and bid–ask spreads.

Because tax treatment varies by account type (taxable accounts, IRAs, 401(k)s, etc.), jurisdiction, and individual circumstances, readers should consult qualified tax professionals for personalized guidance.

Tax laws are subject to change, and future legislation may materially alter investment outcomes.

USE OF INDICES AND BENCHMARKS

Benchmarks such as the S&P 500®, Nasdaq 100®, Dow Jones Industrial Average®, MSCI EAFE®, and Bloomberg US Aggregate Bond Index® are referenced solely for general comparison and educational discussion.

Indices are unmanaged, cannot be directly invested in, and do not include transaction costs, management fees, or expenses.

Mentioning these indices does not imply that any investment or strategy will achieve similar or comparable results.

TRADEMARK AND OWNERSHIP NOTICE

All company names, fund names, trademarks, and ticker symbols appearing in this book are the exclusive property of their respective issuers and owners (including but not limited to Vanguard, Fidelity, BlackRock iShares, Schwab, PIMCO, T. Rowe Price, American Funds, and State Street SPDR).

Their inclusion is for identification and educational purposes only and does not imply sponsorship, endorsement, or affiliation with the author, publisher, or affiliated entities.

REGULATORY STATUS AND PROFESSIONAL RESPONSIBILITY

The author is both a registered investment advisor representative (IAR) of an SEC-registered investment adviser and a registered representative of a FINRA-member broker-dealer.

This book has been prepared in a personal capacity for general financial education and does not constitute advertising, performance marketing, or client solicitation.

All material has been created in good faith and reviewed for accuracy and compliance; however, no warranty is made as to completeness, timeliness, or ongoing accuracy. Readers should rely only on professional advice customized to their financial circumstances before acting on any idea discussed.

READER DUE DILIGENCE

Before investing, investors should thoroughly review official offering documents, including prospectuses, fact sheets, statements of additional information (SAIs), private-placement memoranda, Form ADV Part 2A brochures, and other regulatory filings.

Each investment vehicle carries distinct objectives, risks, liquidity constraints, and fee structures that must be understood individually.

The examples and stories in this book are intended to promote financial awareness and thoughtful decision making—not to prescribe or construct specific portfolios or strategies.

Appendix 7C: Annuities Disclosure

The information and examples in this book that reference annuities—including fixed annuities, fixed indexed annuities (FIAs), variable annuities, deferred income annuities, and immediate annuities—are provided solely for educational and illustrative purposes.

They are intended to help readers understand the general structure, mechanics, and role of annuities within financial planning and retirement-income strategies.

All examples of annuity purchases and how they may have helped particular individuals and families are composites of years of experience and do not represent exact situations. The goal of all such discussions and references is to show examples of when an annuity could benefit an investor.

Nothing in this book should be construed as an offer, solicitation, or recommendation to purchase, sell, exchange, or replace any annuity or insurance contract.

Annuities may offer features such as tax deferral, guaranteed income streams, or death benefits. However, these guarantees are subject to the claims-paying ability of the issuing insurance company, not backed by the US government, the SEC, or FINRA.

All guarantees in annuity products—such as income, withdrawal, or death benefits—are contingent upon the financial strength and claims-paying ability of the issuing insurance company. Annuities often include surrender charges if funds are withdrawn before the end of a contractual holding period. Withdrawals before age fifty-nine and six months may incur IRS penalties and ordinary income tax on earnings.

Variable annuities involve investment risk, and account values will fluctuate with market conditions. Indexed annuities may include caps, participation rates, spreads, or crediting limits, which can reduce the amount of interest credited.

Fees and riders vary by product and can significantly affect performance.

Earnings within an annuity grow tax-deferred, meaning taxes are due only upon withdrawal. Withdrawals are taxed as ordinary income, not capital gains, and early withdrawals (before age fifty-nine and six months) may incur a 10 percent IRS penalty.

Tax rules and interpretations may change over time.

Readers should consult a qualified tax advisor for guidance on their specific circumstances.

Past performance is not indicative of future results, and annuity crediting rates, rider values, and contract provisions vary widely by issuer and state.

Readers should always review the official product prospectus, disclosure statement, or contract illustration provided by the issuing insurance company before making any purchase or replacement decision.

IMPORTANT CONSIDERATIONS AND LIMITATIONS

Annuities are long-term financial instruments not suitable for short-term liquidity needs. Surrendering or exchanging an annuity before the end of its surrender period may result in loss of principal and penalties. Riders providing lifetime income, enhanced death benefits, or market buffers involve additional costs. The purchase of multiple annuities or layered products should be carefully reviewed for redundancy and cost efficiency. Income or return projections should always be viewed as estimates, not guarantees.

Any mention of annuity products, features, or concepts is for educational discussion only and should not be interpreted as a personal recommendation or endorsement of any product, issuer, or strategy.

READER RESPONSIBILITY

Annuities involve complex trade-offs between liquidity, growth potential, risk, and cost. Before purchasing an annuity or making changes to an existing contract, readers should:

- Obtain and review all relevant product literature and state-approved disclosures
- Consult a licensed insurance professional and, if applicable, a registered investment advisor or tax professional
- Confirm that any guarantees, fees, and surrender schedules are fully understood

All annuity- and investment-related discussions and examples in this book are intended to encourage financial literacy and informed decision making—not to promote or endorse any specific product or company.

Appendix 7D: Real Estate Disclosure

Real estate investments involve a range of financial, operational, and market risks, and should be approached with careful analysis and professional guidance.

Any reference in this book to property purchases, rental income, appreciation, capitalization rates, or internal rates of return (IRRs) is illustrative and educational only. The examples are designed to explain financial concepts such as compounding, leverage, diversification, and behavioral decision making—not to represent actual investment outcomes or to recommend any specific property or strategy.

NO GUARANTEE OF PERFORMANCE

The performance of real estate investments varies widely depending on economic conditions, local markets, management skill, financing terms, and regulatory factors. Past appreciation rates, rent growth, or reported returns in the examples provided do not predict or guarantee future performance. Property values can decline, tenants can default, and liquidity can be limited for extended periods.

Real estate is typically illiquid and cyclical. Market downturns, rising interest rates, changes in credit availability, or oversupply of properties may significantly reduce investment value. Investors may be unable to sell properties or recover invested capital when desired.

Use of leverage (borrowing to purchase property) magnifies both gains and losses. If market values fall or rental income decreases, leveraged investors may face loan defaults, margin calls, or foreclosure. Real estate investments are subject to complex tax rules governing depreciation, capital gains, passive activity losses, and 1031 exchanges.

References in this book to cash-on-cash returns, IRRs, cap rates, or appreciation percentages are hypothetical and assume simplified scenarios for clarity. Actual investment performance depends on numerous variables including purchase price, transaction costs, property management, maintenance expenses, financing, and taxes.

NO OFFER OR SOLICITATION

Nothing in this publication constitutes an offer to buy, sell, or invest in any real estate property, limited partnership, private placement, or security.

Notes

Preface

1. Sonja Lyubomirsky, *The How of Happiness: A New Approach to Getting the Life You Want* (Penguin Books, 2008).

Part 1

1. The distinction between first-order desires (what one wants) and second-order desires or *second-order volitions* (what one wants to want) was developed by philosopher Harry Frankfurt in his influential essay "Freedom of the Will and the Concept of a Person." Frankfurt argues that genuine freedom of the will consists not merely in acting on one's desires, but in endorsing the desires that move one to act. See Harry G. Frankfurt, "Freedom of the Will and the Concept of a Person," *Journal of Philosophy* 68, no. 1 (1971): 5–20.

Chapter 1

1. Romans 1:19 (The Passion Translation).
2. Abū Āmid al-Ghazālī, *Freedom and Fulfillment: An Annotated Translation of al-Munqidh min al-Dalāl (Deliverance from Error)*, trans. R. J. McCarthy, S.J. (Twayne Publishers, 1980).
3. Thomas Aquinas, *Summa Theologiae, I, q. 1, a. 1, in Summa Theologica*, trans. Fathers of the English Dominican Province (Benziger Brothers, 1947).

4. Pascal Boyer and Justin L. Barrett are prominent scholars in the cognitive science of religion (CSR), an interdisciplinary field drawing on psychology, anthropology, and evolutionary biology to explain religious belief as an unintended consequence of cognitive systems shaped for survival, such as agency detection and theory of mind. See Pascal Boyer, *Religion Explained: The Evolutionary Origins of Religious Thought* (Basic Books, 2001); Justin L. Barrett, *Why Would Anyone Believe in God?* (AltaMira Press, 2004). For an overview of CSR research, see Ilkka Pyysiäinen, *Supernatural Agents: Why We Believe in Souls, Gods, and Buddhas* (Oxford University Press, 2009).
5. Émile Durkheim, *The Elementary Forms of Religious Life*, trans. Karen E. Fields (Free Press, 1995), esp. bk. 1, chap. 1. Durkheim argues that religious symbols and gods represent society itself and that religion functions as a collective expression of social reality; the formulation "religion is society worshipping itself" is a widely used paraphrase of his central thesis rather than a direct quotation.
6. Pam Wasserman, "World Population by Religion: A Global Tapestry of Faith," Population Education, January 12, 2024, https://populationeducation.org/world-population-by-religion-a-global-tapestry-of-faith/.
7. Richard Dawkins, *The God Delusion* (Houghton Mifflin, 2006), chap. 8. Dawkins discusses religion as a culturally inherited system of beliefs transmitted across generations, drawing on his earlier concept of memes.
8. Kirsten Lesage et al., "Around the World, Many People Are Leaving Their Childhood Religions," Pew Research Center, March 26, 2025, https://www.pewresearch.org/religion/2025/03/26/around-the-world-many-people-are-leaving-their-childhood-religions/.
9. 5Pillars, "Islam Has Highest Retention Rates of Any World Religion," March 27, 2025, https://5pillarsuk.com/2025/03/27/islam-has-highest-retention-rates-of-any-world-religion/.
10. Conrad Hackett et al., "How the Global Religious Landscape Changed From 2010 to 2020," Pew Research Center, June 9, 2025, https://www.pewresearch.org/religion/2025/06/09/hindu-population-change/.
11. Lesage et al., "Around the World."

Chapter 2

1. Mark Twain, *Europe and Elsewhere* (Cosimo Classis, 1923).
2. Twain, *Europe and Elsewhere.*
3. Twain, *Europe and Elsewhere.*

4. USAFacts, "How Many Voters Have a Party Affiliation?," August 29, 2025, https://usafacts.org/articles/how-many-voters-have-a-party-affiliation/.
5. USAFacts, "Party Affiliation."
6. Hannah Hartig et al., "Behind Trump's 2024 Victory, a More Racially and Ethnically Diverse Voter Coalition," Pew Research Center, June 26, 2025, https://www.pewresearch.org/politics/2025/06/26/voter-turnout-2020-2024/.
7. Hartig et al., "Voting Patterns."
8. Hartig et al., "Voting Patterns."
9. USAFacts, "Party Affiliation."
10. USAFacts, "Party Affiliation."
11. Pew Research Center, "The Partisan Divide on Political Values Grows Even Wider," October 24, 2017, https://www.pewresearch.org/politics/2017/10/24/the-partisan-divide-on-political-values-grows-even-wider/.
12. Daniel Cox, "Why Republican Parents Raise Democratic Daughters," Institute for Family Studies, April 18, 2024, https://ifstudies.org/blog/why-republican-parents-raise-democratic-daughters.
13. Hartig et al., "Voting Patterns."
14. Hartig et al., "Voting Patterns."
15. Bocar Ba et al., "Political Diversity in US Police Agencies," *American Journal of Political Science* (February 2025), doi:10.1111/ajps.12945.
16. Luona Lin et al., "What's It Like to Be a Teacher in America Today?," Pew Research Center, April 4, 2024, https://www.pewresearch.org/social-trends/2024/04/04/teachers-views-on-the-state-of-public-k-12-education/.
17. Charles Hewlett and Kelly Mangold, "From Polling Places to Commercial Spaces: Does Real Estate Prefer Trump or Biden?," RCLCO Real Estate Consulting, June 27, 2024, https://www.rclco.com/publication/from-polling-places-to-commercial-spaces-does-real-estate-prefer-trump-or-biden/.
18. AdvisorHub Staff, "Financial Advisors Lean Republican in 2024 Election: AdvisorHub Culture Study," AdvisorHub, July 5, 2024, https://www.advisorhub.com/resources/financial-advisors-lean-republican-in-2024-election-advisorhub-culture-study/.
19. Haylie Shipp, "Agri-Pulse Poll Shows Farmers Support Donald Trump," Ag Information Network of the West, January 12, 2024, https://www.aginfo.net/report/58605/Southeast-Regional-Ag-News/Agri-Pulse-Poll-Shows-Farmers-Support-Donald-Trump.

20. Joseph Copeland, "Military Veterans Remain a Republican Group, Backing Trump over Harris by Wide Margin," Pew Research Center, September 30, 2024, https://www.pewresearch.org/short-reads/2024/09/30/military-veterans-remain-a-republican-group-backing-trump-over-harris-by-wide-margin/.
21. Lars Willnat et al., "Key Findings from the 2022 American Journalist Study," The American Journalist, May 6, 2022, https://www.theamericanjournalist.org/post/american-journalist-findings.
22. Mary Hylton et al., "The Political Ideology and Political Engagement of Licensed Social Workers in the Age of Trump," abstract, paper presented at Society for Social Work and Research 24th Annual Conference: Reducing Racial and Economic Inequality, Washington, DC, January 18, 2020, https://sswr.confex.com/sswr/2020/webprogram/Paper39379.html.
23. Pew Research Center, "Public Praises Science; Scientists Fault Public, Media, Pew Research Center," July 9, 2009, https://www.pewresearch.org/politics/2009/07/09/section-4-scientists-politics-and-religion/.
24. Nili Solomonov and Jacques P. Barber, "Conducting Psychotherapy in the Trump Era: Therapists' Perspectives on Political Self-Disclosure, the Therapeutic Alliance, and Politics in the Therapy Room," *Journal of Clinical Psychology* 75, no. 9 (2019): 1508–1518, doi:10.1002/jclp.22801.
25. Ben Davis, "How Much Do Creative Professionals Donate to Republicans Versus Democrats? Here Are the Numbers," Artnet News, November 3, 2020, https://news.artnet.com/art-world-archives/creative-jobs-political-donations-1920632.

Chapter 3

1. Michael J. Sandel, *The Tyranny of Merit: What's Become of the Common Good?* (Farrar, Straus and Giroux, 2020), 26–27.
2. Muneerah N. Bin-Jumah et al., "Genes and Longevity of Lifespan," *International Journal of Molecular Sciences* 23, no. 3 (2022): 1499, https://doi.org/10.3390/ijms23031499.
3. Giuseppe Passarino et al., "Human Longevity: Genetics or Lifestyle? It Takes Two to Tango," *Immunity & Ageing* 13, no. 12 (2016), https://doi.org/10.1186/s12979-016-0066-z.
4. Aristotle, *Nicomachean Ethics*, trans. Terence Irwin (Hackett Publishing, 1999).
5. Kira M. Newman, "How Much of Your Happiness Is Under Your Control?," *Greater Good Magazine*, February 18, 2020, https://greatergood.berkeley.edu/article/item/how_much_of_your_happiness_is_under_your_control.

6. Newman, "How Much of Your Happiness."
7. Newman, "How Much of Your Happiness."
8. Lyubomirsky, *The How of Happiness.*
9. Mass General Brigham, "Genetic Heart Disease: Inherited Heart Conditions," last accessed December 4, 2025, https://www.massgeneralbrigham.org/en/patient-care/services-and-specialties/heart/conditions/inherited-heart-conditions.
10. National Kidney Foundation, "Your Genes, Your Family, and Kidney Health," last accessed December 4, 2025, https://www.kidney.org/kidney-topics/genetics-and-kidney-disease.
11. Maria Shadrina et al., "Genetics Factors in Major Depression Disease," *Frontiers in Psychiatry* 9 (2018): 334, https://doi.org/10.3389/fpsyt.2018.00334.
12. Sharon Salzberg, *Faith: Trusting Your Own Deepest Experience* (Riverhead Books, 2002), 24.

Chapter 4

1. Carl Hoefer, "Causal Determinism," in *The Stanford Encyclopedia of Philosophy,* Fall 2016 ed., edited by Edward N. Zalta, https://plato.stanford.edu/entries/determinism-causal/.
2. Aristotle, *Nicomachean Ethics,* 1113b5–7.
3. Martin Luther, *On the Bondage of the Will*, trans. Edward Thomas Vaughan (T. Hamilton and T. Combe, 1823), 8.
4. Immanuel Kant, *Critique of Practical Reason*, trans. Lewis White Beck (Macmillan, 1993), 30.
5. Ronald W. Clark, *Einstein: The Life and Times* (World Publishing Company, 1971), 413.
6. Roderick M. Chisholm, *Person and Object: A Metaphysical Study* (Open Court, 1976), 122.
7. Robert M. Sapolsky, *Behave: The Biology of Humans at Our Best and Worst* (Penguin Press, 2017), esp. chaps. 1–4; Robert M. Sapolsky, *Determined: A Science of Life Without Free Will* (Penguin Press, 2023), esp. introduction and chaps. 1–6. Across these works, Sapolsky argues that human behavior is fully determined by biology, developmental history, brain chemistry, and environmental context; that perceptions of willpower and choice are themselves products of those forces; that luck compounds rather than evens

out over time; and that what is commonly called "free will" reflects biological processes not yet fully understood.

8. Robert M. Sapolsky, *Determined,* esp. chaps. 6–9. Sapolsky critiques common attempts to rescue free will through chaos theory, emergent complexity, and quantum indeterminacy, arguing that unpredictability or randomness does not constitute agency or conscious choice and therefore does not restore free will.
9. Brian Greene, *Until the End of Time: Mind, Matter, and Our Search for Meaning in an Evolving Universe* (Knopf, 2020).
10. Chunkai Li et al., "The Freedom to Pursue Happiness: Belief in Free Will Predicts Life Satisfaction and Positive Affect among Chinese Adolescents," *Frontiers in Psychology* 7, no. 2027 (2016): 2027, https://doi.org/10.3389/fpsyg.2016.02027; Tom St Quinton and A. William Crescioni, "Free to be Healthy? Free Will Beliefs are Positively Associated with Health Behavior," *Psychological Reports* (2024), https://doi.org/10.1177/00332941241260264.
11. Daniel Kahneman, *Thinking, Fast and Slow* (Farrar, Straus and Giroux, 2011), esp. chaps. 1–2. Kahneman introduces "System 1" and "System 2" as two interacting modes of thought: an automatic, fast, intuitive system and a slower, effortful, analytical system that requires conscious attention.
12. Nate Silver, *The Signal and the Noise: Why So Many Predictions Fail—But Some Don't* (Penguin Press, 2012), esp. introduction and chaps. 1–2. Silver argues for probabilistic thinking—replacing categorical predictions with probability estimates that reflect uncertainty and degrees of confidence.

Chapter 5

1. Albert Einstein, quoted in Walter Isaacson, *Einstein: His Life and Universe* (Simon & Schuster, 2007), 525.
2. Donald D. Hoffman, *The Case Against Reality: Why Evolution Hid the Truth from Our Eyes* (W. W. Norton & Company, 2019), esp. chaps. 1–3. Hoffman argues that natural selection favors perceptions that enhance fitness rather than veridical representations of objective reality, likening perception to a user interface—such as a computer desktop—that hides underlying complexity while enabling effective action. His evolutionary game-theoretic models suggest that organisms tuned to fitness-relevant simplifications tend to outcompete those that perceive reality more accurately.
3. Lesley Kennedy, "The Prehistoric Ages: How Humans Lived Before Written Records," History, last updated May 28, 2025, https://www.history.com/articles/prehistoric-ages-timeline.

4. Yuval Noah Harari, "Ecology," Yuval Noah Harari, last modified 2025, https://www.ynharari.com/topic/ecology/.

5. "Galileo Galilei," in *Oxford Essential Quotations*, 6th ed., edited by Susan Ratcliffe (Oxford University Press, 2018), https://doi.org/10.1093/acref/9780191866692.001.0001/q-oro-ed6-00004705.

6. John Locke, *Two Treatises of Government*, ed. Peter Laslett (Cambridge University Press, 1988), bk. II, §§95–99.

7. Immanuel Kant, "'Dare to Know,' from *What is Enlightenment?* 1784," in *Tolerance*, ed. Caroline Warman (Open Book Publishers, 2016), https://books.openedition.org/obp/2962.

8. Mary Wollstonecraft, *A Vindication of the Rights of Woman: With Strictures on Political and Moral Subjects* (London, 1792; repr., Oxford University Press, 1999), esp. chaps. 2–4.

9. Adam Smith, *An Inquiry into the Nature and Causes of the Wealth of Nations* (W. Strahan and T. Cadell, 1776).

10. Carmen Ang, "Visualized: The Growth of Global Internet Users (1990–2025)," Visual Capitalist, March 19, 2024, https://www.visualcapitalist.com/visualized-the-growth-of-global-internet-users-1990-2025/.

11. World Bank, "Life Expectancy at Birth, Total for the World," retrieved from FRED, Federal Reserve Bank of St. Louis, February 5, 2026, https://fred.stlouisfed.org/series/SPDYNLE00INWLD, based on data from the United Nations Population Division and national statistical offices, showing an increase in global life expectancy from approximately 66.8 years in 2000 to 73.33 years in 2023.

12. "Levels and Trends in Child Mortality." UNICEF, March 24, 2025, accessed December 10, 2025, https://data.unicef.org/resources/levels-and-trends-in-child-mortality-2024/.

13. World Bank, *Poverty, Prosperity, and Planet Report: Pathways Out of the Polycrisis* (World Bank Group, 2024), https://www.worldbank.org/en/publication/poverty-prosperity-and-planet.

14. United Nations Conference on Trade and Development (UNCTAD), "Global Trade Hits Record $33 Trillion in 2024, Driven by Services and Developing Economies," UNCTAD News, March 14, 2025, https://unctad.org/news/global-trade-hits-record-33-trillion-2024-driven-services-and-developing-economies.

15. Our World in Data, "GDP per capita, 2024," chart, last modified September 8, 2025, https://ourworldindata.org/grapher/gdp-per-capita-worldbank.

16. Estimated deaths and population data compiled from multiple sources including Matthew White, *Atrocities: The 100 Deadliest Episodes in Human History* (W.W. Norton, 2011); Milton Leitenberg, *Deaths in Wars and Conflicts in the 20th Century* (Cornell University Peace Studies Program, 2006); Uppsala Conflict Data Program (UCDP), "UCDP Battle-Related Deaths Dataset," Department of Peace and Conflict Research, Uppsala University, accessed December 4, 2025, https://ucdp.uu.se/; United Nations, Department of Economic and Social Affairs, "World Population Prospects 2022," accessed December 4, 2025, https://population.un.org/wpp/.

17. Bastian Herre et al., "War and Peace," Our World in Data, 2024, https://ourworldindata.org/war-and-peace.

18. Herre et al., "War and Peace."

19. Steven Pinker, *The Better Angels of Our Nature: Why Violence Has Declined* (Viking, 2011).

20. Lauren Collins, "Was Jeanne Calment the Oldest Person Who Ever Lived—or a Fraud?," *The New Yorker*, February 17, 2020, https://www.newyorker.com/magazine/2020/02/17/was-jeanne-calment-the-oldest-person-who-ever-lived-or-a-fraud.

21. Ray Kurzweil, *The Singularity Is Near: When Humans Transcend Biology* (Viking, 2005), 58–60.

22. Aubrey D. N. J. de Grey and Michael Rae, *Ending Aging: The Rejuvenation Breakthroughs That Could Reverse Human Aging in Our Lifetime* (St. Martin's Press, 2007).

23. Morgan E. Levine, "Modeling the Rate of Senescence: Can Estimated Biological Age Predict Mortality More Accurately Than Chronological Age?," *The Journals of Gerontology: Series A* 68, no. 6 (2013): 667–674, https://doi.org/10.1093/gerona/gls233.

24. Kevin Daly et al., *The Path to 2075—The Positive Story of Global Aging* (Goldman Sachs, 2025), https://www.gspublishing.com/content/research/en/reports/2025/05/20/2d3fe290-10b1-44be-8d0e-77b8d303928f.html.

25. Daly et al., *The Path to 2075.*

26. International Monetary Fund Research Department, "Chapter 2: The Rise of the Silver Economy: Global Implications of Population Aging" in *World Economic Outlook: A Critical Juncture amid Policy Shifts* (International Monetary Fund, 2025).

27. Lydia Belanger, "Warren Buffett's 3 Top Pieces of Advice for Entrepreneurs," *Entrepreneur,* August 30, 2016, https://www.entrepreneur.com/leadership/warren-buffetts-3-top-pieces-of-advice-for-entrepreneurs/277648.

Chapter 6

1. Danny Vena, "Is This Nvidia's iPhone Moment?," *The Motley Fool,* June 1, 2023, https://www.fool.com/investing/2023/06/01/is-this-nvidias-iphone-moment/.
2. OpenAI, "GPT-4 Technical Report," March 2023, https://openai.com/research/gpt-4; Jacob Browning and Yann LeCun, "AI and the Future of Work," *Scientific American*, March 2023, https://www.scientificamerican.com/article/the-future-of-work-in-the-age-of-ai/; Erik Brynjolfsson et al., "Generative AI at Work," Stanford Digital Economy Lab, September 2023, https://digitaleconomy.stanford.edu/research/generative-ai-at-work/.
3. Andrea Vacchiano, "Artificial Intelligence 'Godfather' on AI Possibly Wiping Out Humanity: 'It's Not Inconceivable,'" Fox News, March 25, 2023, https://www.foxnews.com/tech/artificial-intelligence-godfather-ai-possibly-wiping-humanity-not-inconceivable.
4. Sam Altman, testimony before the US Senate Judiciary Subcommittee on Privacy, Technology, and the Law, *Oversight of A.I.: Rules for Artificial Intelligence*, May 16, 2023.
5. Yoshua Bengio, statement in "Statement on AI Risk," Center for AI Safety, May 30, 2023, https://www.safe.ai/statement-on-ai-risk.
6. Camila Domonoske, "Elon Musk Warns Governors: Artificial Intelligence Poses 'Existential Risk,'" NPR, July 17, 2017, https://www.npr.org/sections/thetwo-way/2017/07/17/537686649/elon-musk-warns-governors-artificial-intelligence-poses-existential-risk.
7. Stephen Hawking, quoted in Rory Cellan-Jones, "Stephen Hawking Warns Artificial Intelligence Could End Mankind," *BBC News*, December 2, 2014, https://www.bbc.com/news/technology-30290540.
8. Daniel Quinn, *Ishmael* (Bantam, 1995), 96–99.
9. "CDC Museum COVID-19 Timeline," CDC, accessed February 3, 2026, https://www.cdc.gov/museum/timeline/covid19.html.
10. UN News, "UN Continues to Support Pakistan Flood Response," March 7, 2023, https://news.un.org/en/story/2023/03/1134302.
11. Quinn, *Ishmael*, 137–140.

12. Intergovernmental Panel on Climate Change (IPCC), *Climate Change 2023: Synthesis Report, Summary for Policymakers* (Geneva: IPCC, 2023), https://www.ipcc.ch/report/ar6/syr/; "2023 Was the Hottest Year on Record, by a Large Margin," Copernicus Climate Change Service, January 9, 2024, https://climate.copernicus.eu/global-climate-highlights-2023.

13. Steven E. Koonin, *Unsettled: What Climate Science Tells Us, What It Doesn't, and Why It Matters, Expanded and Updated Edition* (BenBella Books, 2024).

14. Ian Tufts, "Fact of the Week: China's Share of US Goods Imports Has Fallen by 8 Percentage Points Since the 2018–2019 Tariff Hikes," Information Technology and Innovation Foundation (ITIF), May 28, 2024, https://itif.org/publications/2024/05/28/chinas-share-us-goods-imports-fallen-by-8-points-since-2018-2019-tariff-hikes/.

15. Graham Allison, *Destined for War: Can America and China Escape Thucydides's Trap?* (Houghton Mifflin Harcourt, 2014).

16. World Bank national accounts data and OECD National Accounts data files. "GPD (Current US$)—China, 1990–2024," World Bank Group, accessed 2024, https://data.worldbank.org/indicator/NY.GDP.MKTP.CD?locations=CN.

17. World Bank national accounts data and OECD National Accounts data files.

18. World Bank, "Poverty Headcount Ratio at $2.15 a Day (2017 PPP) (% of Population)—China," accessed 2024, https://www.worldbank.org/en/country/china/overview.

19. Kathryn Palmer, "Report: Impact of Chinese Research 'on Par' with US," Inside Higher Ed, December 8, 2025, https://www.insidehighered.com/news/government/science-research-policy/2025/12/08/report-impact-chinese-research-par-us.

20. Data compiled from World Bank, International Monetary Fund (IMF), Stockholm International Peace Research Institute (SIPRI), World Intellectual Property Organization (WIPO), and UNESCO Institute for Statistics. Figures from 1990–2024 reflect the latest available data and projections as of 2024.

21. Justin Pope, "The U.S. Just Imposed Sweeping Tariffs on All Imports. Here's How Walmart Stock Might Be Affected," Nasdaq, April 04, 2025, https://www.nasdaq.com/articles/us-just-imposed-sweeping-tariffs-all-imports-heres-how-walmart-stock-might-be-affected.

22. Office of the US Trade Representative (USTR), "US–China Trade Facts," updated 2024, https://ustr.gov/countries-regions/china-mongolia-taiwan/peoples-republic-china.
23. US Department of the Treasury, "Major Foreign Holders of Treasury Securities," 2025, https://ticdata.treasury.gov/resource-center/data-chart-center/tic/Documents/slt_table5.html.
24. A Zen koan is a paradoxical statement, question, or short story used in Zen Buddhist practice to provoke deep reflection and transcend conventional thinking.
25. Thomas L. Friedman, *The World Is Flat: A Brief History of the Twenty-First Century* (Farrar, Straus and Giroux, 2005).

Chapter 7

1. Carl Sagan, *Cosmos* (Random House, 1980), 45.
2. The saying is a *Hadīth* (reported saying) attributed to Muhammad (peace be upon him) and recorded in the most authoritative collections of Sunni Islam. It appears in Muhammad ibn Ismail al-Bukhari, *Sahīh al-Bukhārī*, and also in *Sahīh Muslim*. Al-Bukhārī (810–870 CE) was a Persian-born Islamic scholar whose compilation of authenticated sayings of the Prophet is regarded by Sunni Muslims as the most reliable collection of hadīth. The saying teaches moral accountability, emphasizing that every individual bears responsibility for those entrusted to their care, whether in family, leadership, or society.
3. This saying is a *hadīth* attributed to Muhammad (peace be upon him) and recorded in Muslim ibn al-Hajjaj, *Sahīh Muslim*, *Kitāb al-Birr wa'l-Silah wa'l-Ādāb* (The Book of Righteousness, Maintaining Ties, and Good Manners), no. 2699 (according to standard numbering). Muslim ibn al-Hajjāj (821–875 CE) was a leading ninth-century Islamic scholar whose compilation of rigorously authenticated prophetic sayings is regarded by Sunni Muslims as one of the two most authoritative hadīth collections, second only to *Sahīh al-Bukhārī*. The tradition emphasizes moral responsibility, compassion, and service to others, teaching that acts of relieving human suffering carry spiritual consequence beyond this life.
4. Patrick Olivelle, "Moksha," *Encyclopaedia Britannica*, last modified April 15, 2021, https://www.britannica.com/topic/moksha-Indian-religion.
5. Wat Pah Nanachat, "What Is Buddhism?," accessed June 10, 2025, https://www.watpahnanachat.org/what-is-buddhism.
6. Paul Dundas, *The Jains*, 2nd ed. (Routledge, 2002), 28–45.

7. Laozi, *Tao Te Ching,* trans. D.C. Lau (Penguin Classics, 1999), chap. 33.
8. Confucius, *The Analects*, trans. James Legge, in *The Confucian Analects, The Great Learning & The Doctrine of the Mean* (Oxford University Press, 1971).
9. Confucius, *The Great Learning.*
10. Confucius, *The Analects.*
11. Confucius, *The Analects.*
12. Confucius, *The Analects.*
13. Confucius, *The Analects.*
14. Albert Camus, *The Myth of Sisyphus* (Gallimard, 1942), p. 123.
15. Viktor E. Frankl, *Man's Search for Meaning: An Introduction to Logotherapy* (Beacon Press, 2006), 99.

Chapter 8

1. Brian Hare and Vanessa Woods, *Survival of the Friendliest: Understanding Our Origins and Rediscovering Our Common Humanity* (Random House, 2020), 34–36.
2. Charles Darwin, *The Descent of Man, and Selection in Relation to Sex* (John Murray, 1871).
3. Dunbar, R. I. M., "Coevolution of Neocortical Size, Group Size and Language in Humans," *Behavioral and Brain Sciences* 16, no. 4 (1993): 681–694; Robin Dunbar, *How Many Friends Does One Person Need? Dunbar's Number and Other Evolutionary Quirks* (Harvard University Press, 2010).
4. Miller McPherson et al., "Social Isolation in America: Changes in Core Discussion Networks over Two Decades," *American Sociological Review* 71, no. 3 (June 2006): 353–75, https://doi.org/10.1177/000312240607100301.
5. YouGov, "How Many Close Friends Do Americans Have?," YouGov Poll, 2021, https://today.yougov.com/topics/society/trackers/how-many-close-friends-do-americans-have.
6. US Census Bureau, "Census Bureau Releases New Estimates on Families and Living Arrangements," press release, May 30, 2024, https://www.census.gov/newsroom/press-releases/2024/families-living-arrangements.html.
7. Administration for Community Living, *2023 Profile of Older Americans* (Administration for Community Living, May 2024), https://acl.gov/sites/default/files/Profile%20of%20OA/ACL_ProfileOlderAmericans2023_508.pdf.

8. Sarah E. Taylor and Gina C. Gonzaga, "Evolution, Relationships, and Health: The Social Shaping Hypothesis," in *Evolution and Social Psychology*, edited by Mark Schaller, Jeffry A. Simpson, and Douglas T. Kenrick (Psychology Press, 2006), https://taylorlab.psych.ucla.edu/wp-content/uploads/sites/5/2014/11/2006_Evolution-Relationships-and-Health_The-Social-Shaping-Hypothesis.pdf.
9. Shelley E. Taylor and Gonzalo G. Gonzaga, "The Social Shaping Hypothesis: How Social Relationships Regulate Stress," in *Social Psychology: Handbook of Basic Principles*, 2nd ed., ed. Arie W. Kruglanski and E. Tory Higgins (Guilford Press, 2007), 632–645.
10. Robert J. Waldinger and Marc S. Schulz, *The Harvard Study of Adult Development: Insights into Human Flourishing and Well-Being* (Harvard Medical School, 2023), accessed October 2025, https://www.adultdevelopmentstudy.org.
11. Robert Waldinger, "What Makes a Good Life? Lessons from the Longest Study on Happiness," TED Talk, TED, April 2015.
12. Robert Waldinger and Marc Schulz, *The Good Life: Lessons from the World's Longest Scientific Study of Happiness* (Simon & Schuster, 2019), 45.
13. Waldinger, "What Makes a Good Life?"
14. Waldinger and Schulz, *The Good Life*, 77.
15. George E. Vaillant, *Aging Well: Surprising Guideposts to a Happier Life from the Landmark Harvard Study of Adult Development* (Little, Brown and Company, 2002), 5.
16. Jeremiah D. Landvatter et al., "Partner's Perceived Social Support Influences Their Spouse's Inflammation: An Actor-Partner Analysis," *International Journal of Environmental Research and Public Health* 19, no. 2 (January 12, 2022): 799, https://doi.org/10.3390/ijerph19020799.
17. National Institute on Aging (NIA) et al., *Growing Older in America: The Health and Retirement Study* (US Government Printing Office, 2017), https://www.nia.nih.gov/sites/default/files/2017-06/health_and_retirement_study_0.pdf.
18. Silvia E. Jackson et al., "The Influence of Partner's Behavior on Health Behavior Change," *JAMA Internal Medicine* 175, no. 3 (March 2015): https://doi.org/10.1001/jamainternmed.2014.7554.
19. Anna Miller, "Can This Marriage Be Saved?," *Monitor on Psychology* 44, no. 4 (April 2013): 42, https://www.apa.org/monitor/2013/04/marriage.

20. United Nations Population Fund (UNFPA), "Nearly Half of All Pregnancies Are Unintended—a Global Crisis, Says New UNFPA Report," press release, March 30, 2022, https://www.unfpa.org/press/nearly-half-all-pregnancies-are-unintended%E2%80%94-global-crisis-says-new-unfpa-report.

21. David Benatar, *Better Never to Have Been: The Harm of Coming into Existence* (Oxford University Press, 2006).

22. David Benatar, *The Human Predicament: A Candid Guide to Life's Biggest Questions* (Oxford University Press, 2017).

Chapter 9

1. Max Rust et al., "See How the Average US Worker Has Changed Over 250 Years," *Wall Street Journal*, October 27, 2025, https://www.wsj.com/economy/jobs/see-how-the-average-u-s-worker-has-changed-over-250-years-b04ffb45.

Chapter 10

1. Marcus Tullius Cicero, *De Officiis*, trans. Walter Miller (Harvard University Press, 1913), book 1, sec. 22.

2. Robert A. Emmons, *Thanks! How the New Science of Gratitude Can Make You Happier* (Houghton Mifflin Harcourt, 2007), 4.

3. Waldinger and Schulz, *The Good Life*.

4. Lyubomirsky, *The How of Happiness*, 41–42.

5. Robert A. Emmons and Michael E. McCullough, "Counting Blessings Versus Burdens: An Experimental Investigation of Gratitude and Subjective Well-Being in Daily Life," *Journal of Personality and Social Psychology* 84, no. 2 (2003): 377–389.

6. Emmons and McCullough, "Counting Blessings Versus Burdens."

7. Philip Brickman et al., "Lottery Winners and Accident Victims: Is Happiness Relative?," *Journal of Personality and Social Psychology* 36, no. 8 (1978): 917–927.

8. David G. Blanchflower and Andrew J. Oswald, "Is Well-Being U-Shaped over the Life Cycle?," *Social Science & Medicine* 66, no. 8 (2008): 1733–1749; Elizabeth Dunn et al., "If Money Doesn't Make You Happy, Then You Probably Aren't Spending It Right," *Journal of Consumer Psychology* 21, no. 2 (2011): 115–125; National Marriage Project, *The State of Our Unions 2021* (University of Virginia, 2021), https://stateofourunions.org/.

9. Emmons, *Thanks!,* 63.
10. Marcus Aurelius, *Meditations,* trans. Gregory Hays (Modern Library, 2002), 7.27.
11. *The Holy Bible,* New Revised Standard Version, 1 Thess. 5:18.
12. *The Qur'an*: English Translation and Parallel Arabic Text, trans. Saheeh International (2010), Surah Ibrahim 14:7.
13. *The Qur'an:* English Translation and Parallel Arabic Text, trans. Saheeh International (2010), Surah Al-Luqman 31:18.
14. Eknath Easwaran, *The Bhagavad Gita* (Nilgiri Press, 2007), chap. 2, 6; Swami Sivananda, *Practice of Santosh*a (Divine Life Society, 2004).
15. Confucius, *Analects*, trans. Arthur Waley (Vintage Books, 1989), 4.16.

Chapter 11

1. Raj Chetty et al., "The Association Between Income and Life Expectancy in the United States, 2001–2014," *JAMA* 315, no. 16 (April 26, 2016): https://doi.org/10.1001/jama.2016.4226.
2. Substance Abuse and Mental Health Services Administration (SAMHSA), *Key Substance Use and Mental Health Indicators in the United States: Results from the 2022 National Survey on Drug Use and Health* (SAMHSA, 2023).
3. Centers for Disease Control and Prevention (CDC), "Physical Activity and Health: Socioeconomic Factors and Activity Levels," *MMWR*, 2020, https://www.cdc.gov/physicalactivity/data/income.htm.
4. US Department of Health & Human Services, Administration for Children and Families, Children's Bureau, *Child Maltreatment 2021 Report* (US Department of Health & Human Services, 2023), https://www.acf.hhs.gov/cb/report/child-maltreatment-2021.
5. Board of Governors of the Federal Reserve System, *Changes in U.S. Family Finances from 2019 to 2022: Evidence from the Survey of Consumer Finances* (Federal Reserve Research & Analysis, 2023), 12, https://www.federalreserve.gov/publications/files/scf23.pdf.
6. Board of Governors of the Federal Reserve System (US), "Share of Net Worth Held by the Bottom 50% (1st to 50th Wealth Percentiles) (WFRBSB50215)," Federal Reserve Bank of St. Louis, accessed December 4, 2025, https://fred.stlouisfed.org/series/WFRBSB50215.

7. Congressional Research Service (CRS*), United States Bankruptcy Courts: Overview and Analysis of Bankruptcy Filings in 2024,* Insight IN12536 (Library of Congress, 2024), https://www.congress.gov/crs-product/IN12536.

8. Eviction Lab, "Preliminary Analysis: Eviction Filing Patterns in 2024," Eviction Lab (2025), accessed June 11, 2025, https://evictionlab.org/ets-report-2024/.

9. Urban Institute, "71 Million US Adults Have Debt in Collections," Urban Wire, accessed June 11, 2025, https://www.urban.org/urban-wire/71-million-us-adults-have-debt-collections.

10. US Department of Housing and Urban Development, "HUD Releases January 2024 Point-In-Time Count Report," press release, December 27, 2024, https://www.hud.gov/press/press_releases_media_advisories/hud_no_24_327.

Chapter 12

1. S&P Dow Jones Indices LLC, "SPIVA® US Mid-Year 2025 Scorecard," 2025, https://www.spglobal.com/spdji/en/spiva/article/spiva-us/.

Chapter 13

1. Discover Financial Services, "Discover Survey: Save More, Earn More and Spend Less Are Top 2025 Financial Resolutions for American Consumers," press release, December 11, 2024, https://investorrelations.discover.com/newsroom/press-releases/press-release-details/2024/Discover-Survey-Save-More-Earn-More-and-Spend-Less-Are-Top-2025-Financial-Resolutions-for-American-Consumers/default.aspx.

Chapter 14

1. DALBAR, Inc., "Quantitative Analysis of Investor Behavior (QAIB) 2022," 2022, https://dalbar.com/ProductsAndServices/QAIB; Part of the difference can be from fee and cost related to investment management while the S&P 500 index is simply the return of the index and does not account for any cost.

2. J.B. Maverick, "S&P 500 Average Returns and Historical Performance," Investopedia, last modified September 22, 2025, https://www.investopedia.com/ask/answers/042415/what-average-annual-return-sp-500.asp.

3. S&P Dow Jones Indices (Various Years), SPIVA® US Scorecard. https://www.cnbc.com/2019/03/15/active-fund-managers-trail-the-sp-500-for-the-ninth-year-in-a-row-in-triumph-for-indexing.html
4. Daniel Kahneman and Amos Tversky, "Prospect Theory: An Analysis of Decision Making under Risk," *Econometrica* 47 (1979): https://doi.org/10.2307/1914185.
5. J.P. Morgan Asset Management, *Guide to the Markets* (J.P. Morgan Asset Management, 2025), data as of March 31, 2025, 2025, https://am.jpmorgan.com/us/en/asset-management/adv/insights/market-insights/guide-to-the-markets/.
6. Josh Howarth, "Startup Failure Rate Statistics (2025)," *Exploding Topics* (blog), last updated June 5, 2025, https://explodingtopics.com/blog/startup-failure-stats.

Chapter 15

1. Paul Coelho, *The Alchemist* (HarperCollins, 1993).
2. Hypothetical illustration for educational purposes only. Assumes consistent contributions and compound growth; not a guarantee of future results. Your actual investment results will be different. Investments involve risk, including the risk of loss of capital. Consult your financial advisor and undertake your own analysis before investing. This is not intended to be investment advice.
3. J.P. Morgan Asset Management, *Guide to the Markets: US 4Q 2025* (J.P. Morgan Asset Management, 2025), data as of September 30, 2025, https://am.jpmorgan.com/us/en/asset-management/adv/insights/market-insights/guide-to-the-markets/.
4. J.P. Morgan Asset Management, *Guide to the Markets: US 4Q 2025*.
5. "S&P 500—100 Year Historical Chart & Data," Macrotrends, https://www.macrotrends.net/datasets/2324/sp-500-historical-chart-data.
6. Warren E. Buffett, *To the Shareholders of Berkshire Hathaway Inc.* (Berkshire Hathaway Inc., 1988), https://www.berkshirehathaway.com/letters/1988.html.
7. Brad M. Barber and Terrance Odean, "The Behavior of Individual Investors," in *Handbook of the Economics of Finance*, vol. 2, ed. George M. Constantinides, Milton Harris, and René M. Stulz (Elsevier, 2011), https://doi.org/10.1016/B978-0-44-459406-8.00022-6.

8. Alice Henriques et al., "Changes in US Family Finances from 2016 to 2019: Evidence from the Survey of Consumer Finances," *Federal Reserve Bulletin* 106, no. 5 (September 2020): https://www.federalreserve.gov/publications/files/scf20.pdf.

9. Jasica Usman, "Average Home Appreciation Per Year: What You Need to Know," *Redfin Blog*, June 16, 2025, https://www.redfin.com/blog/average-home-appreciation-per-year/.

Comprehensive Investment Guide

1. For illustration purpose only. This example is to describe the past performance and the power of compounding. Past performance is not a guarantee of future returns.

2. Benjamin Graham, *The Intelligent Investor* (Harper & Brothers, 1949).

3. J.P. Morgan Asset Management, *Guide to the Markets: US 4Q 2025* (J.P. Morgan Asset Management, 2025), data as of September 30, 2025, https://am.jpmorgan.com/us/en/asset-management/adv/insights/market-insights/guide-to-the-markets/.

4. According to data compiled from the S&P SPIVA® scorecards (as summarized by Apollo Global Management's chief economist), over the ten years through December 31, 2024, 98 percent of active Treasury fixed-income managers underperformed their benchmark, as did 82 percent of public investment-grade credit managers, and 79 percent of high-yield managers, https://www.apolloacademy.com/public-fixed-income-managers-underperforming-their-benchmark/.

5. Plante Moran, "Private Equity's Long-Term Performance Can Make It Worth the Risk," Plante Moran, July 17, 2024, https://www.plantemoran.com/explore-our-thinking/insight/2024/07/private-equitys-long-term-performance-can-make-it-worth-the-risk.

6. Hamilton Lane, "Has Private Credit Lost Its Shine?," April 17, 2025, https://www.hamiltonlane.com/en-us/insight/private-credit-2025.

7. World Bank, "Listed domestic companies, total—United States," World Bank Data, accessed December 4, 2025, https://data.worldbank.org/indicator/CM.MKT.LDOM.NO?locations=US.

8. Any reference in this book to property purchases, rental income, appreciation, capitalization rates, or internal rates of return (IRRs) is illustrative and educational only. The examples are designed to explain financial concepts

such as compounding, leverage, diversification, and behavioral decision-making—not to represent actual investment outcomes or to recommend any specific property or strategy.

9. "Cost of Car Ownership." Edmunds, https://www.edmunds.com/tco.html#.
10. AAA, "Annual Cost of New Car Ownership Crosses $10K Mark," AAA Newsroom, August 11, 2022, https://newsroom.aaa.com/2022/08/annual-cost-of-new-car-ownership-crosses-10k-mark/.
11. "Cost of Car Ownership."
12. LIMRA, "2024 Retail Annuity Sales Grow 13% to a Record $434.1 Billion," news release, March 17, 2025, https://www.limra.com/en/newsroom/news-releases/2025/limra-2024-retail-annuity-sales-grow-12-to-a-record-$434.1-billion/.
13. LIMRA, *Life Insurance Awareness Month 2023 Fact Sheet* (LIMRA, 2023), https://www.limra.com/siteassets/newsroom/liam/2023/0859-2023-liam-fact-sheet-2023_final.pdf.
14. Social Security Administration, *Social Security Fact Sheet* (Social Security Administration, 2025), https://www.ssa.gov/news/press/factsheets/basicfact-alt.pdf.
15. Administration for Community Living, "How Much Care Will You Need?," LongTermCare.gov, last modified February 18, 2020, https://acl.gov/ltc/basic-needs/how-much-care-will-you-need.
16. Ryan Clark, "Genworth and Carescout Release Cost of Care Survey Results for 2024," Genworth, March 04, 2025, https://investor.genworth.com/news-events/press-releases/detail/982/genworth-and-carescout-release-cost-of-care-survey-results/.
17. Wells Fargo Investment Institute, "The Perils of Trying to Time Volatile Markets," Wells Fargo Advisors, 2025, https://www.wellsfargoadvisors.com/research-analysis/reports/policy/volatile-markets.htm.

Appendix 5

1. J.P. Morgan Asset Management, *Guide to the Markets: US 1Q 2026* (J.P. Morgan Asset Management, 2025), data as of December 31, 2025, https://am.jpmorgan.com/us/en/asset-management/adv/insights/market-insights/guide-to-the-markets/.

Appendix 6

1. Vanguard, *Advisor's Alpha: A Measure of the Value of Financial Advice* (Vanguard Research, 2019), https://ptmwealth.com/articles/vanguard-working-with-an-advisor-can-add-about-3-in-net-returns; Vanguard, *Putting a Value on Your Value: Quantifying Vanguard Adviser's Alpha* (Vanguard, 2020), https://www.ch.vanguard/content/dam/intl/europe/documents/en/putting-a-value-on-your-value-quantifying-vanguard-adviser-alpha-eu-en-pro.pdf.

Acknowledgments

I am deeply grateful to the many individuals whose insights, support, and thoughtful feedback helped shape this book into its final form. I want to especially thank the following people for reviewing the manuscript, often multiple times, and offering valuable suggestions to improve clarity, tone, and structure:

- Richard Cisakowski, who generously read the manuscript and shared thoughtful ideas through many engaging conversations.
- Alya Haq, whose candid feedback, particularly her comment that the book's tone in the Preface felt like it was "scolding me," led to important revisions in both voice and approach.
- Asma Furniturewala, whose concept of a LIVING360 arc helped sharpen the book's overall framework.
- Salman Safdar, for encouraging me to highlight early on that personal financial planning is integral to the LIVING360 philosophy.
- Farooq Ansari, who meticulously reviewed each line, ensuring accuracy in both data and calculations.
- Ali Ansari, whose philosophical perspective helped make several sections more grounded and relatable.

- Professor Chris Schwarz, for helping me distill the book's core themes with greater clarity.
- Mona Abbasi, for her narrative guidance and suggestions that encouraged a more open and personal tone in key sections.
- Irfan Furniturewala, whose feedback reassured me that the book's content was accessible and coherent.
- Imran Ansari, for his thoughtful review and meaningful comments throughout the manuscript.
- Javaid Ansari, who kindly spent part of his vacation in Hawaii reviewing the manuscript and offering ideas to make the narrative more inclusive and engaging.
- Avi Gorasia, for her meticulous research and diligence in assembling the endnotes.
- Panav Gogte, for his early review and valuable research contributions.
- Michelle Heyne, for multiple rounds of review and feedback that strengthened the composite narratives and helped align the content with the most thoughtful and current ideas in the financial industry.
- Nadeem Ahmedi, for offering suggestions that made the content more approachable for younger readers.
- Emil Ali, for reviewing the manuscript, especially the financial section, and for his guidance on details and disclosures.

A heartfelt thank you to the team at Greenleaf Book Group, especially Dee Kerr, Brian Welch, Morgan Robinson, Amanda Hughes, Diana Coe, Chase Quarterman, and Jared Dorsey, for their dedication, professionalism, and care in bringing this book to life.

Finally, I am deeply indebted to my wife, Fauzia Ansari, whose unwavering encouragement and support over the past two years made it possible for me to dedicate countless evenings and weekends to this project. Her belief in this work kept me going.

About the Author

FEROZ ANSARI is an adjunct professor at the University of California–Irvine and a senior principal and portfolio manager at a registered investment advisory firm. He also serves as chair of the Todd & Lisa Halbrook Center for Investment and Wealth Management at UC Irvine's Paul Merage School of Business, a center of excellence for financial education and wealth management research.

For more than three decades, Feroz has helped thousands of clients and students discover meaning, purpose, and financial security. His work centers on the development of Total Wealth—the integration of Awareness, Action, and Acceptance—as a pathway to both emotional fulfillment and long-term financial security. He is a Certified Financial Planner® (CFP®) professional and holds a Master of International Management (MIM) from Arizona State University's Thunderbird School of Global Management, along with an MBA from the Institute of Business Administration in Karachi, Pakistan.

Feroz has completed advanced programs in portfolio management, leadership, and finance at Oxford University (UK), INSEAD (France), Harvard Business School, Citi Training Center (Singapore), and Euromoney. He has also led training programs in treasury management and foreign exchange for financial institutions in Dubai.

He is the creator of LIVE360, a life-satisfaction and purpose-development program featured in *The Wall Street Journal.* Feroz is also the founder of the Investment, Financial Planning & You (IFPY) summer program, which delivers financial literacy and life-planning education to students nationwide. Each year, he volunteers four weeks of his time to teach financial literacy programs at UC Irvine. Under his leadership, IFPY has generated more than $1 million to support financial-literacy initiatives for underserved youth, including the LifeVest program, impacting more than four hundred students annually.

Beyond his professional work, Feroz is passionate about golf, travel, books, and lifelong learning. He enjoys traveling with his wife of thirty years and playing golf with his two sons—content now to break ninety, though he once celebrated a proud seventy-nine.